Discovery Travel Ad

WILD WEST

Nicky Leach
Editor

John Gattuso
Series Editor

Discovery Communications, Inc.

Discovery Communications, Inc.
John S. Hendricks, *Founder, Chairman, and Chief Executive Officer*
Judith A. McHale, *President and Chief Operating Officer*
Michela English, *President, Discovery Enterprises Worldwide*
Raymond Cooper, *Senior Vice President, Discovery Enterprises Worldwide*

Discovery Publishing
Natalie Chapman, *Publishing Director*
Rita Thievon Mullin, *Editorial Director*
Mary Kalamaras, *Senior Editor*
Maria Mihalik Higgins, *Editor*
Kimberly Small, *Senior Marketing Manager*
Chris Alvarez, *Business Development & Operations*

Discovery Channel Retail
Tracy Fortini, *Product Development*
Steve Manning, *Naturalist*

Insight Guides
Jeremy Westwood, *Managing Director*
Brian Bell, *Editorial Director*
John Gattuso, *Series Editor*
Siu-Li Low, *General Manager, Books*

Distribution
United States
Langenscheidt Publishers, Inc.
46-35 54th Road, Maspeth, NY 11378
Fax: 718-784-0640

Worldwide
APA Publications GmbH & Co.
Verlag KG Singapore Branch, Singapore
38 Joo Koon Road, Singapore 628990
Tel: 65-865-1600. Fax: 65-861-6438

Discovery Communications produces high-quality nonfiction television programming, interactive media, books, films, and consumer products. Discovery Networks, a division of Discovery Communications, Inc., operates and manages the Discovery Channel, TLC, Animal Planet, and Travel Channel. Visit Discovery Channel Online at http://www.discovery.com.

Although every effort is made to provide accurate information in this publication, we would appreciate readers calling our attention to any errors or outdated information by writing us at: Insight Guides, P.O. Box 7910, London SE1 1WE, England; fax: 44-171-403 0290; email: insight@apaguide.co.demon.uk

Printed by Insight Press Services (Pte) Ltd., 38 Joo Koon Road, Singapore 628990.

Wild West / Nicky Leach, editor.
    p. cm.––(Discovery travel adventures)
    Includes bibliographical references (p.   ) and index.
    ISBN 1-56331-833-4
    1. West (U.S.) Guidebooks. 2. West (U.S.)––History.
3. Frontier and pioneer life––West (U.S.)   I. Leach, Nicky J. II. Series.
    F590.3.W553 1999
    917.804'33—dc21   99-26078
                                           CIP

*W*ild West combines the interests and enthusiasm of two of the world's best-known information providers: **Insight Guides**, whose titles have set the standard for visual travel guides since 1970, and **Discovery Communications**, the world's premier source of nonfiction television programming. The editors of Insight Guides provide both practical advice and general understanding about a destination's history, culture, institutions, and people. Discovery Communications and its website, www.Discovery.com, help millions of viewers explore their world from the comfort of their home and encourage them to explore it firsthand.

About This Book

This book reflects the contributions of dedicated editors and writers familiar with the West's wildest destinations. Managing editor **John Gattuso**, of Stone Creek Publications in New Jersey, worked with Insight Guides and Discovery Communications to conceive the series and selected stunning images from some of the biggest names in western photography. Gattuso, editor of several western guides, quickly brought on board writer and editor **Nicky Leach** as project editor. A longtime drylander in the desert Southwest now "relearning the color green" in Seattle, she has written a number of books on the West's most magical places and covered Grand Canyon and southern Utah's Canyon Country for this guide. "Westerners have had to learn to adapt to the landscapes they settled in, not the other way round," she says. "The stories of how they succeeded – and failed – are as intriguing to me as the landscape itself."

All the writers in this book are personally caught up in these unfolding human sagas. **Julie Fanselow**, who penned chapters on Lewis and Clark, the Oregon Trail, Jackson Hole, the Northern Rockies, and West Texas, is a Midwesterner by birth and an Idahoan by choice. A travel writer specializing in history, her road guide to the Lewis and Clark Trail received kudos from a fellow trail buff, historian Stephen Ambrose, and she still recalls her reason for coming West. "I was lured by its open spaces and lingering sense of possibility," she says.

Also heeding the siren call of open spaces is cowboy-at-heart **Peter Fish**, a California writer and magazine editor. "I've admired cowboys ever since I was a kid – when my favorite musical group was Sons of the Pioneers and my favorite possession Roy Rogers' autograph," he recalls. Here he brings alive the colorful but hard lives of the West's cowboys in chapters on buckaroos and rodeo and guides readers through the Gold Rush Country of his home state.

Another desert rat-turned-wetlander, Seattle writer **Lawrence Cheek** writes often about New and Old West and has authored guides to Arizona, northern New Mexico, and southwestern prehistoric cultures. He offers an incisive look at our nation's fixation on the mythic West and northern New Mexico's deeply satisfying adobe architecture and mix of cultures. Cheek grew up speaking English and Spanish in El Paso, Texas, and sees the western experience as a collision of cultures. "The West is a work in progress," he says. "I find it fascinating to explore how one culture is layered upon another."

Susan Hazen-Hammond's nine nonfiction books include three on Native Americans and two on southwestern history. Born in Washington State and now living in Santa Fe, New Mexico, she presents a clear-eyed and affectionate look at the state of Native America today, then takes us to Lincoln County on the trail of the infamous Billy the Kid.

Writer **Rose Houk** has made the Southwest her home and subject for 20 years. She didn't have to go far to explore northern Arizona's Indian Country, which sprawls at the back door of her Flagstaff home. "I consider it a great privilege to be a neighbor to the Navajo, Hopi, and other Native American groups," she says. "To visit them is to remove to another time and place." The Lakota Sioux and their nemesis, George Armstrong Custer, fascinate Colorado Springs writer **Conger Beasley**, whose piece on the Black Hills of South Dakota examines how each side viewed that ancient landscape. The author of the award-winning *We are a People in this World*, which wove historic accounts of the 1890 Wounded Knee massacre with a personal account of the 1990 Bigfoot Memorial Ride, he is particularly struck by one irony: "Custer and Crazy Horse had starkly contrasting mentalities – militarily, though, they were alike."

Tucson writer **Philip Varney**'s obsession is "ghosts" – ghost towns, that is. He has written several guides to the West's ghost towns and each year takes a lucky few to explore these old haunts. Here, he offers a ghost town primer and lists the best ghosts in the West. "Exploring these old mining camps is as close to traveling back to the Old West as you can get," he says. Varney also gives us an insider's look at Arizona's Sonoran Desert, home of ghostly and mortal mining towns, Spanish missions, Indian homelands, and Tombstone's infamous O.K. Corral.

Mining towns also feature strongly in Wyoming writer **Jeremy Schmidt**'s wild ride through the Colorado Rockies. Author of several National Geographic guides and publisher of his own successful series of western guides, he takes readers to visit revivified mining ghosts, remnants of ancient Indian cultures, and the contemporary Indian, Hispanic, and Anglo populations of southwest Colorado today.

Texan historian **Bill O'Neal**, author of several books on western history, has always had a taste for epic tales of the Old West. He covers San Antonio's Spanish heritage and the trail north to famed cowtown Fort Worth, with a side trip to the famous King Ranch, one of the Old West's biggest spreads. O'Neal is quick to point out the Spanish influence on the West. "Spain had a presence in Texas a century before the pilgrims landed in New England, and it was the Spanish vaqueros who planted the seeds of cowboy culture in the West."

Mythmakers like Buffalo Bill and early western pioneers are the longtime subjects of writer **Gregory Lalire**, editor of *Wild West* magazine, who tries to separate myth from reality in his two chapters on those subjects. Ranching, rodeo, the Old West, and Native America crop up often in Wyoming writer **Candy Moulton**'s books and articles. A regular contributor to *Wild West* and *Ranch* magazines, she delves here into the gentle (and ancient) art of horse whispering.

Finally, thanks to Nez Percé author Beth Hege Piatote for her insights into the Indian West, and to members of Stone Creek's editorial team: Edward A. Jardim, Michael Castagna, Nicole Buchenholz, and Judith Dunham.

Potsherds (opposite), remnants of ancient Indian ceramics found throughout the Southwest, help date archaeological sites.

A pioneer and his rifle (above) were rarely parted. Rifles were more accurate than handguns for hunting and fighting at long range.

Boot spurs (left), used by cowboys to control horses, retain many flourishes from those of 18th-century Spanish vaqueros.

Cowboy boots (following pages) traditionally have pointed toes to fit stirrups, high leather tops for protection against brush and rocks, and sharp heels to steady the rider during roping.

Table of Contents

SECTION THREE: WILD WEST DESTINATIONS

MAPS

Picture this. You're out West, driving an empty highway bolted straight to a forever horizon, one hand on the wheel, coffee cup in the other. A map lies strewn across the passenger seat. Bach's *Double Violin Concerto* soars to a crescendo on the stereo just as the sun dips behind the mountains. The smell of sagebrush and smoky pinyon wafts through the open window. As the last strains of sunset and Bach fade, you pull over and begin walking a dirt track with no particular destination in mind. Elk and deer haunt the shadows. Just over the rise, a coyote soprano breaks into a short aria. The *koyaanisqatsi* thrum of the big city feels like a lifetime away. And you think: Perhaps I'll never go back. ◆ Sound familiar? Epic fantasies underlie almost everyone's experience of the West. We measure ourselves against that flat sagebrush plain, **Saddle up for a wild ride** the hypnotic, blue bowl-shaped sky, the **through the myths,** battered summits of mountain ranges, the bright **history, and adventure** shock of rivers surging through desert canyons, **of the Old West.** and understand suddenly why a joyful Walt Whitman wrote, "I am immense. I contain multitudes." For all the talk of heroics, manifest destiny, and national wealth that has driven settlement of the West, the simple truth is that it is a place of personal reverie, only lately learning how to cooperate and build communities of many individual destinies. ◆ The West is young country, both physically and mentally, only now moving from willful teenage whim to patient adult understanding of the world and its processes. Today, this boundless place is learning that freedom means finding the balance between possibility and self-imposed boundaries. The West is defined by water – or lack of it – a fact appreciated by all its Indian residents and early

"Cowboys," wrote Walt Whitman, "are a strangely interesting class ... with their swarthy complexions and broad-brimmed hats."

Preceding pages: Texas cowpunchers, circa 1907; *Where the Desert Meets the Mountain* (detail), by Walter Ufer; horse roundup, Idaho.

Deer's Skull with Pedernal, 1936 (detail, right), by Georgia O'Keeffe, is typical of the artist's inspired interpretations of the New Mexico landscape.

The tin star (below) was a fragile symbol of law and order in the often-violent frontier.

A Zuni religious leader (left) photographed in 1903 by Edward S. Curtis, whose haunting images of American Indians documented a disappearing way of life.

cattle was king even as they explore different grazing practices, reintroduction of dryland-adapted species like the buffalo, and a little heritage tourism of their own.

More than half the West is publicly owned and, therefore, sparsely populated, making this the best place in America to have a direct experience of many different natural and cultural landscapes. You can visit preserved Ancestral Pueblos in the Four Corners and sacred Indian sites in every state; Spanish missions in southern Texas, southern Arizona, northern New Mexico and California; gold-mining ghosts in the Black Hills, northern California, Nevada, southern Arizona, Colorado, Idaho, and Montana; historic westward trail sites from Nebraska to Oregon; and breathtaking natural treasures like Yellowstone, Yosemite, Grand Canyon, Canyonlands, Death Valley, and many, many more.

arrivals such as the Spanish, John Wesley Powell, and the Mormons. Dubbed an "oasis civilization" by Professor Walter Webb, this is a land shaped by aridity, where 86 percent of its residents now live in cities along the Pacific, the Rockies, and major rivers like the Rio Grande and Colorado. The lessons of cooperation, size limitation, and shared resources in the Indian villages were lost on 19th-century arrivals. The interior West is littered with the ghosts of boom-and-bust mining towns thrown up haphazardly without civic thought and abandoned when an insatiable appetite for more drew their residents away.

But the mythic idea of the West remains as important as grittier realities, helped along by all those willing to buy into the fantasy. Hardworking cowboys with time on their hands cling to the image of the "rugged individual" created for them by greenhorn easterners like Zane Grey and Owen Wister. Indian tribes, struggling to overcome unimaginable cultural losses, use a combination of reality and romance to promote Indian heritage tourism and show how they have survived and adapted to every century's demands. Those ranchers who haven't sold their land for ranchettes yearn for the days when

Be ready to meet a place of great paradox and unearthly beauty. Open your heart and mind, strap on your sense of adventure, and come on in.

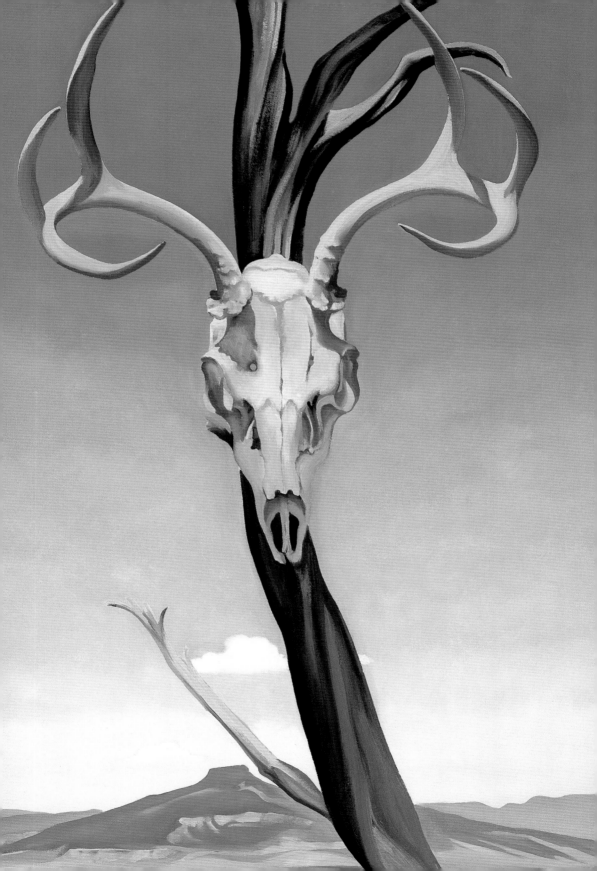

Western Lives

To understand the West, look beyond easy definitions and simple notions to a magnificently diverse land where place shapes perception, myths inform reality, and the threads of various cultures are woven into a rich living tapestry.

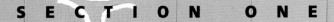

Gammons Gulch, the quintessential Old West ghost town, snores in the sun beside a desolate back road in the Sonoran Desert west of Tucson, Arizona. Hardly anyone goes there; the road serves mainly a few hardscrabble ranches. You meander the town's main street alone and absorb the eerie silence, which is broken only by the distant rasp of cicadas. You stare through the window of the blacksmith's shop, wondering if that drill press of a century past still works. ◆ And then, like dawn fragmenting a dream, reality intrudes. The sun-bleached WANTED posters are photocopies. The general store, closed and deserted, has a wheelchair ramp. Yes, Gammons Gulch is a fabrication, the fantasy of a contemporary ghost-town enthusiast named Jay Gammons. He's been building the place for the past 30 years with lumber and antique hardware scrounged from old **Today's image of** buildings being demolished around **the Wild West is shaped by** Arizona. "I call 'em spirits," he says. "Nails and **romantic myths, literary** timbers and boardwalks that actually **fiction, and movie cliches.** come from old places." ◆ Well, we're all a little like Jay Gammons. We collect the spirits of the historic West, real and mythical, and hammer them into modern American culture. What Frederick Jackson Turner wrote famously in 1893 still holds more or less true: the United States is a frontier nation. And the history, landscape, and characters of the historic West continue to shape our image of ourselves. ◆ "A person puts on a cowboy hat anywhere in the world, even if alone in a room, and starts acting differently," Timothy Egan observed in his book *Lasso the Wind*. "Sometimes stupidly, sometimes nobly, but it is a new personality." An off-duty cop touring the Roy Rogers–Dale Evans Museum in California told Jane and Michael Stern of

The Madonna of the Prairie, 1922, by William Henry David Koerner, captures the weariness of weeks on the trail for thousands who migrated west.

Preceding pages: Pack Creek Ranch, Moab, Utah.

The Atlantic Monthly that his father had been an abusive drunk, so while growing up he adopted the television cowboy as his role model. "Even today, when I am faced with a predicament on the job," he said, "I ask myself, What would Roy do?"

Fantasies of the West

Well, what *would* Roy do? What is the spirit of the Old West? Or, to pose a more pertinent question, what do we imagine it to be?

First, adventure. From Coronado's thrust into New Mexico way back in 1540 to John Wesley Powell's 1869 expedition through the Grand Canyon, the people who explored the West never fully knew what they were getting into. Even with topographical maps, a cell phone, and a Global Positioning System, an excursion into backcountry anywhere in the West today is still a flirtation with the unknown; the land remains too fierce to domesticate. When Santa Fe writer Douglas Preston began planning to retrace Coronado's route on horseback, an experienced wilderness guide warned: "There is a fair probability that this trip will actually kill you." That was in 1989.

Second, virtue. Here is the power of myth in its full glory. One after another, we have turned each of the key players in the Old West into national heroes, their charac-

ter and motivation as pure as a mountain spring. Spanish conquistadores and missionaries, Indians and Indian fighters, trappers, cowboys, lawmen, even outlaws. Davy Crockett, martyred at the Alamo, stands as a symbol for independence, self-reliance, courage, and freedom, not the dark current of American

Hi-ho, Trigger! Hollywood cowboy Roy Rogers and his horse, Trigger, (left) symbolized the honor code of the Old West during the 1940s and '50s.

The Herd Quitter, 1897 (right), by Charles M. Russell, illustrates the artist's skill at depicting the romance and drama of cowboy life.

imperialism. Jean Baptiste Lamy, the bullying bishop of 19th-century New Mexico, becomes a humble saint without a trace of arrogance in Willa Cather's historical novel *Death Comes for the Archbishop*. Chief Seattle is celebrated today for the profound and prescient environmentalist speech he is supposed to have made in 1854: "Man did not weave the web of life, he is merely a strand in it. Whatever he does to the web, he does to himself ...." These wise words actually were written in 1972 by a Texas screenwriter named Ted Perry. To venerate Seattle, we've had to slip him a script.

It isn't that we deliberately set out to distort the record. Every culture needs its heroes, and heroes serve best when they are without complexities and contradictions. And because the West is so big, its history so vast, and its landscapes so colossal, we need to cut it down to size, recast it into manageable images, in order to grasp it. So the virginally pure Roy Rogers stood

John Wayne takes a swing at Montgomery Clift (left) in 1948's *Red River*, a western version of *Mutiny on the Bounty*, with cowboys instead of sailors rising up against the bossman.

in for the 19th-century cowboy, and the pink howling coyote on a T-shirt came to symbolize the entire western wilderness.

The Role of Myth

That wilderness, too, has played a profound role in the individual and collective American dream. Thoreau never ventured any farther west than Minnesota, but whenever he went walking in New England, he instinctively turned westward. "The future lies that way to me, and the earth seems more unexhausted and richer on that side," he wrote. "Eastward I go only by force; but westward I go free." The fact that there was so much unexplored territory out there literally and symbolically expanded Americans' horizons. Anything and everything seemed possible in the West of the 19th century, and much of that belief lingered through the 20th century, even after the West was paved and urbanized and species began to disappear. Where

else could Sasquatch – the ultimate symbol of wildness – exist but in the dark forests of the Northwest?

Wilderness, of course, exists to be conquered and exploited, and it was the West's bad luck to be chockfull of natural resources as well as vast horizons. It was a cornucopia of gold, silver, copper, uranium, timber, oil, gas, buffalo, salmon, rangeland, and hydroelectric power, all awaiting harvest. And because there seemed to be so *much* of everything, the myth of unlimited resources became imprinted on the American consciousness. And there it has stayed, even as the resources dwindle and disappear.

Myths have a way of shaping reality, which may be the Old West's most profound influence on the nation as a whole. "As people accept and assimilate myth," wrote historian Richard White, "they act on the myths, and the myths become the basis for actions that shape history."

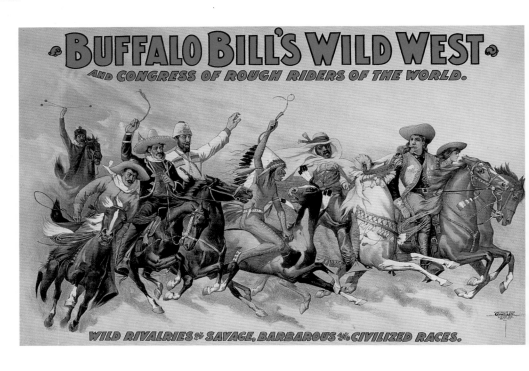

Ronald Reagan was a perfect example of how myth and real life energize each other. Reagan was no cowboy, but he had played one on television. He wore boots, rode horses, and chopped wood, so he seemed invested with the attributes of the mytho-logical cowboy: rugged individualism, loyalty, courage. Even where objective measurements of his policies and judgment left him wanting, most Americans found it impossible to dislike him personally. When John Hinckley tried to assassinate him, Reagan lived his role to perfection: he cracked jokes and healed with blinding speed. The western myth helped elect him; in return he polished its tarnishing image.

True West

It's a wonder that the Old West never burned itself out through sheer overexposure. In 1959, no fewer than 30 westerns clotted prime-time television; White suggests that the genre eventually died from "a severe case of cultural indigestion." In the 1980s, "Santa Fe Style," a far-rago of Spanish Colonial, western, and Indian motifs, spread like brushfire across the country. Rustic hand-painted furniture turned up in chic Manhattan apart-ments; R. C. Gorman posters of aerodynamic Navajos flooded galleries everywhere. Pepperidge Farm created a Santa Fe cookie, explaining, more than a little desperately, that its chunky oatmeal tex-ture evoked New Mexico's craggy terrain.

But this is only natural. The West is a land of excess, so the cultural trends that grow out of it are themselves pumped to excess.

There is also a more subtle and deeper way in which the West continues to inform the American character. History is alive in thousands of

Mythmakers

Buffalo Bill Cody's Wild West (left) was called "the most animated equestrian spectacle ever seen."

Sitting Bull and Buffalo Bill in 1885 (right): The great Sioux leader toured with Cody's Wild West show, but gave away most of his pay to hoboes and needy children.

Homesteaders and timber barons (bottom, left) had cut down many of the biggest and most beautiful old-growth trees by the late 1800s.

Yes, Virginia, there really was a Wild West, complete with cowboys, Indians, stagecoaches, and all the rest. And then there's that other version, cooked up in dime novels and on celluloid. The trouble is, telling them apart is not always easy.

Take, for example, the fabulous Deadwood Dick. He was entirely a creature of imagination, the fictional subject of 33 dime novels churned out in an eight-year span, but you'd never know it from all the people who actually ventured out to the Dakota Territory to see him in the "flesh." He even rated a mention in Calamity Jane's creative "autobiography" of 1896. Others, like Dakota settler Richard Clarke and the black cowboy Nat Love, claimed not only to know Deadwood Dick but to be him.

Yes, a lot of tall tales were spun, and the dudes back East ate them up. Newspapers and popular periodicals such as *Leslie's* and *Harper's* made the West seem a far more dangerous place than in fact it was. And the myths were in large measure encouraged by the principals themselves, who self-promoted shamelessly. The professional storytellers also had a big impact. Owen Wister's best-selling *The Virginian* of 1902 was hugely influential in creating an image of the cowboy as romantic hero, and the novels of ex-dentist Zane Grey and his successors were peopled by supermen in white hats besting villains in black hats.

Of course, the West's mythmaker par excellence was Buffalo Bill Cody, a flamboyant showman who actually had been a legitimate frontier hero. His highly popular Wild West show capitalized on his own exploits but also included real-life Indians like Sitting Bull, real buffalo and bucking horses, and top-notch shooters like Annie Oakley. In one form or another, the show's version of the Wild West would appear in countless motion pictures: attacks by bloodthirsty Indians, thrilling buffalo hunts, Custer's courageous fade-out, and endless thwarted robberies of the Deadwood stage. Deadwood Dick, if there ever was one, would have been proud. – *Gregory Lalire*

venues across the West, and even where it says less about who Americans are than who we imagine ourselves to be, as one writer put it, it has the power to energize us, to prime us for a run at the next frontier – whatever that may be.

We feel it inside the mission of San Xavier del Bac near Tucson, where some obscure Franciscan priests and itinerant craftspeople created a dazzling evocation of Spain's baroque glory – literally in the middle of nowhere. Their audacity can be claimed by all of us, proudly, as a piece of the multicultural American heritage.

We sense it in the pioneer musical *Texas*, staged on summer nights in Palo Duro Canyon near Amarillo. Americans now know enough history to separate myth and fact, but in this musical both retain the power to move us. We see it in the Georgia O'Keeffe Museum in Santa Fe. O'Keeffe, a pioneer of the arts in the 20th century, demonstrated that miracles remain to be explored even in the commonplace landscapes of the West. We may go out and do likewise.

Even Jay Gammons' fake ghost town has something to say. On an outside wall of the saloon, a hand-lettered sign advises that "This place is dedicated to all pioneers past and future. Anyone can be a pioneer. Believe in yourself and your ideas, work hard, and never give up."

The pioneer story was never as simple nor even remotely as idealistic as this motto. But few of us will walk past that sign without some small shiver of pride, and perhaps even a tingle of inspiration.

Come autumn, Rod McQueary rides the range north of Elko, Nevada, hiring himself out to the ranches that spread across this still lonesome country. His workday is a long one. He and his fellow cowboys gather at four in the morning to head up toward the mountains, where they'll spend the next 13 or 14 hours in the saddle as they cajole ornery cattle from the summer range toward winter pastures. ◆ It's not an easy life, but it's a life that McQueary loves and one that he feels lucky to be leading. Northeastern Nevada is one of the few corners of the West where cattle ranching remains an economically viable activity and cowboying a possible career path. Even here, though, McQueary warns that the going is tough for many a cowpoke. "You can make it if you don't have a family," he says, explaining that a cowboy's pay is $400 a month plus board, and "all the horses you can ride." But if you acquire a wife or children, you need to diversify. That's what McQueary has done. He's a published author, a storyteller, a humorist who has appeared on television; these other careers enable him to continue cowboying. ◆ That just goes to show the draw that cowboy life has on Americans, whether they're working wranglers like Rod McQueary or the other millions of us who have never been closer to the open range than our last Clint Eastwood movie, but who are certain that we have some cowboy in our soul. From the day the first lasso was draped around the first longhorn, cowboying has been as much ideal as occupation. The vaquero, the cowboy, the buckaroo: they were, and are, America's knights errant, sagebrush Sir Galahads. As such they have come to symbolize the American West throughout the world.

Their livelihood was dangerous, their pay a pittance, but buckaroos were eventually regarded as western heroes.

Arizona cowboys: With its emphasis on stock handling, ranch chores, and long days outdoors, cowpunching is a lifestyle with more sweat than glamour.

Buckaroo Beginnings

Where did the buckaroo come from? The trio of terms – vaquero, buckaroo, cowboy – testifies to mixed ancestry. Most historians agree that classic cowboy culture emerged first on the plains of south Texas shortly after the Civil War. That was the beginning of the large ranches, which raised cattle to be driven north to railheads like Dodge City for shipment to eastern slaughterhouses. Ranchers needed men to round up cattle and move them north. Texas' proximity to Mexico ensured that early cowboys were hybrid creatures. They may have spoken English, but they drew gear, skills, and terminology from south of the border. The Spanish *cincha* became cinch;

la reata, lariat; *rancho*, ranch. And the Mexican *vaquero* became the western cowboy or buckaroo.

Many of the earliest buckaroos were former soldiers from the fallen Confederacy. Later their ranks were joined by farm boys looking for adventure, even by immigrants from the Old World. Some historians estimate that as many as one-third of the West's cowboys were black or Hispanic. Buckaroos were, in short, a varied bunch. But they did have some traits in common. Most were young – in their late teens and early 20s. And while Hollywood cowboys like John Wayne may have been larger than life, the

The jingle of silver spurs announces a cowboy long before he is seen.

average cowboy tended to be smaller in stature, well muscled but wiry. E. C. "Teddy Blue" Abbott, who rode on trail drives in the 1870s (and whose memoir, *We Pointed Them North*, remains a classic of cowboy literature), put it bluntly: "A heavy man was hard on horses."

And after all, riding horses is what being a buckaroo is all about. Horsemanship is the single most important trait shared by all working cowboys. Granted, many cowboys in the past did not own their own horses (some trail bosses discouraged it), and in the course of a cattle drive, a

cowboy might often switch mounts. Nevertheless, the horse is still central to a cowboy's existence. As Teddy Blue wrote, there are only two things a cowboy is afraid of: "a decent woman and being set afoot."

The Legendary Roundup

During the era of the great cattle drives, the buckaroo's life had a rhythm defined by the seasons. Come spring, cowboys would fan across a ranch's open range, rounding up cattle to assemble a herd of thousands that would then be branded and castrated for that year's trail drive. In fall, a second roundup caught new calves and stragglers missed in spring. But it was what came in between – the cattle drive itself – that was the high point of the cowboy's working life. These epic journeys could stretch 1,200 miles, from the rangelands of Texas to the cattle towns of Kansas, and could take as long as four months. Heroic in retrospect, the drives were brutal on those who participated in them. Hazards included Indian attack, swollen rivers,

and stampede. As Andy Adams recounted in his *Log of a Cowboy,* "Outfits eagerly started north, only to reach their destination months later with half of their cattle gone, some of their men lying in shallow graves along the trail or lost in the water of angry rushing rivers."

When at last buckaroos reached the end of the trail – the railhead at Dodge City, Kansas; Cheyenne, Wyoming; or Miles City, Montana – it was time to blow off some steam. That might include a visit to one of the West's "soiled doves," prostitutes like Squirrel Tooth Alice or Big Nose Kate Elder. But for many cowboys, the highlight of a trip to town was a visit to a clothier like Jacob Karatofsky's Great Western Store in Abilene, Texas, or Meyer Goldsoll's Old Reliable House in Ellsworth, Kansas.

Indeed, as things worked out, the legend of the buckaroo became inseparable from his clothing. The cowboy

developed a uniform both practical and stylish. His wide-brimmed hat – like the most famous model, Stetson's "Boss of the Plains" – gave him shelter from the prairie sun. The cowboy boot looked sleek but was also practical. Its high leather tops protected the buckaroo from brush and rocks; its sharp heels steadied him during roping. For such duds, the cowboy was willing to pay a substantial portion

Texas longhorns (top, right) are driven to a railhead in Dodge City in this Edward Rapier sketch.

California Vaqueros, 1876–77 (left), by James Walker, portrays the hidalgo flair and colorful dress of Spanish vaqueros.

Chaps and a cowboy hat (right) are cowboy essentials; chaps protect legs from thorns and brush and a broad-brimmed hat shields the face from the sun.

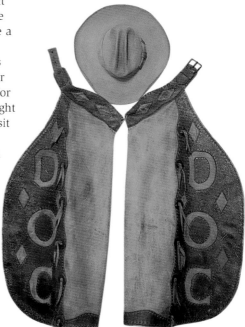

of his paycheck – $25 for a good pair of boots, or a full month's pay. But then, as W. S. James wrote, "The cowboy's outfit, as a rule, is of the very best from hat to boots. He may not have a dollar in the world, but he will wear good, substantial clothing, even if he has to buy it on a credit."

Objects of Disdain and Curiosity

As the cowboys of the 1870s swaggered across the West, they inspired a mixed response from civilians. Some solid citizens of western cities looked upon the cowboy's revelries with disdain. Even though Cheyenne,

Wyoming, was economically dependent on cowboys and cattle drives, the *Cheyenne Daily Leader* editorialized: "Morally, as a class, they are foul-mouthed, blasphemous, drunken, lecherous, utterly corrupt. Usually harmless on the plains when sober, they are dreaded in towns, for then liquor has the ascendancy over them."

Yet at the same time, the American public increasingly thrilled to tales of western buckaroos. In the industrial cities of the East, life on the open range looked romantic and heroic. New York publishers like Erastus Beadle churned out series of cheap books – "dime novels" – fea-

turing gripping but factually dubious exploits of supposed western cowboys. Buckaroo life even began to lure well-bred young men from good eastern families. In 1884, a 26-year-old Harvard man, Theodore Roosevelt, came west to start a cattle ranch in Dakota Territory. He was duly impressed with the men he saw working around him. As he later wrote, "A cowboy will not submit tamely to an insult, and is ever ready to avenge his own wrongs; nor has he an overwrought fear of shedding blood ... He does possess, to a very high degree, the stern, manly qualities that are invaluable to a nation." Roosevelt so valued those "stern, manly qualities" that when it came time to round up volunteers to fight the Spanish-American War, he turned to cowboys. A substantial number of the Rough Riders who charged up San Juan Hill were Arizona and New Mexico buckaroos.

By the turn of the century, the cowboy's position in American life had become so exalted that it became hard to separate buckaroo myth from reality. In 1902, a Harvard friend of Teddy Roosevelt, Owen Wister, published a novel set in Wyoming cowboy country. An immediate best-seller, *The Virginian* established the image of the brave, taciturn cowboy that lingers today. Another friend of Roosevelt, Yale-educated Frederic Remington, similarly immortalized cowboy life in paintings and bronzes that made him one of the most popular artists in turn-of-the-century United States.

Cowgirls (left) work ranches alongside men and have adopted similar dress to protect themselves from the weather and terrain.

Cowboy poetry gatherings (right) like the annual event at the Western Folklife Center in Elko, Nevada, are gaining in popularity.

Cowboy singers and poets (below) enthrall audiences with tales of life on the range.

Cowboy Poetry Gathering

I went to the first annual ever convention of cowboy bards.

(I woulda said poets, but poet's a word that sure makes a rhymer's job hard.)

– Baxter Black, from "The Cowboy Poetry Gathering"

Maybe the images don't dance in perfect iambic pentameter, and the rhyme scheme doesn't obey a sonnet's rigorous rules. What the heck. When it comes to expressing heartfelt emotion in language pungent and sweet as mesquite smoke curling up from a campfire, the works of the cowboy poets who gather each January in Elko, Nevada, can hardly be beat.

When folklorist Hal Cannon founded the Cowboy Poetry Gathering in 1985, he was giving new life to a venerable tradition. Cowboy poetry harks back to the ballads composed on long cattle drives or on winter nights in some remote ranch bunkhouse. Now, for a week at the end of each January, as many as 8,000 visitors convene at Elko's Western Folklife Center to listen to the rhymes of cowboys (and cowgirls and ranchers and veterinarians) from all over the West.

The poems recited before the admiring crowds are by turns funny and poignant, hard-edged and wistful. Some poets paint the cowboy's world as an ideal, honoring the beauty and independence of life on the western range. But the best poems also acknowledge grittier realities: the hard work, the low pay, the struggle to maintain ranching and cowboying as viable ways of life in an increasingly urban, populous, and technologically oriented West.

Elko's Cowboy Poetry Gathering has launched some of its cowboy poets, like Baxter Black and Waddie Mitchell, to nationwide prominence. It has also inspired numerous other cowboy poetry festivals around the West. But Elko's gathering remains the granddaddy of them all, the Stratford-upon-Avon of the buckaroo bard.

Real Cowboy Life

In both art and literature, the most authentic portraits of cowboy life came from men who had been real working buckaroos. Charles Marion Russell began working as a Montana cowboy at age 16; in winter he would paint pictures in exchange for food and lodging. Eventually, Russell's oils, watercolors, and bronzes would be considered the most accurate yet beautiful representations of life on the western plains. Charlie Siringo's book, *A Texas Cowboy*, was based on his experiences working for famed Texas rancher Shanghai Pierce on his Rancho Grande in the 1870s. Indiana-born Andy Adams ran away from home to become a cowboy, making his first cattle drive in 1883. His *Log of a Cowboy* is fictionalized but so thoroughly detailed as to be among the best accounts of the buckaroo's world. And it is Adams who probably delivered the final verdict on the buckaroo's career: "No harder life is lived by any working man."

In fact, cowboying never provided much of a living. Average pay was a meager $25 or $30 a month. The career was short. As Texas cowboy James McCauley wearily conceded, "For a man to be stove up at thirty may sound strange to some people,

Cowboy Hall of Fame

The Cowboy Hall of Fame and Western Heritage Center in Oklahoma City celebrates America's most durable folk figure in all his (and her) many guises. Buffalo Bill Cody is honored there, of course, and pioneering Texas cattleman Charles Goodnight. But so is cowboy author Zane Grey, and 10 soundstages' worth of Hollywood cowboys, from Tom Mix to Roy Rogers – not to mention some Hollywood cowgirls, like Big Valley's Barbara Stanwyck and *Gunsmoke's* Amanda Blake.

Opened in 1965, the Cowboy Hall of Fame was the dream of businessman Chester Reynolds. His initial idea was to honor the West's buckaroos and other notables with a series of commemorative plaques and busts. Since then, the Hall of Fame has grown enormously in size and ambition. Spacious galleries display spurs and saddles and other cowboy tools of the trade, Plains Indian clothing and beadwork, and substantial holdings of western art – notably the Atherton Gallery Permanent Art Collection, which has a superb collection of 20th-century western painters. Kids get an entire wing where they can learn what a longhorn is, how a chuck wagon worked, and the words to every verse of "Git Along Little Dogie."

Big as it is – it sprawls for 200,000 square feet on a green hillside overlooking Interstate 44 – the Hall of Fame is in the midst of major expansion. Set to open soon are additional galleries devoted to the American Cowboy, Rodeo, and Native American life – not to mention an entire Frontier Town. Like the West itself, the Cowboy Hall of Fame and Western Heritage Center is an institution in constant motion.

The Cowboy Hall of Fame (left) in Oklahoma City pays homage to the West's most enduring folk heroes.

Actor Tom Mix (below), known for his authentic, rough-and-tumble stunts, was known as the "man who never fakes."

but many a cowboy has been so banged up that he has to quit riding that early in life ... My advice to any young man or boy is to stay at home and not to be a rambler, as it won't buy you anything. And above everything stay away from a cow ranch, as not many cowpunchers ever save any money and 'tis a dangerous life to live."

Here and there buckaroos even tried to organize to improve pay and working conditions. Despite their independent nature, cowboys banded together to strike in the Texas panhandle in 1883, then again in Wyoming in 1886. But these strikes weren't successful. And by the turn of the century, the era of the big cattle drives was over; the West no longer needed tens of thousands of working cowboys. Some cowboys were able to buy small ranches of their own – become "nesters," in the parlance of the day. Others made a living on that new institution, the dude ranch. Or they abandoned homes on the range for life in western towns and cities.

In a strange way, none of this mattered. The economics of buckaroo life had changed, but not the power of the buckaroo myth. At the same time the cowboy was dwindling on the American prairie, he was riding high in American literature, and, soon, on the American movie screen. *The Virginian*

inspired countless other cowboy best-sellers. As silent films began to flicker across the nation's theater screens, they gave Americans cowboy movies starring William S. Hart and Tom Mix, founders of a line that would lead to John Wayne and Gary Cooper and Clint Eastwood.

Today the buckaroo is both legend and reality. Any video store stocks shelves full of Clint Eastwood westerns, and *The Virginian* is still in print. The real working buckaroo has not vanished, either. True, there are fewer buckaroos than there were a hundred years ago. They may spend as much time in a four-

wheel-drive pickup as on horseback, and instead of being schooled on a cattle drive they may have earned a degree in range science from some western university. But head out to a western emporium like King's Saddlery in Sheridan, Wyoming, or Capriola's in Elko, Nevada. There you'll see tourists shopping for leather belts and cowboy boots. But you'll also see a lot of genuine working cowboys testing lassos, talking cattle prices and weather – proof, if you needed it, that the buckaroo has not vanished from the wide open spaces of the West... and probably never will.

The Indian West

n northwestern Nevada, in an isolated part of the Great Basin, the Pyramid Lake Paiutes live near a shimmering, 240-square-mile freshwater sea. It's set in a stark, rugged desert that seems so unlikely to contain a natural lake that, even with map in hand, it's hard to believe the lake exists until it comes into sight. ◆ Unbelievably beautiful, Pyramid Lake is all that remains of Lake Lahontan, a vast, ancient sea that once stretched across 8,700 square miles. Sacred to the Native peoples who have lived along its shores for at least 10,000 years, it is known to outsiders as one of the best fly-fishing lakes in the world – and as a source of precious water. During the past century, water-starved non-Indian farmers have plundered the lake repeatedly. ◆ Native America is like Pyramid Lake. Until you've actually been there, it's hard to believe **Indians are reclaiming** it exists. Exotic, mysterious, full of surprises, **places that once belonged** Native America today is a mere fragment **to them and preserving** of what it once was. And it remains **native languages, ceremonies,** threatened by outside forces. ◆ By the mid- **and artistic traditions.** 1800s, many eastern tribes had either been annihilated or pushed westward. Today three out of four of the nation's two million Native Americans – or Indians, as they call themselves – live in the West. The four states with the highest Indian populations are Oklahoma (252,000), California (236,000), Arizona (203,000), and New Mexico (134,000). More than half of the West's Native Americans live in Indian Country – that is, on or near reservations. ◆ In general, the 550 recognized tribes have enough treaty-mandated sovereignty to earn the title "nations within a nation," and tribes often call themselves nations. That's a concept Indians and non-Indians

A dancer wears traditional dress at the annual Navajo Nation Fair in Window Rock, Arizona; the event is attended by more than 50,000 Navajos and members of neighboring tribes.

across the West chew on all the time. Indian sovereignty is why you have to buy a permit to drive to Hilltop in the high country of the San Carlos Apache reservation in Arizona. It's also why, when Navajo politicians considered closing the part of Interstate 40 that runs through the Navajo Nation, people took them seriously.

Although outsiders tend to see the West's Native Americans as a monolithic block, every tribe has its own culture and customs. Some groups, like the 19 Pueblo tribes of New Mexico, do have much in common. The traditional worldview of San Ildefonso Pueblo scarcely differs from that of nearby Tesuque Pueblo. But no one from San Ildefonso would ever confuse himself or herself with someone from Tesuque. And the Pueblo peoples still speak six different native languages. A Keresan-speaking native of Cochiti Pueblo communicates with a Towa speaker from Jemez Pueblo in English or Spanish.

Cultural Dissipation

The strongest common bond that links Indians across the West is that the life of every single one is irrevocably different from what it would have been if whites had not arrived five centuries ago. As U.S. Senator Ben Nighthorse Campbell, a Northern Cheyenne and the chairman of the Senate's Indian Affairs Committee, puts it, "It is difficult to comprehend the magnitude of the atrocities – intentional, neglectful, or accidental – perpetrated on Indian people by the conquering culture."

In the 1600s, Spanish colonists in northern New Mexico saw Native peoples as an endless supply of servants. By the 1800s, U.S. government officials were moving entire Indian nations of the West around as casually as if they were rock piles.

In 1867 Ten Bears, a Comanche leader, lamented, "I was born upon the prairie, where the wind blew free, and there was nothing to break the light of the sun. I was born where there were no enclosures, and where everything drew a free breath. I want to die there, and not within walls."

Tall Bull, a Cheyenne leader, pointed out that same year that his braves fought

Apache dancers (left) with painted bodies and black hoods personify mountain spirits, or *Ga'an*.

only when attacked. "We never did the white man any harm; we don't intend to," he said.

Still, across the West, pioneers saw Indians as a nuisance and a danger, best eliminated. In 1864, Arizona rancher and volunteer soldier King Woolsey spoke for many when he said, "I fight on the broad platform of extermination." In the Bannock War and the Modoc War of the 1870s, non-Indian soldiers rationalized killing Native children with the slogan, "Nits make lice."

Native Americans have endured discrimination and stereotypes into the 20th century. In Pomo territory in northern California, businesses once routinely posted signs that said, "No dogs or Indians allowed." As a result, most Native cultures have been battered. Even a people like the Crow of the Great Plains, who fight every day to preserve their language and traditions, have seen enormous cultural loss since 1800. And no wonder. In the first half of the 19th century, 50 percent of them died of smallpox. In the second half, non-Indians stole 95 percent of the land granted the Crow in the 1851 Fort Laramie treaty. Meanwhile, non-Indian hunters slaughtered so many buffalo that the sacred animal – around which Crow lives, culture, and beliefs revolved – vanished. In 1884, the U.S. government made it a crime to hold a traditional giveaway, to perform the Sun Dance, to marry more than one wife, to

sell a horse to a fellow Indian, or to be a medicine man. It was even a crime to leave the reservation without permission. Under such circumstances, it's surely remarkable that the Crow people retained any culture at all.

Reclaiming Sovereignty

Across the West, changes and upheavals continue for Native America, but now Indians can often choose their changes, at least at the tribal level. Typical questions tribes struggle with include: Shall we build a casino? Shall we allow our timber to be clear cut? Shall we permit a nuclear-waste repository to be built on our sacred lands?

Such questions tear tribes apart, leading to another characteristic common to Indian nations around the West: internal conflicts. They began with the arrival of missionaries, whose teachings created a division between traditional Indians and Christians. They continued through the 19th century,

Hopi pottery
like this seed jar display utilitarian beauty and a connection to the natural world.

when people disagreed about how to deal with non-Indian intruders – that's why Apaches hunted Apaches in Geronimo's day. Conflicts persisted in the 20th century, as tribes were forced to abandon tradition and elect leaders by democratic vote. Today, elected leaders often disagree with traditional spiritual leaders.

Casinos are a major cause of conflict. Many see them as a final defeat of tradition. Yet tribes that choose casinos often find themselves in the historically ironic position of taking non-Indian money in great fistfuls. Such tribes have become the new Have's, while tribes which don't own casinos often remain Have-Not's. A Tohono O'odham woman in southern Arizona said: "We're making over a million dollars a month, and it terrifies us.

A Navajo girl wears a traditional velveteen blouse, broomstick skirt, and heavy silver jewelry popular at the Navajo Nation Fair.

Inlaid jewelry like this bola tie (left) is a specialty of the Zuni.

We all grew up so poor, and now there's all this money."

But there's also good news from Indian country. Tribes across the West are resurrecting and preserving endangered traditions, including Native languages. Among the Comanches of the southern Great Plains, for instance, only 250 people, all elderly, still spoke the language fluently by 1993. But a program sponsored by the tribe and the University of Oklahoma is reviving the language among young people. The Cahuilla Indians of southern California are restoring ancient funeral traditions and other sacred rites. The Coquille people of Oregon are strengthening storytelling traditions and have resurrected the ancient midwinter World Renewal Ceremony. Many Navajo girls still undergo a puberty ceremony at menarche. Across the West, tribes are rebuilding buffalo herds and resurrecting traditions and practices related to the sacred animal.

A spectacular renaissance in traditional Indian arts is also under way. Artisans among people as diverse as the Utes and the Lakota (Sioux) are known for their fine beadwork. Kiowas paint images taken from their visions onto leather shields. California artisans weave intricate baskets as their ancestors did. And Pueblo potters produce superb pots, using traditional techniques and materials.

Chief Joseph's People

Even the battered Nez Percé have exciting news. The story begins on one of those tragic notes found in every tribe's history. In the spring of 1877, General Oliver O. Howard forced the Wallowa band of Nez Percé from their homes in Oregon's Wallowa Valley. Led by Chief Joseph, 700 Nez Percé men, women, and children fled across 1,700

Shaking The Earth

Drums throbbed. Sparks flew. Flames leaped from giant bonfires and cast an orange glow on the dancers as they wove among the fires.

The moving feet, the drums, the flickering light – it seemed as if the earth itself were shaking. As if the past 500 years had vanished. As if, at any moment, the ancestors and the spirits would appear and dance side by side.

But this remarkable moment in Carlsbad, New Mexico, was not a private ceremonial. It was public, open to all, in honor of the spring agave harvest. "Some people call events like this powwows," Mescalero Apache elder Evelyn Martine said. "But no matter what you call it, it's a time when Indians and non-Indians can connect with each other."

That's true of such events throughout the West. Originally *pau-wau*, an Algonquian word, meant medicine man; as a verb it meant to perform a healing ceremony. By the 1800s, however, it applied to any gathering of Indians, and today it refers to hundreds of public events in which dancers, singers and other followers of the powwow trail come to celebrate Indian culture.

Most powwows welcome spectators, but it's best to keep a few rules in mind. Before pulling out your camera, check to see if photography is allowed or if a permit is required, and always ask permission before snapping the shutter. Try to be unobtrusive; don't ask unnecessary questions about traditions and customs, and don't join a dance unless invited. Non-Indians may be encouraged to participate in the Round Dance, which celebrates the universality of all humankind.

Fancy dancers (right), known for their elaborate outfits and energetic steps, are the colorful stars of powwows like this one in Gallup, New Mexico.

miles of rugged countryside. For months soldiers under General Howard and General Nelson Miles chased and attacked them. "All along the trail was crying," one refugee said. Finally, just south of Canada and safety, the starving, freezing band found themselves surrounded again by soldiers.

General Miles promised Chief Joseph that he and his people could return to their homeland, about which Chief Joseph said, "My father sleeps there, and I love it as I love my mother." Instead, they were shipped in boxcars like cattle and forced to live on inhospitable land in Kansas. Many died of malaria and other diseases. Chief Joseph later said it was worse to die there than to die fighting in the mountains.

Chief Joseph kept his famous promise, made the day he surrendered, "From where the sun now stands, I will fight no more forever." But he spent the rest of his life petitioning to return to his beloved land.

His band's descendants, scattered, broken, in turmoil, continued his struggle. Today the Nez Percé of Idaho, who include some descendants of Chief Joseph's band, have

Crow Fair (left), an annual powwow in Montana, offers a chance to wear finery, meet friends, share stories, and dance.

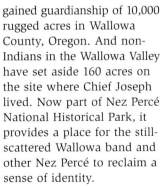

gained guardianship of 10,000 rugged acres in Wallowa County, Oregon. And non-Indians in the Wallowa Valley have set aside 160 acres on the site where Chief Joseph lived. Now part of Nez Percé National Historical Park, it provides a place for the still-scattered Wallowa band and other Nez Percé to reclaim a sense of identity.

If you can understand Chief Joseph's plight, and what his people have gone through, if you can understand what it means to his descendants to reclaim the

land where their ancestors stood, you're ready to experience the adventure, poignancy, and complexity of travel in Indian country. You're ready to understand why tribes across the West have wistful prophecies of a happier future, free of non-Indians, like the distant past.

When you stand on Indian soil – which was once, after all, every inch of the West – you breathe the air of other nations and other times. Literally and metaphorically, you stand on the bones of the ancestors.

Judging by old movies and outdated history books, you'd think the only folks who came out west were white and spoke English. It just wasn't so. African-Americans, Asians, Hispanics, and a great variety of Europeans were a part of the Old West from the very beginning. ◆ Black homesteaders, liberated from slavery, set up colonies on the Kansas frontier, and black soldiers joined the U.S. Army. Chinese immigrants worked with the Irish to build the first transcontinental railroads. And Mexican vaqueros, the original cowboys, rode alongside their Anglo counterparts. These unsung westerners were a varied bunch – explorers, traders, missionaries, prospectors – but most had one thing in common: a desire to escape their old lives and start anew. ◆ Slaves were among the first blacks to experience the unexplored West. In 1528, a Moor named Esteban, part of a Spanish expedition to discover the fabled Seven Cities of Cíbola, survived a shipwreck off Florida with his commander, Cabeza de Vaca,

History has not forgotten the former black slaves, European homesteaders, and Chinese miners and laborers who settled the West.

and two others. He found himself wandering with his compatriots through what would later become Texas, New Mexico, and Arizona. Eight years later, the bedraggled survivors stumbled into Mexico City, telling tales of fantastical country, friendly Indians, and, most importantly, enormous wealth in the Pueblo cities of the Southwest. ◆ Smelling gold and glory, the Spanish sent Esteban and a missionary, Fray Marcos de Niza, back north in search of this El Dorado. This time, however, Esteban was not so lucky. The once friendly natives, now encountering newcomers of a more mercenary bent, angered quickly, and Esteban was killed at Cíbola by outraged Puebloans.

Immigrant families from Germany and Russia gather at a church picnic in Montana in 1913.

Misled by de Niza's hazy account of events, a Spanish expedition mounted by nobleman Francisco Vasquez de Coronado returned in 1540, still intent on finding the Seven Cities of Cíbola, but again returned empty-handed. In 1605, Spain decided that Indian labor and natural resources made colonization of the Southwest worthwhile. Don Juan de Oñate rode into New Mexico and established a colonial government north of present-day Santa Fe, taking with him a large force that included half a dozen Africans and mulattos. Blacks played a prominent role throughout the Spanish period. A census in 1790 indicated that 18 percent of California's population was of African descent.

Blacks on the Frontier

People of color were also part of the earliest American expansion into the West, despite Horace Greeley's pronouncement that the West "shall be reserved for the benefit of the white Caucasian race." On the Lewis and Clark expedition, Captain William Clark's black slave Ben York distinguished himself as hunter, trader, and scout, and, along with Sacagawea, the Shoshone woman who acted as guide, was treated as an equal by members of the Corps of Discovery, as they were called. York was considered "great medicine" by Indians they encountered along the way. Slavery was still in full force when Lewis and Clark returned from their expedition in 1805. Nevertheless, York was eventually freed by Clark, who helped him get started in a freight-hauling business.

One of the first African-Americans to see the country as a free man was Jim Beckwourth, born in 1798 in St. Louis, Missouri, the son of

a mulatto mother and a titled English father. Beckwourth went west at an early age and became one of the most feared Indian fighters on the frontier. In 1824, he was adopted by the Crow Indians, given the name Morning Star, and later became a tribal leader. A restless, rough-and-ready character, he worked as a trapper, prospector, Indian fighter, and army scout. He is remembered best for establishing the route through California's Sierra Nevada that still bears his name: Beckwourth Pass.

After the Civil War, newly freed black homesteaders took their chances on the frontier but often found themselves competing with whites for land, and suffering continued discrimination. In remote southeastern Utah, when Mormon colonists founded Moab in the 1870s, a black settler nicknamed Negro Bill was already homesteading by the Colorado River. He was accepted by the Utes there, though their people had driven out the Mormon Elk Mission in 1851. One successful black colony in Kansas, named Nicodemus after a legendary black prophet, was founded in July 1877. About a dozen black colonies sprang up across Kansas in 1877–78, setting the stage for the so-called Black Exodus of 1879, in which thousands of black

Ho for Kansas!

Brethren, Friends, & Fellow Citizens:
I feel thankful to inform you that the
REAL ESTATE
AND
Homestead Association,
Will Leave Here the
15th of April, 1878,
In pursuit of Homes in the Southwestern Lands of America, at Transportation Rates, cheaper than ever was known before.
For full information inquire of
Benj. Singleton, better known as old Pap,
NO. 5 NORTH FRONT STREET.
Beware of Speculators and Adventurers, as it is a dangerous thing to fall in their hands.
Nashville, Tenn., March 18, 1878.

Benjamin "Pap" Singleton (right), an ex-slave from Tennessee, led 300 black Exodusters to Kansas after the Civil War. His promotional leaflets (above) encouraged thousands of others to join them.

homesteaders, or "exodusters," came to Kansas. As one emigrant said: "Every black man [was] his own Moses."

Other African-Americans won fame, and occasionally notoriety, in western settings. During the Indian Wars of the 1870s, the U.S. Army employed free black men to fight Indians, who admiringly dubbed the dark-skinned newcomers "buffalo soldiers" because their physique and character reminded them of buffalo. Black cowboys sometimes stood out, even among their hardworking, hard-living, colorful companions. Rodeo star Bill "Bulldog" Pickett was known for sinking his teeth into the upper lip of steers to subdue the animals and was associated late in life with such luminaries as ex-Apache leader Geronimo and a young Tom Mix. Another black cowboy, Isom Dart, was shot dead in 1903 for cattle rustling, a

hazardous profession in remote cattle country that knew no racial boundaries but was universally condemned by ranchers.

Even the tradition of the American cowboy was a Spanish invention. Many decades before Texan cowboys sealed the image of the cowboy in the American imagination, vaqueros, the working cowboys of Spanish missions and ranches, were winning admirers. Most of the vaqueros were Indians or mestizos (mixed Indian and Spanish ancestry) from Mexico. Wearing colorful ponchos, sombreros, and jingling spurs, they relied more on knives and ropes than tools and weapons. They valued courage, perseverance, and stoicism – qualities that came to be associated with the Anglo cowboys to whom they passed on their skills, lingo, and way of life.

Western Women

Frontier women faced hardships they never could have imagined back East. They chopped wood and broke sod. They ate food they would have tossed to the pigs back home. They lost children to illness, flash floods, and Indian attacks. Many were forced into prostitution merely to survive.

But for some women, the frontier offered freedom and opportunity. The comforts of civilization may have been far away but so too were stifling mores and conventions. Take Esther Morris. She was a Wyoming transplant from New York who, in 1870, became one of the nation's first female judges. Clara Brown, an ex-slave, used the money that she made as a laundress in a Colorado mining town to help other freed slaves settle on the frontier.

Countless other women left their mark on the West – some famous, others unknown. There was an Ohio farm girl who showed the world that a woman could shoot as well – Hell, much better! – than any man. Her name was Annie Oakley, and her skill as a "dead shot" made her a star in Buffalo Bill's Wild West Show. Nellie Cashman, the so-called "Angel of Tombstone," was celebrated for her care of down-and-out miners as well as for her own exploits as a prospector. And such notorious figures as Belle Starr and Cattle Annie proved that women outlaws could raise hell as well as any male desperado.

For most women, however, frontier life was devoted to building homes, raising families, and tending crops and livestock. History books tend to focus on big events and flamboyant characters, but it was this sort of thankless, everyday work that really settled the West.

Home on the range: Rancher and photographer Evelyn J. Cameron (above) kneads dough at her Montana home in 1904.

Ranch woman (below, left) reflects a depth of character forged by a lifetime of independent living and dedication to family and work.

Earlier, around 1832, vaqueros had introduced the tricks of the ranching trade to Hawaii, where British navigator George Vancouver had first brought cattle in 1793. *Paniolos*, or Hawaiian cowboys, adopted Mexican dress to suit local conditions and added a few uniquely Hawaiian touches, such as leis and feathers. "Even the roughest, toughest, rowdiest, and most rugged and most manly of us wear leis," said one longtime *paniolo*.

Mormon State

For many, the West represented spiritual as well as physical freedom. The Shakers, the Amish, and the Mennonites found sanctuary from European oppression in eastern states. The religious group that had the most lasting impact on the West was the Church of Latter-day Saints, whose members are known as Mormons. The church was founded in 1830 by Joseph Smith after the teachings of the *Book of Mormon* were revealed to him through a series of visions. In 1844, Smith was killed by a mob in Carthage, Illinois, and succeeded by the energetic and visionary new head of the church, Brigham Young. The new leader studied explorer John C. Frémont's recently published report on the western lands and realized that an independent Mormon homeland, which they named Deseret, might be carved out of the vast Great Basin region, stretching west from the Wasatch Mountains all the way to California.

The advance party

reached Salt Lake valley in July 1847 and was quickly followed by thousands of converts – many newly arrived in the United States and pushing handcarts piled with their belongings across a thousand miles of rough and dangerous country. Hand-picked skilled laborers, craftsmen, farmers, ranchers, and teachers, working closely with one another, quickly laid out orderly communities; built places of worship, homes, schools, and stores; and dammed the rivers, planted crops, and raised stock. The Mormons then fanned outward and did the same thing in southern Utah, Nevada, Arizona, Idaho, and California. Despite droughts, dam breaks, crop infestations, Indian hostilities, and continued antipathy from outsiders, the hard-working, well-organized Mormons succeeded in cultivating dry desert country and becoming self-sufficient within just a few years of their arrival. Husbands took more than one wife, and populations quickly grew, swelled by immigrants from Britain, Scandinavia, Greece, and later the South Sea Islands and other far-flung missions. In 1888, the U.S. government banned polygamy and took legal action against polygamous Mormons. The church relented on that issue, and Utah was admitted to the United States, allowing the Beehive State to become part of the shared vision of Manifest Destiny then driving the country.

Chinese Laborers

The Mormons arrived in Utah just before gold fever had hit California and were quickly able to finance their growing empire by selling necessities to those headed for the gold-fields. Also determined to benefit were Chinese immigrants, lured to California by promises of gold in the Golden Mountains. By 1852, some 25,000 Chinese had made the steamship journey east across the Pacific. Many borrowed money for passage from agents who charged high rates of interest, forcing the new arrivals to hire themselves out as laborers. More than half of the 200,000 who came between 1876 and 1890 returned home, most still poor.

Chinese and Irish labor helped build the railroad system that connected West Coast markets with those back East. The Chinese workers, however, were treated as expendable by the railroad and often given jobs considered too dangerous or demeaning for whites. The Chinese reworked mining districts abandoned by American miners who, backed by various anti-Chinese state and municipal laws, frequently killed the Chinese workers or took their gold with little fear of reprisals. Against all odds, one Chinese immigrant did succeed in

Chinese immigrants like this one, photographed in California in 1851, came in search of gold but faced violent opposition from white miners whose term "Not a Chinaman's Chance" summed up their feelings.

making a fortune. Chin Lin bought a mine in southern Oregon, treated his employees fairly, and was so successful that he managed to deposit more than $1 million worth of gold in the bank.

After the Chinese Exclusion Act was passed in 1882, violence against the Chinese escalated. For their own protection, the Chinese formed tight communities in San Francisco and elsewhere: the modern-day Chinatowns. With work opportunities for the Chinese severely restricted, laundries and restaurants replaced mines and railroads as the primary places of employment by the turn of the century.

New immigrants continue to pour into the West. Many residents of rural towns in the region speak only Spanish, and Asians continue to have a major impact on western cities. The new West, like the old, is still looked on as a place of promise. And where promise lies, diversity is never far behind.

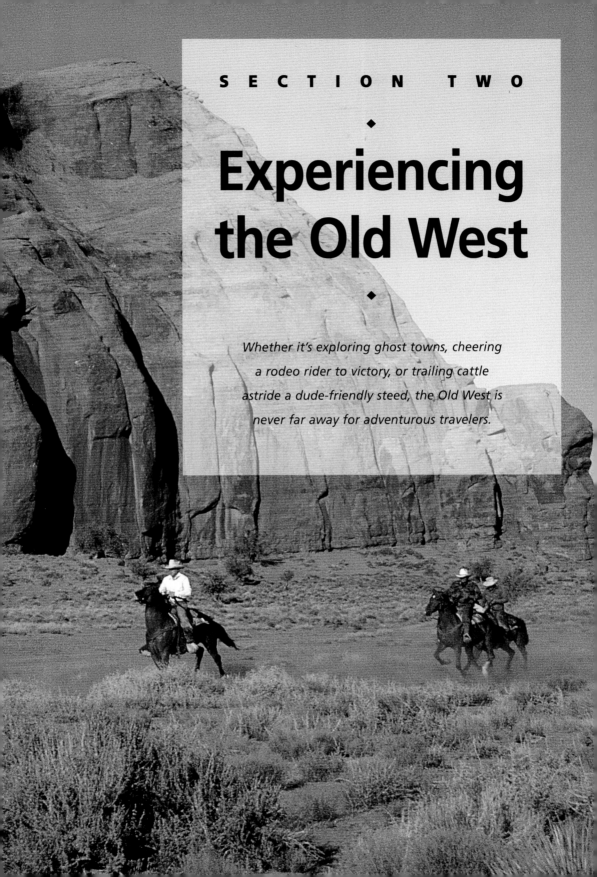

SECTION TWO

Experiencing the Old West

*Whether it's exploring ghost towns, cheering
a rodeo rider to victory, or trailing cattle
astride a dude-friendly steed, the Old West is
never far away for adventurous travelers.*

Their century-old boards bleach in the sun, their corrugated tin roofs bend and clatter with the occasional dust devil, and their abandoned cemeteries recline silently on forgotten hillsides. They are ghost towns, pallid reminders of bygone mining bonanzas that brought hordes of dream-seekers to the American West. ◆ Once they were spectacularly alive, swarming with miners and merchants, clergymen and saloonkeepers, lawmakers and lawbreakers. Well-dressed dudes from back East brought in capital for the expensive machinery required to dig deep into the earth for hidden and elusive riches. But the towns they created were destined to fail. When all the precious stuff was tapped out, the settlements were doomed. ◆ The bonanzas that fueled the boom towns were dramatic, the decline often catastrophic. As mineral deposits played out and miners moved on to new fields of dreams, fortunes won turned quickly to fortunes lost, and boom town became ghost town. ◆ There are hundreds of ghost towns in the West.

Abandoned mining camps and forgotten outposts are frozen in time, offering insights into the lives of their long-gone inhabitants.

Most are mere traces on the landscape or a site on a topographic map, but every state has several worth visiting. ◆ A true ghost town has two characteristics: Its population has precipitously decreased, and the initial reason for its settlement, usually a mine, no longer supports the community. The pure ghost town is completely deserted, but most have a few residents who keep the buildings and artifacts from vanishing. If, then, a ghost town can have residents, how will you know if you're in one? A large majority of the buildings will be dilapidated and vacant, and municipal buildings like schools, churches, and courthouses will either be empty or used

The ruins of a mill cling to a rocky ledge in Crystal City, an abandoned mining town in the Colorado Rockies.

for other purposes. If a town of several thousand people has dwindled to a couple of hundred, it's a ghost.

For some, the quintessential ghost town is a mining camp with the saloon door creaking in the wind and the playing cards still on the table. Your best bet for this kind of experience is on a movie set. Movies have been filmed in real ghost towns many times. Grafton, Utah, was used for the classic *Butch Cassidy and the Sundance Kid*. Mogollon and Cabezon, both in New Mexico, were locales for Henry Fonda's *My Name is Nobody*. Some of the best buildings in Mogollon and Cabezon are not genuine at all – they were constructed by Universal Studios to give the towns an authentic look.

Vanished Communities

If you're not likely to find that saloon door or the playing

cards, what are you going to find in a ghost town? Bodie, California, the West's best ghost town, features 170 buildings, including a schoolhouse with desks, textbooks, and cut-out Easter bunny decorations on the wall. Homes have dishes on tables and toys in children's bedrooms. The morgue still has a ready supply of caskets. Now a California park, Bodie has been preserved in a state of "arrested decay": buildings are protected, repaired, and propped up if necessary, but

they are not restored or painted to try to recapture Bodie's boom times, which occurred during the 1870s and 1880s. The resulting effect is eerie indeed. With tourists' autos safely out of view, Bodie looks as if it has been waiting, abandoned, for you to discover.

If Bodie looks serene and ghostly now, it belies its past, when it was known as one of the West's most raucous, lawless places. When one little girl was told by her family that they were moving from Aurora, Nevada, to nearby Bodie, she summed up her feelings in her prayers that night with "Goodbye, God, I'm going to Bodie." When that prayer, overheard by her parents, made it into the Aurora newspapers, the boosters in the Bodie press searched for a rejoinder. In a fit of creativity, they claimed the little girl's statement was actually a joyful exclamation: "Good! By God, I'm going to Bodie!"

Ghost towns smaller than Bodie still offer much to

enjoy. St. Elmo, Colorado, for example, sits among dramatic mountain peaks and has one of the most photogenic main streets in the West. St. Elmo was typical of gold and silver boomtowns – it grew so fast that tents standing one day were replaced by hand-hewn log cabins within the week. A few months later, many of those cabins were supplanted by milled-lumber false-front buildings. In the early days of St. Elmo, a guest arrived at a not-quite-complete hotel and asked for a private room. The hotelier drew a chalk line around one of many beds and told him that he had even given him a suite.

Once the supply center for nearby mines during the gold strikes of the early 1880s, St. Elmo was a favorite Saturday night "blow-off" town for miners, freighters, and railroad workers. Now the town is somnolent. Miners' cabins have become summer residences and the main activity centers around insatiable chipmunks that cadge handouts from visitors.

An even smaller ghost town is Shakespeare, New Mexico. It features only a few buildings, but each provides a sense of history. In the kitchen of the two-story Stratford Hotel, you can stand where Billy the Kid, then really a kid, washed dishes. The Grant House, a former stage stop, has two nooses dangling from a beam, reminders of a time when startled stagecoach travelers gaped at two bodies hanging in that very room. The passengers were informed that one, Russian Bill, was a horse thief. The other, Sandy King, was "just a damned nuisance." Russian Bill's mother later wrote to the postmaster at Shakespeare, worried about the lack of communication from her son. The postmaster replied as tactfully as possible, "I regret to inform you, madam, that your son has died of throat trouble."

Bodie, St. Elmo, and Shakespeare are three of the West's best ghost towns, but even deserted, decrepit ghosts offer much to see and photograph. Some showcase old railroad depots. Others feature mills, smelters, headframes, tramways, and other mining-related buildings and equipment. Often a boarded-up courthouse or school dominates the site. In many cases, the sole reminder that a town ever existed is its forlorn cemetery, with weathered markers and picketless fences.

Risen from the Grave

Although most western ghost towns were mining camps, there are other reasons communities die. Some ghosts started out as railroad towns

"Hang 'em high." Frontier justice was often swift, violent, and definitive.

only to be doomed when diesel fuel replaced coal, allowing locomotives to make fewer stops. Other places dried up because of the urbanization of the West; they were farming and ranching centers on wind-blown prairies whose hard ways of life became unattractive to people lured to the cities. Water has created several ghost towns: some had too much, disappearing beneath reservoirs; others had too little, like Keeler, California, which once was a vital shipping port on Owens Lake. When Los Angeles appropriated the area's water, however, Keeler was left high and dry next to a parched and barren desert.

Still other towns died for miscellaneous reasons: a lumber camp where the timber gave out, a farming community engulfed by expanding suburbs, a highway town bypassed by a new interstate road. Llano, a ghost town in southern California, was a socialist utopia undone by the realities of human nature.

Not all ghost towns have remained dead. Some former mining towns have rebounded with another source of gold, one that never seems to run

Tomboy (left), a once-bustling mining camp in the 1890s, now stands in ruins in the San Juan Mountains outside Telluride, Colorado.

out. Crested Butte, Aspen, and Breckenridge, all in Colorado, are now sparkling ski resorts. Georgetown, Colorado, is enjoying a renaissance as an expensive retreat for the wealthy. In California, the summer tourist trade has brought the entire 1849 Gold Rush region back to life. In southern California, Calico has been transformed from a genuine ghost into the tourist-destination Calico Ghost Town, complete with so many added-on shops, attractions, and rides that the original town has receded into a mere footnote. The pockets of gold and silver in the hills above Cripple Creek, Central City, and Black Hawk, Colorado, have been replaced with silver and gold in the pockets of gamblers at multistory casinos. Even as gaming dollars help to preserve the historic mining towns, however, the casinos so alter the face of the cities that their historic charm has been seriously besmirched.

Although some ghost towns are difficult to reach and others have been commercialized or vandalized, visitors continue to seek them out. Why are so many people fascinated by ghost towns? Mystery writer Tony Hillerman put it perfectly: "To me, to many of my friends, to scores of thousands of Americans, these ghost towns offer a sort of touching-place with the past. We stand in their dust and try to project our imagination backward into what they were long ago. Now and then, if the mood and the light and the weather are exactly right, we almost succeed."

The morgue (top) in Bodie, California, saw lively business during the town's raucous heyday.

An assay office in Chloride, Arizona (below). The town was established in the 1860s and named after the silver-chloride ore that was mined in the surrounding mountains.

THE GHOST	The Setting	Claim to Fame

Bodie State Park, California
Preserves more than 170 buildings from an 1870s gold camp, including more than 65 saloons and brothels. One of the best authentic ghost towns in the country.

Twenty miles southeast of Bridgeport, California, in the desert mountains on the California-Nevada border. Access by snowmobile only in winter.

Famous for violent characters like Rough-and-Tumble Jack, any of whom may have been the legendary "Bad Man from Bodie." Said one undertaker, "As soon as the local talent get to thinking they're tough, they go to try it out in Bodie, and Bodie undertakers get the job of burying 'em."

St. Elmo, Colorado
An 1880s mining camp and rowdy "Saturday night town," with a lovely main street of wooden false-front buildings, including a hotel, a town hall, a miner's exchange, and a combination general merchandise store and post office.

About 24 miles southwest of Buena Vista in the mountainous Colorado mining country.

When Mark Twain rode the railroad down to St. Elmo, the brakeman "had some difficulty" after the perilous journey, and Twain declined a return trip. Eccentric brothers Roy and Tony Stark and their sister Annie protected the town for decades in its ghost-town years.

Shakespeare, New Mexico
A 19th-century mining town with seven adobe buildings, now part of a family-owned working ranch. Tours on weekends; occasional historic reenactments.

About three miles south of Lordsburg, in southwestern New Mexico's rolling ranch country.

Originally Mexican Springs, the town was renamed Shakespeare in 1879 by its new owner, an Englishman, who also rechristened the main street Avon Avenue. Billy the Kid was a dishwasher here.

Victor, Colorado
A gold-mining town from the 1890s with paved streets, rare brick-and-mortar buildings, including a two-story school, depot, church, newspaper office, and a once elegant miners club.

Six miles southwest of Cripple Creek in the mountainous Colorado mining country.

Victor's streets, dug up during the Depression, had been laid with mine "waste" – literally paved with gold. Before becoming a boxing legend, Jack Dempsey was a mucker in the Portland Mine.

Ruby, Arizona
A lead, zinc, and silver-mining town that died in 1941, Ruby features more than two dozen buildings, including a store, jail, and school.

Thirty miles northwest of Nogales, near the U.S.–Mexico border.

Banditos from across the Mexican border killed four people during robberies in 1920 and 1921 in the now-crumbling adobe store. Only one murderer was captured, and it's conceivable that one or more are alive today.

Vulture Mine, Arizona
An 1860s gold-mining camp with two schools, a dormitory, an assay office, a dining hall with old stove, and lots of strewn mining equipment.

Thirteen miles southwest of Wickenburg in southern Arizona's Sonoran Desert.

Vulture has only one tree – a hanging tree, next to the jail. The mine was an important supplier of Union bullion during the Civil War. Miners "high-graded" (stole) 20–40 percent of the mine's gold. Eighteen were hanged for it.

THE GHOST	The Setting	Claim to Fame
Cerro Gordo, California An 1860s silver and lead-mining town that still contains an old hoist house, a two-story hotel, brothel cribs, and a madam's house. Open for group outings. 	About 22 miles southeast of Lone Pine in the southern Inyo Mountains.	At one point, silver ore production so outpaced shipping that creative miners stacked 30,000 ingots into cabins – perhaps the most valuable "housing development" in California history.
 **Bannack State Park, Montana** Became Montana's first gold-rush town in 1862, later territorial capital. More than 60 buildings remain, including a two-story combination Masonic Lodge and school. Best in summer; winter temperatures are frigid.	About 85 miles southwest of Butte, in the high northern Rockies.	The little jail was built by Sheriff Henry Plummer, notorious for pretending to pursue holdup men while actually being their leader. He was eventually caught and hanged on his own gallows.
Silver City, Idaho A charming 1870s silver-mining town that died in 1940 but still has a few residents. Features several outstanding structures, including a Masonic hall, a two-story schoolhouse, a church known as Our Lady of Tears, and the rambling Idaho Hotel, which still serves meals. The Owyhee County Cattlemen's Association meets annually in the old schoolhouse.	About 70 miles southwest of Boise in the mountains bordering Nevada.	The booming silver camp had Idaho's first telegraph service, sent from Winnemucca, Nevada. An unusual feature of the hotel is its second-story outhouses perched on stilts, connected by rickety catwalks to the hotel itself.
Rhyolite, Nevada A 1905 gold-mining town with an elaborate train depot, a house made of bottles, and the dramatic stone-and-masonry ruins of the John S. Cook Bank Building. 	About 120 miles northwest of Las Vegas, in the Amargosa Desert at the edge of Death Valley.	Rhyolite swelled to 6,000 residents in 1907, dropping to 700 three years later. It became a ghost soon after. Its famous bottle house is actually a reconstruction, but from the 1920s – it was rebuilt for the Zane Grey western movie *Wanderers in the Wasteland*.
Grafton, Utah An abandoned 1859 Mormon settlement, with a church, a schoolhouse, a store, several cabins, and a poignant little cemetery. Still farmed and cared for by locals.	Thirty-eight miles northeast of St. George, near Zion National Park, in Utah's dramatic redrock country.	Famous as the setting for the bicycle scene in *Butch Casssidy and the Sundance Kid* and the locale for other movies. Repeated flooding of the Virgin River drove residents away in the early 1900s. The cemetery contains the graves of the Berrys, killed in an 1866 massacre by southern Paiutes.
Silver Reef, Utah An unusual 1870s silver-mining town, with only the John Rice House and Wells Fargo Bank building on the main street still standing. The bank, on the National Register of Historic Places, houses a museum and gallery. A scale model of the old town can be seen in the old powder house. 	Two miles north of Leeds, near St. George, in the redrock country of southern Utah.	Silver Reef shipped more than $10.5 million in silver from its mills. The town once had 2,000 residents and mills, schools, laundries, bakeries, butcher shops, saloons, gambling houses, a brothel, even a Chinatown (for railroad workers). Silver, copper, and uranium were processed here until the 1960s.

The chute opens. A fiery bronco, snorting and mean, lunges out, and hanging on top of him, bareback, a cowboy waves one hand as if fear were the last thing on his mind. But even from the bleachers, you can almost feel the adrenaline pumping out of man and horse. The announcer starts the count. Everyone holds his or her breath. The cowboy must stay atop the bronco for only eight seconds. Only eight seconds? Right now, it's a lifetime. ◆ Welcome to rodeo. The setting could be a dusty county fairground or a makeshift corral on an Indian reservation. Tonight it's the University of Nevada at Las Vegas's Thomas and Mack Center, just a roll of the dice from the neon and lounge acts of the Strip. The month is January. Here, in the shadow of Glitter Gulch, the country's best bull-riders, calf-ropers, and steer wrestlers are competing for the most lucrative prizes rodeo has to offer at the annual PRCA National Final Rodeo.

Whether roping a steer or riding a bull one-handed, today's rodeo cowboy needs to be strong, quick, and precise.

Elsewhere in town, high rollers are crowding the poker tables and low rollers the slot machines. But in this stadium, the stakes are just as high – and everyone wants a piece of the action. ◆ It's all a far cry from rodeo's origins, out among the lonesome ranches of the West. But like the West itself, rodeo has survived by inventing and renewing itself, while hanging on to its traditions like a bareback rider to his bronco. The roots of rodeo (from the Spanish *rodear*, "to go round") date back more than a century to a time when, after a week's backbreaking work on the ranch, cowboys would amuse themselves by competing to see who was the fastest at roping a calf or who could ride the toughest horse.

Bull riding requires balance, strength, and nerves of steel. A cowboy must stay atop the snorting, thrashing, 2,000-pound beast for at least eight seconds.

These informal competitions grew into community events and then into rodeo. Numerous western towns have claimed to be the first to hold an official rodeo. The two most accepted contenders are Pecos, Texas, which held its first rodeo on July, 4, 1883, and Prescott, Arizona, which awarded the first rodeo trophy, on July 4, 1888. That July 4 date set a tradition; even now, while the professional rodeo season stretches through most of the year, July 4 is filled with so many rodeos that riders call it "cowboy Christmas." In the 1890s, rodeo was taken up by showmen like Buffalo Bill Cody, who added rodeo events to his Wild West show.

By the 1920s, rodeos were drawing big crowds in sophisticated East Coast venues like Madison Square Garden.

Over the years, rodeo has attracted more than its share of characters. One of the most fascinating was Bill Pickett, a black cowboy from Texas who became something of a legend. Bill starred in the 101 Ranch Wild West Show, where he developed his unique method of steer wrestling. Riding his horse, Spradley, Pickett would chase down a longhorn, then slide down his horse's side to come within a whisper of the galloping steer. He'd grab the bovine's head, twist it toward him, then render the steer helpless by biting it on the

lip. Pickett called this technique bulldogging, because it was akin to the way cattle dogs controlled steers. Even today steer wrestlers perform a kind of bulldogging, although they don't subdue the calf with their teeth.

Today, rodeo is big business. The Professional Rodeo Cowboy Association (PRCA), based in Colorado Springs, Colorado, sanctions about 800 rodeos a year in the United States and Canada. Together, these PRCA-sanctioned rodeos award $21 million in prize money. For the select few, rodeo can be a lucrative calling. A champion rodeo cowboy, like Montana's Don Mortensen, four-time world champion saddle bronc rider

Bronc riding (left) is a rodeo classic in which stylish moves and staying power atop a lively mount carry the day.

Bulldoggers (right) try to beat the clock, using a quarter horse to ride behind a steer, then wrestling the animal to the ground.

and a World Champion All Around Cowboy, can earn as much as $180,000 in one year.

Skills in Competition

Rodeo events fall into two categories. In timed events, cowboys compete against both the animal and the clock. Team roping, which is the only team event in rodeo, draws on techniques cowboys employed when they had to catch a steer for branding. Two cowboys urge their quarter horses after the steer. One of the riders – the header - ropes the steer around the horns, then rides to the left, turning the steer around so that his partner – the heeler - can rope the steer's hind feet. It's a unique division of labor: not only do many cowboys specialize in working as header or heeler but their horses specialize, too, with the header horse being generally taller and heavier, the heeler horse being smaller and more agile.

Solo calf roping combines accuracy and speed. Here a single cowboy rides after a calf, then tosses his lasso around the calf's shoulders. As soon as the calf is caught, the cowboy's horse halts and

the cowboy dismounts. He runs toward the calf, throws it to the ground, then ties three legs together. Throughout this process, his horse obediently stands at the other end of the rope, taking up slack while making sure the rope isn't tight enough to drag the calf. In the last timed event, steer wrestling, a cowboy rides behind a steer on his quarter horse, then slides down and attempts to wrestle the steer to the ground.

Roughstock events comprise the second category of rodeo events. Each requires that the cowboy hang onto an animal (horse or bull) for a minimum of eight seconds. The judges award extra points if he hangs on with skill and style. Bareback riding is often considered the most physically demanding of rodeo events. Seated saddle-less on

a bucking horse, the cowboy must use one hand (and one hand only) to hang on; if he touches the animal (or himself) with the other, he'll be disqualified. As for saddle bronc riding, it's sometimes considered rodeo's classic event, and to observe a skilled saddle bronc rider in action is indeed to observe athleticism at its most graceful.

The last roughstock event is bull riding. The cowboy climbs onto a 2,000-pound bull, wraps a rope around his hand, then tries to hang on as the bull spins, jumps, and lunges. But the bull rider is not the only person in jeopardy. An integral part of this event is the bullfighter – formerly called the rodeo clown – whose job it is to distract the bull once it has bucked off its cowboy, giving the cowboy time to escape being gored.

Hard-Knock Life

Today's rodeo contestants may not be quite as larger-than-life as Bill Pickett. But it still takes a special kind of man to be a rodeo cowboy.

Young cowboys (right), known as wooly riders, do timed rides atop lambs at the Navajo Nation Fair.

Most start young – five-time all-around rodeo champion Ty Murray said he knew he wanted to be a rodeo star at age five – and hone their skills at 4-H and college rodeos. From here they move to county fair competitions, where a first prize could garner them $400 or so, and then into the ranks of the PRCA. Even at the upper levels, though, rodeo's a hard way to make a living. The PRCA estimates that there are 400 cowboys who do rodeo full time and about another 8,000 part-timers. Unless they belong to the rodeo elite, they are likely to travel from rodeo to rodeo, crowded four or five to a car, sharing cheap motel rooms with four or five fellow cowboys.

And it is, mainly, cowboys, although in the early days of rodeo, women were frequent competitors. Prairie Rose Henderson was the first woman to enter a rodeo competition, competing in bronc riding at the Cheyenne Frontier Days Celebration in 1901. The judges balked at first, but could find no rules excluding women. Prairie Rose performed so well that "cowgirls bronc riding" became a regular part of many rodeos. Today, however, the ranks of professional rodeo riders include only men. Women are relegated to one event – barrel-racing – or to non-PRCA all-women rodeos.

As for rodeo animals, they're the most essential participants of all. There would be no rodeo without well-trained horses – or without untrained broncos and bulls. Events like team roping and solo roping depend on the cowboy's ability to work with his horse. In bronc riding and bull riding, the animal's mettle is

Horse Whisperers

When horse trainers talk to horses, they use a method first developed by Xenophon, a Greek cavalry officer who lived some 2,300 years ago. The practice is made popular today by American horse trainers Monty Roberts and Buck Brannaman. They are the modern-day horse whisperers.

Treating horses with respect, compassion, and quiet skill, horse whisperers train animals not with whips and spurs but with gentle actions and empathy. True horse whisperers communicate with body language and other nonverbal means. And they recognize the horse's responses: the way it holds its head or body, twitches its ears, or twists its tail.

Trainers start with a process known as "join-up," or getting to know the horse. Horse and trainer "talk" to each other by exchanging body signals that soothe the animal and let the trainer know when to begin saddling. Though it takes years of practice to become a skilled horse whisperer, those who have learned the technique can often enter a corral with an untrained horse and have the animal responding to commands within 30 minutes. The art of horse whispering is part instinct, part psychology, and extremely effective.

An increasing number of people are using at least some of these techniques in horse training – a process formerly called breaking. Horse whispering became internationally known in 1989 when Queen Elizabeth II invited Roberts to demonstrate his technique at Windsor Castle. Individual trainers have known about horse whispering for years, but the practice seized the imagination of the public following Nicholas Evans's best-selling novel *The Horse Whisperer* and the 1998 movie by Robert Redford. – *Candy Moulton*

Rodeo clowns (top), or bullfighters, must distract the maddened bull after it has unseated its rider, giving the cowboy time to escape goring.

Horse sense (left): Some trainers rely more on subtle cues and body language than on traditional horse-breaking methods.

A cowboy (opposite) bows his head during the playing of the national anthem at the beginning of an Arizona rodeo.

judged along with the cowboy's. The judges will award
the rider more points if he
rides a tough aggressive
bronco than they would if he
rode a more docile steed.
Some of the greatest bucking
horses, animals like Midnight
and Five Minutes to Midnight,
became stars themselves.

But rodeo's treatment of
animals has brought controversy to the sport. Animal-
rights groups have attacked
rodeo, claiming that animals
are mistreated – that broncs
and bulls are subjected to the
pain of wearing a flank strap
across their loins, that animals
suffer being transported from
one rodeo to the next. Rodeo's
defenders argue just as
strongly that cowboys and
stockmen have a substantial
economic incentive to make
sure the animals stay healthy.

Despite competition from
television and video games
and the Internet, the annual
rodeo remains the high point
of the year in many western
cities. Frontier Days in
Cheyenne, for example, is
over a hundred years old –
and still going strong. Held in
late July, it regularly brings
visitors by the tens of thousands to the Wyoming city,
and volunteers work year-
round to assure that the
Daddy of 'Em All (as Frontier
Days styles itself) remains a
rodeo to remember. Other
major rodeos include the
National Western Stock Show
Rodeo in Denver, Colorado,
held each January; the Reno
Rodeo in Reno, Nevada, in
June; and the Pendleton
Round-Up Rodeo in Pendle-

ton, Oregon, and Calgary
Stampede in Alberta, Canada,
held, like Cheyenne Frontier
Days, in July. And of course
January's National Finals in
Las Vegas.

In an era of big bucks and
media deification, top rodeo
riders acquire at least some
of the perks of major athletes:
a decent income from prize
money, along with product

endorsements for boots and
blue jeans and snuff. But
despite all the big-money
trappings, rodeo is still the
West's down-home test of
cowboy skill. Here, the contests between man and
horse, man and steer offer
reassurance that, at least in
some ways, the more the
West changes, the more it
remains the same.

H e may not rank with Kit Carson or Wild Bill Hickok, but in the annals of western history, some place of honor must be reserved for one Mr. Burt Rumsey of Buffalo, New York. In 1882 Mr. Rumsey visited Howard Eaton's ranch in the Dakota badlands. Mr. Rumsey wanted to live the rugged and exciting life of a western cattle rancher. For this privilege he paid Howard Eaton $10 a week, duly signed his name in Eaton's new guest book, and became the first guest at the world's first dude ranch. Thus, an American institution was born. ◆ In all the world, there is no vacation spot quite like the dude ranch of the American West – a place where sophisticated travelers willingly turn themselves into hired ranch hands. In the beginning, especially, most guests at dude ranches were well-bred, well-off easterners with the money and leisure to spend months away from home. They could have been summering in Newport or soaking up high culture on a European Grand Tour, but instead they helped round up cattle in Wyoming or urged a balky horse across a Montana mountainside. And they paid dearly for the privilege. ◆ The first dude ranch, Howard Eaton's, began almost by accident. Eaton was a young Pennsylvanian of good family who ventured out into the Dakotas in the 1870s. He was not alone. During the cattle boom of the 1870s and 1880s, the West attracted numbers of adventurous easterners – including Eaton's neighbor and friend, Teddy Roosevelt. But Eaton and many of these new ranchers quickly found themselves in a quandary. They were besieged by friends and relatives who wanted a taste of life in the Wild West. The code of western hospitality mandated that these interlopers be

For a taste of the real West, would-be cowboys eagerly mount a horse, learn to rope, or join a cattle drive.

City slickers enjoy a trail ride in Colorado's scenic San Juan Mountains. Some dude ranches offer activities such as fly-fishing, bird-watching, and hiking, but the main attraction remains horseback riding.

treated well. But that was mighty expensive: Eaton figured that over the course of one year he served 2,200 free meals. Out of desperation, Eaton decided to charge guests for their stays.

That decision proved to be Eaton's salvation. The blizzards of 1886–87 pushed many cattle ranchers into bankruptcy, but Eaton stayed solvent via the profit he earned from his guests. Indeed, dudes rather than cattle became the main focus of Eaton's ranch, and early in the 1900s he moved his operation to the Big Horn Mountains of Wyoming, more convenient for leading pack trips into Yellowstone National Park.

Charming and savvy, Howard Eaton proved an enormously successful publicist for this new phenomenon, the dude ranch. But there were larger societal reasons for its popularity as well. As cities in the East and Midwest grew more crowded and more industrialized, western ranch life was seen as an ideal antidote to the

Nostalgia reigns at ranches like this one (left) in the Hill Country of central Texas.

Accommodations range from log cabins (right) and bunkhouses to plush lodges more akin to fancy resorts.

strains of urban living. Meanwhile, railroads like the Southern and Union Pacific and the Great Northern had discovered that dude ranches could lure paying passengers on westbound trains. They promoted the ranches in their tourist brochures. Dude ranches began sprouting up all over the West, with particular concentrations in places like Jackson Hole, Wyoming, and, a bit later, the desert around Wickenburg, Arizona.

During the golden age of dude ranching, from about 1910 to World War II, guests would head west on the train to spend entire summers learning to rope and ride. The

dude ranch had something for the entire family. On the ranch, tired businessmen swapped boardroom pressures for bunkhouse pleasures. Children got to live the life they saw in Tom Mix or Gene Autry movies. Women, in particular, were seen to benefit from the regimen of the dude ranch. In more staid eastern resorts, women were left to endure social chitchat while their husbands played golf; out on the ranch, they could ride and hike and fish, just like the men.

Recipe for a Dude Ranch

Turning a working cattle ranch into a resort for visiting dudes was no easy matter. Ranchers had to acquire an understanding of how to coddle sometimes persnickety guests. Ranchers' wives had to learn how to cook for people with more discriminating palates than the average cowboy's. No rancher analyzed the challenges more keenly than did Strothers Burt, pioneer dude rancher in Jackson Hole, Wyoming. Calling the dude business "a very pleasant one and in other ways a very trying one," Burt added: "You have, you

Elements of style: Pendleton blankets and lodgepole pine furniture (left) lend a touch of rustic comfort.

see, upon your hands a number of people most of whom are in an entirely new and rather bewildering environment. You give them horses and teach them to ride, you beg and argue with them not to over-ride, you outfit them and send them out on pack trips, you flirt occasionally, if you have to, with some of the younger or, as you get older, youngish ones, and you try to prevent some of the still younger ones from breaking up discipline by flirting with your cowboys, you tell innumerable stories, so that at times your voice becomes hoarse and your mind wanders and you answer an infinite number of questions."

What were the ingredients of a successful dude ranch?

There was, of course, the horse – a dude ranch without horses was like a beach resort without the ocean. A good dude horse possessed a capable trot and gallop, and notably patient disposition. Some ranches began to breed their own horses to promote those qualities.

With the horse came the wrangler. Many a dude-ranch wrangler began his career as a working cowboy. Indeed, as cattle ranches consolidated, the dude ranch proved a refuge where a wrangler could still be paid for his cowboying skills. But other skills were required, too. A good dude-ranch wrangler had to be charming to the ladies, pals with the men, and a hero to the children. He needed a mix of rusticity and social graces. As one ranch manager said, "There is a real future here for a cowhand who can ride, play the guitar, and still smell nice." The duties could be arduous indeed, as one cowboy song laments: "I'm a tough, hard-boiled old cowhand with a weather-beaten hide,/But herdin' cows is nuthin' to teachin' dudes to ride./I can stand their hitoned langwidge and their hifalutin' foods,/But you bet your bottom dollar I am fed up on wranglin' dudes."

Defining a Dude

Above all, of course, a dude ranch required dudes. The term was controversial. To some the word *dude* was used to condemn the kind of

Campfire sing-alongs (left) make for friendly, folksy entertainment at the Double Diamond X in Cody, Wyoming.

Cowboy chili (right), a chuckwagon special, is typical of the simple but hearty fare served at dude ranches.

ming pools spreading alongside the stables. The Alisal in California's Santa Ynez Valley was, and is, a working cattle ranch. But proximity to Hollywood meant that a certain show-business glamour rubbed off on it – especially when guests like Clark Gable were in residence. Some ranches developed even narrower niches – with Nevada dude ranchers lassoing a particularly lucrative specialty. In an era when divorces were impossible to come by in much of the country, the state of Nevada permitted them to anyone who had established a six-week residency. That inspired the brainstorm of socially well-connected ranch owner Cornelius Vanderbilt, Jr., who operated two ranches near Reno. He designed a dude-ranch package divorce, six weeks for $795, including a pack of cigarettes a day and a bottle of liquor a week.

Ranch Experiences

Today, the dude ranch is going strong. Many of the classic ranches, including Eaton's in Wyoming, most venerable of all, are still thriving. There have been a few changes, of course. Few guests have the leisure to spend an entire summer away from work, so dude ranches have switched to week-long

eastern visitor who knew the West only through Hollywood movies. Two of those kind of dudes were described this way by one grizzled wrangler: "One wore lavender angora chaps, the other bright orange, and each sported a tremendous beaver sombrero and wore a gaudy scarf knotted jauntily about his throat."

Other dude ranchers maintained that the word *dude* was an affectionate nickname for honored guests. They also took pains to say that many an eastern dude could outride many a westerner. "For

some reason that completely eludes me," wrote Spike VanCleve, pioneering Montana dude rancher, "most westerners have the idea that a dude can't ride. Over the years I have seen a lot of guests at the ranch who will stack up right along with any horsehands in the West."

As the dude-ranch movement blossomed, regional variations developed. Traditionally the Rocky Mountain resorts were more rough and rustic, while Arizona dude ranches verged on the posh, with golf courses and swim-

packages. And some ranches have become even more plush, offering conference facilities and spa programs.

Dude-ranch vacations don't come cheap. A stay at a good ranch can cost a couple of thousand dollars per week or a family of four. How do you choose the right one? Two good sources of information are the Dude Ranchers Association in LaPorte, Colorado, and *Gene Kilgore's Ranch Vacations*.

Once you've made your selection and are saddling up for your first ride, you begin to understand that you haven't just embarked on any ordinary vacation. You're living a legend. You're going to start off your week a city slicker and end it a ridin', ropin' western hero. Horseback riding is still the main activity at most dude ranches. But you don't have to be an expert rider – in fact, you don't have to have ever climbed into a saddle at all. A good ranch, like Eaton's, will maintain a stable of horses suited to all levels of riding ability. It will also have an ample number of wranglers capable of instructing riders from novice to expert.

Most ranches offer numerous daily trail rides; many also offer longer two- or three-day horse-packing trips for guests who really

want to gallop far from the madding crowd. While guests at the earliest ranches regularly herded dogies, rode fences, and performed other ranch chores, such work is harder to come by these days. But some ranches still let guests who are good riders participate in the working life of the ranch – a few, like Hunewill's Circle H in California's Eastern Sierra, even hold cattle drives which qualified guests can join.

Although horses still reign over the dude ranch, many ranches have branched out to offer other activities. The growing popularity of fly-fishing in the West has inspired some ranches – especially those along trout-rich streams in Montana, Wyoming, and Colorado – to offer instruction in the sport. Other outfits offer courses in bird-watching, photography, even paleontology. The TA Ranch in Buffalo, Wyoming – itself a historic site, having played a big part in the famed Johnson County range war – sponsors programs in western history. And in recent years, many ranches have taken pains to beef up their children's activities.

Montana's Mountain Sky Guest Ranch offers a week-long children's program that includes riding and crafts; California's Alisal likewise works hard to make sure that young buckaroos are happy, with special campfire and riding programs.

As for amenities, those can vary greatly. Some good old-time ranches maintain a simple but comfortable rusticity. That means cozy cabins grouped along a stream, and grub that tends towards the western classics: barbecued steak, beans, corn on the cob. But many Arizona dude ranches long ago bloomed into full-service resorts, with tennis courts, golf courses, and cocktails by the pool. And some of the newest Rocky Mountain ranches – places like the Home Ranch, near Steamboat Springs, Colorado – are downright luxurious, with guest suites that might have been decorated by Ralph Lauren, and the kind of haute cuisine you'd expect to savor in Beverly Hills or Manhattan – and we don't mean Manhattan, Montana.

Paint ponies (right), known for their calm disposition and flashy colors, are a popular dude horse.

◆

Wild West Destinations

◆

From pueblos to missions, revived gold camps to lonely battlegrounds, epic scenery to wind-blown ghost towns, landscape and history intertwine in the Old West.

San Antonio and Fort Worth

Texas

CHAPTER 8

t's the silence you notice first. A lingering silence, despite the crowds in the stone chapel of the **Alamo**. Everyday noises float up from bustling downtown **San Antonio**: a chaotic symphony of car horns, the perpetual thrum of traffic, a radio tuned to an AM station blaring scratchy mariachi music. But beyond the intricately carved entryway to this sanctuary, there is only the shuffle of feet and the occasional whisper disturbing a peace that has lasted more than a century. It's a place that seems twice consecrated: first by God and now by humans.   ◆   The Battle of the Alamo had all the elements one associates with Texas: big characters and big dreams fueled by guns and glory and heroic exploits – a romantic combination, no matter how historians dissect the tale.   ◆   Inside this crumbling Spanish mission in the late winter of 1836, an ailing Jim Bowie and **A place of big dreams and big** fellow frontiersman Davy Crockett, **country, the Lone Star State** acting commander William Barrett Travis, and **attracted early Spanish** their cobbled-together band of raggle- **missionaries, frontier fighters,** taggle Texas volunteers faced down absentee **and cattle barons.** landlord Mexico – and made it into the history books. Vastly outnumbered by General Santa Anna's troops, the 180 or so would-be heroes, accompanied by frightened women and children, fought with guns and then went hand to hand, meeting bayonets with bowie knives and tomahawks, inflicting devastating casualties on Santa Anna's men, before being martyred to their cause. It's the rare Texan who can hear the rallying cry "Remember the Alamo!" without feeling the prick of pride in his countrymen.

Mission Nuestra Señora de la Purísima Concepción (left), established by the Spanish in San Antonio in 1731, is called the "twin of the Alamo."

Preceding Pages: Lightning illuminates the sky above the Mittens in Monument Valley, Arizona.

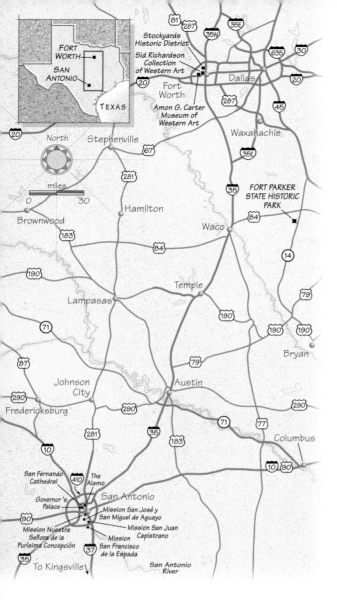

Norte during the colonial era. The Spanish hoped to convert the Indians to Catholicism and transform them into *gente de razon*, "people of reason," who would farm and be productive taxpayers. Between 1690 and 1792 they founded more than two dozen Franciscan missions throughout Texas, the largest concentration of which may be found along the tree-lined San Antonio River.

The trees lining the San Antonio River yielded a nickname, the "Alamo" (cottonwood), for **Mission San Antonio de Valero**, the first of the missions. The Alamo was originally built downstream in 1718, then moved upriver to its present location in the 1720s, a quarter-mile from the plazas where the Governor's Palace and San Fernando Cathedral and the homes and businesses of early San Antonio sprang up. The renovated 1744 chapel and the adjoining *convento* (now known as the Long Barracks Museum) are the Alamo's only two surviving buildings. The DRT Research Library, the Museum/Souvenir Shop, and other structures were added by the Daughters of the Republic of Texas, which bought the dilapidated mission in 1903. The 1936 Alamo Cenotaph, inscribed with the names of the fallen heroes, dominates the busy chapel plaza. It is now known that the plaza contains the mass grave of numerous missionized Indians, sparking debate over how best to respect the dead in the face of modern tourism.

Visitors can follow a self-guided tour or join a 30-minute guided tour of the old mission. A diorama of the battle, a collection of early guns, and Sam Houston memorabilia are on display in the **Museum/Souvenir Shop**, along with "Remember the Alamo" bumper stickers, coonskin hats, and other kitschy sales items. The **Long Barracks Museum** also has battle exhibits and automated slide shows, which may play less well with the kids than the IMAX film *Alamo: The Price of Freedom*, an

Early Spanish Stronghold

San Antonio, the Cradle of Texas Liberty, retains much of the charm of its colorful past: a lovely river setting; a lively blend of Hispanic and Anglo cultures resonating through its food and music; and plenty of larger-than-life characters who have left their mark on this part of Texas.

When the Alamo fell, San Antonio was already an old settlement. Founded by Spanish colonists in 1718 as a mission center and presidio and originally christened San Antonio de Bejar, San Antonio became the headquarters for Spanish operations in El

extravaganza of oversized sight and sound at the six-story IMAX Theater across the street. Shows go on every 45 minutes.

San Antonio's Mission Trail

A few miles south of the Alamo is San Antonio's second mission, **San José y San Miguel de Aguayo**, founded in 1720. Unlike its more famous neighbor, this mission has been entirely restored, and visitors can stroll through several acres of single-story Indian apartments, workshops, fortified gates and towers, an impressive two-story cloister archway, and a large granary supported by flying buttresses. The flour mill, built in 1790, was the first in Texas. The photogenic chapel of San Antonio's "Queen of Missions" features an ornate facade, a domed roof, and the intricately sculpted *Rosa's Window*.

Between San José and the Alamo lies **Mission Nuestra Señora de la Purísima Concepción**, founded in 1731 and completed in 1755. Its massive chapel is the oldest unrestored stone church in the United States. Mission Concepción is called "the twin of the Alamo" because of the close resemblance of the chapel facade to the original appearance of the Alamo chapel. Both chapels had a dome (the Alamo dome was structurally unsound and collapsed), and Concepción has two bell towers. It was near here, on November 26, 1835, that Jim Bowie led a party of Texans in a murderous attack on a Mexican mule train.

Known as the "Grass Fight," the bloody battle earned its nickname when the Texan scouts discovered that the mule train they thought was carrying a payroll for the Mexican garrison in San Antonio was, in fact, hauling freshly cut grass for the garrison's starving cavalry horses.

Two other missions were built in the same year as Concepción: **Mission San Juan Capistrano** and **Mission San Francisco de la Espada**. Capistrano and Espada, like San José, still hold services open to the public. Not far from Espada are the remains of an extensive irrigation system, including an arched aqueduct and a dam on the San Antonio River. The river, lovely today, was not so well cared for during the early years of colonization and eventually became an unsightly sewer. In recent decades, however,

A memorial at Milam Park (left) in San Antonio commemorates the freedom fighters whose martyrdom at the Alamo sparked the Texas Revolution.

River Walk, or Paseo del Rio (right), is lined with shops, galleries, and restaurants.

this river that sustained generations of San Antonio pioneers has been restored as a delightful part of the modern city and is now one of San Antonio's premier attractions. Located one level below teeming city streets, **River Walk** takes in several miles of flowing water and tropical foliage, making it a godsend during the dog days of summer. Sidewalk cafes, gift shops, cabarets, hotels, and riverboats sit elegantly, and invitingly, side by side.

Rough Rider Hangout

In 1772, with as many as 200 Indians living and working at each mission, Spanish officials designated San Antonio the Texas seat of government and constructed a 10-room, L-shaped adobe **Governor's Palace** that has today been fully restored and furnished. Moses Austin came here in 1820 to obtain a colonization grant for Anglo settlers, and several years later Jim Bowie moved in when he married the governor's oldest daughter, Ursula de Veramendi. The enterprising Bowie engaged in a variety of land and business speculations with his father-in-law, the state's most influential official, and during the same period fathered two children. Tragically, an 1833 cholera epidemic killed Bowie's young wife, children, and both parents-in-law. Bowie became a drunk and, spoiling for a fight, seems to have set into motion the tragic events at the Alamo by refusing to follow orders to blow it up before Mexican troops reached San Antonio.

A block from the Governor's Palace is **San Fernando Cathedral**, constructed in 1738. One of San Antonio's oldest and most historic structures, San Fernando is the last resting place for the defenders of the Alamo, whose ashes repose in a large container inside the vast, cool cathedral.

Across the street from the Alamo is the historic **Menger Hotel**, now a luxury hotel. The oldest section of the Menger was constructed in 1859. Be sure to drop by the quaint Teddy Roosevelt Bar. The future president and his colorful Rough Riders drilled in San Antonio, and Roosevelt and his officers made the Menger their headquarters. Roosevelt rode off to war on a horse named

The King Ranch

Texas cowboys (opposite, top) were the original American buckaroos.

Texas longhorns (below), introduced by the Spanish, are adapted to desert conditions but have tough hides, stringy meat, and bad tempers.

"Buy land and never sell" was the single-minded principle pursued by cattle baron Richard King. Over three decades, he bought more than a million acres of Texas rangeland in a rugged region originally known as the Wild Horse Desert, and built his fabled King Ranch, headquartered at Kingsville, about 130 miles southeast of San Antonio. The King Ranch was the foundation of the western cattle industry, developing, among other contributions, the first American breed of cattle and the quarter horse.

King began purchasing land along Santa Gertrudis Creek in 1852. The cattle baron stocked his growing ranch with cattle from Mexico and also brought in Kineños, skilled vaqueros and their families, who provided the ranch with generations of loyal employees. The big frame house built by King burned in 1912 and was replaced by a striking 25-room mansion that still commands the site. A popular bus tour of the ranch leaves from the King Ranch Museum near Kingsville.

Other sites in Texas chronicle the rich heritage of western ranching. The largest ranch ever under fence, the three-million-acre XIT, was headquartered in Channing, where the red-brick office building has been handsomely restored. The Pitchfork Ranch maintains a museum west of Guthrie, and the Ranching Heritage Center in Lubbock preserves more than 30 historic structures.

"Texas." Dozens of photos of the Rough Riders line the bar's dark wood paneling. Another notable feature of the old section of the Menger is the lavish King Ranch Suite, once used by members of the famous ranching family and now open to the public.

Along the Chisholm Trail

The King Ranch and many smaller outfits trailed longhorns in vast numbers from the San Antonio area. The most famous route pointed toward Kansas from San Antonio through **Waco**, which was known as "Six-Shooter Junction" during its heyday as a stopover on the **Chisholm Trail**. In 1870 a toll bridge was built across the Brazos River to accommodate cattle herds and other traffic. Constructed by the Roebling Company of New York City, the 475-foot span was the longest suspension bridge in the world – until the Roeblings built the Brooklyn Bridge a few years later. Today Waco's Old Suspension Bridge is the center of a charming city park.

The world's most famous law enforcement body, the Texas Rangers, played a prominent role on the frontier, from developing the Colt revolver to battling war parties to halting the depredations of such outlaws as Sam Bass and Wes Hardin. The **Texas Ranger Hall of Fame** in Waco offers a superb gun collection, eye-catching exhibits, an excellent library, and a film that depicts the epic story of the Rangers. During an 1860 raid on a Comanche encampment, Texas Rangers rescued Cynthia Ann Parker, who had been abducted by a war party during a famous attack on what is now **Fort Parker State Historical Park**, east of Waco. The beautifully

The lariat (right), from the Spanish *la reata*, is used to rope cattle and requires a high level of skill.

Cowpunchers working a round-up in 1890 (opposite, bottom) "whoop it up" for a photographer.

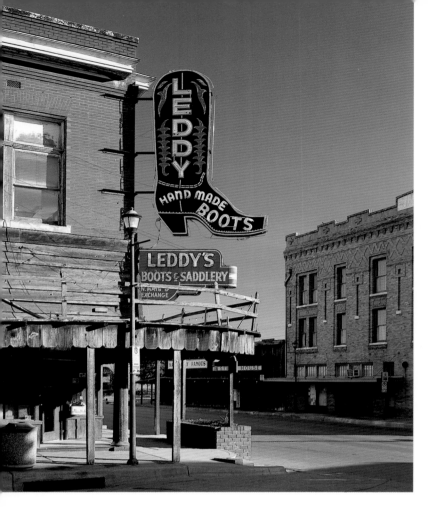

Antonio. Farmers and ranchers supplied the forts with food and grain and horses, and Fort Worth grew into a thriving settlement. The parade ground of the 1849 military post is defined by the modern courthouse square. The army soon left, and after the Civil War, Fort Worth became a lively stopover on the Chisholm Trail. The frontier cowtown proudly boasted the nickname "Panther City," because a Dallas newspaper claimed that Fort Worth's rowdy Main Street was the "noonday lair of the panther." Cowboys and gunfighters roistered through the streets of Fort Worth, and as late as the turn of the century, the red-light district, "Hell's Half-Acre," was visited by such western outlaws as Butch Cassidy, the Sundance Kid, and other members of their Wild Bunch.

A marker on Main Street designates the site of one of the West's most famous gunfights, the shooting gallery where gambler Luke Short killed former city marshal Longhair Jim Courtright on February 8, 1887. Both men were deadly shooters, but Courtright took the initiative by jamming a six-gun into Short's stomach. When Short, a dapper dresser, bent over, his long watch chain caught in the hammer of Courtright's gun. Short produced his own revolver from his right pants pocket, specially tailored with soft leather so that his outfit would not be

reconstructed log fort, erected in 1834 by the Parker clan and reinforced with sturdy blockhouses, a recessed double gate, and firing platforms with loopholes, fell to Comanches one day in 1836 when the gates were accidentally left open. Nine years old when she was abducted, Cynthia Ann Parker eventually became the wife of Chief Peta Nocona and bore three children, including the last great Comanche chief, Quanah Parker, before she and one of her children were reluctantly "rescued." She never got over being separated from her beloved Comanche family and, grief-stricken, died of influenza in 1870.

Cowtown Outlaws and Gunfighters

After Texas joined the Union in 1846, the U.S. Army built more than 30 military outposts across the Lone Star State. One of the first was **Fort Worth**, 240 miles north of San

spoiled by an unseemly gunbelt. Short's first shot shattered Courtright's pistol, then Longhair Jim was drilled three times. This classic shootout is re-enacted each year at 7 P.M. on February 8.

Both Courtright and Short, and many of Fort Worth's most noted citizens, are interred in the grassy, rolling hills of **Oakwood Cemetery**, the "Westminster Abbey of Fort Worth," across the Trinity River from downtown. The West's premier assassin, Killin' Jim Miller, a longtime resident of Fort Worth, also is buried at Oakwood. No other western cemetery provides final rest for three gunfighters of the front rank.

Another view of the West can be seen in the matchless collections of paintings and bronzes by Charles Russell, Frederic Remington, and other western artists at the **Amon G. Carter Museum of Western Art** and downtown at the **Sid Richardson Collection of Western Art**. Decades ago, Fort Worth had the opportunity to acquire a cache of Russell's art, and far more works of the "Cowboy Artist" are displayed in Fort Worth than in his beloved Montana (to the chagrin of Montanans). Russell's *In Without Knocking*, for example, is on exhibit at the Amon Carter; so is Remington's *A Dash for*

the Timber and his bronze, *The Bronco Buster*. Among the many treasures at the Sid Richardson Collection are Remington's *The Cow Puncher* and *Among the Led Horses* and Russell masterpieces such as *Buffalo Hunt* and *When Blackfeet and Sioux Meet*.

The fullest flavor of "Cowtown," as Fort Worth is still proudly known, can be found north of downtown in the **Stockyards Historic District**. Renovated western-style shops and restaurants are fronted on old-fashioned boardwalks. A nine-mile antique railroad heads out from Stockyards Station. The handsome old **Livestock Exchange Building** features a cowboy museum, and the **Stockyards Hotel** offers quality accommodations. The Stockyards District is at its best each September during Pioneer Days, with such lively activities as western cook-offs, hay-hauling contests, trail rides, and parades – just the place to let off steam and hoot and holler after the long drive from San Antonio.

TRAVEL TIPS

DETAILS

When to Go

Spring and fall are warm and pleasant; summer can be uncomfortably hot. Winter is mild, with temperatures in the 40s and low 50s.

How to Get There

Commercial airlines serve San Antonio and Dallas-Fort Worth International Airports.

Getting Around

You can walk around downtown historic districts, but you'll need a car to get into the surrounding area; rentals are available at the airports.

INFORMATION

Fort Worth Convention and Visitors Bureau

415 Throckmorton Street; Fort Worth, TX 76102; tel: 800-433-5747 or 817-336-8791.

San Antonio Convention and Visitors Bureau

203 South St. Mary's Street, P.O. Box 2277; San Antonio, TX 78205; tel: 800-447-3372 or 210-207-8700.

LODGING

PRICE GUIDE – double occupancy

$ = up to $49 $$ = $50–$99
$$$ = $100–$149 $$$$ = $150+

Fairmount Hotel

401 South Alamo Street; San Antonio, TX 78205; tel: 800-996-3426 or 210-224-8800.

Built in 1906, this brick Victorian house is completely renovated in period style. Luxurious suites and double rooms are available, all with private bath, some with balcony. A popular restaurant specializes in Southwestern food. $$$$

Menger Hotel

204 Alamo Plaza; San Antonio, TX 78205; tel: 800-345-9285 or 210-223-4361.

This 350-room hotel across from the Alamo was built in 1859 and has an impressive history. Famous lodgers have included Sam Houston, Robert E. Lee, and Ulysses S. Grant; Theodore Roosevelt recruited his Rough Riders in the bar. Two restaurants, a health club, and a sauna are on the premises. $$$

Running R Ranch

Route 1, Box 590; Bandera, TX 78003; tel: 830-796-3984.

This dude ranch, adjacent to the 5,700-acre Hill Country State Natural Area, offers 13 efficiency cabins, each with private bath, cedar furniture, and Western decor. Horseback riding, hayrides, and a swimming pool are available. $$$–$$$$

St. Anthony Hotel

300 East Travis Street; San Antonio, TX 78205; tel: 800-338-1338 or 512-227-4392.

Built in 1909, this elegant landmark hotel has more than 350 rooms, with period furniture, oriental rugs, and private baths. A restaurant, nightclub, health club, and swimming pool are on the premises. $$$

Stockyards Hotel

109 East Exchange Avenue; Fort Worth, TX 76106; tel: 800-423-8471 or 817-625-6427.

Built in 1907 and renovated in 1983, this hotel offers more than 50 rooms with Old West ambience. It's set in the Stockyards Historic District and has a restaurant and bar. $$–$$$

TOURS & OUTFITTERS

Mission City Tours

1319 Vista del Monte; San Antonio, TX 78216; tel: 210-493-2454.

Bus tours of San Antonio's Spanish missions.

San Antonio City Tours

217 Alamo Plaza; San Antonio, TX 78216; tel: 210-212-5395.

Customized walking tours explore historic downtown San Antonio.

MUSEUMS

Amon G. Carter Museum of Western Art

3501 Camp Bowie Boulevard; Fort Worth, TX 76107; tel: 817-738-1933.

The museum exhibits a large collection of Western masterpieces, with an emphasis on the paintings and sculptures of Charles M. Russell and Frederic Remington.

King Ranch Museum

405 North 6th Street, P.O. Box 1090; Kingsville, TX 78363; tel: 512-595-1881.

This museum interprets the 19th-century ranch of cattle baron Richard King, whose many achievements include the development of the first American quarter horse.

National Cowgirl Hall of Fame and Western Heritage Center

111 West 4th, Suite 300; Fort Worth, TX 76102; tel: 817-336-4475.

Exhibits trace the history of the women of the West.

Sid Richardson Collection of Western Art

309 Main Street; Fort Worth, TX 76102; tel: 817-332-6554.

Works by Remington and Russell are the big attractions here. Highlights include Remington's *The Cow Puncher* and *Among the Led Horses*, and Russell's *Buffalo Hunt* and *When Blackfeet and Sioux Meet*.

Stockyards Museum

131 East Exchange Avenue, Suite 110; Fort Worth, TX 76106; tel: 817-625-5087.

Fort Worth's cowtown history is traced in an Old West setting.

Texas Ranger Hall of Fame and Museum

Fort Fisher Park, P.O. Box 2570; Waco, TX 76702; tel: 254-750-8631.

This museum features a superb gun collection, eye-catching exhibits, an excellent library, and a film that depicts the epic story of the Rangers.

PARKS

Mission San Antonio de Valero (The Alamo)

300 Alamo Place; San Antonio, TX 78205; tel: 210-225-1391 or 210-207-6748.

A renovated chapel and adjoining *convento* (now known as the Long Barracks Museum) are all that remain of the 18th-century mission where Davy Crockett, Jim Bowie, and a band of Texas volunteers were overrun by Mexican soldiers.

Old Fort Parker State Historical Park

c/o City of Groesbeck, RR 3, Box 746; Groesbeck, TX 76642; tel: 254-729-5253.

The park features a reconstructed log fort originally built in 1834 and attacked by Comanches in 1836.

San Antonio Missions National Historical Park

2202 Roosevelt Road; San Antonio, TX 78210; tel: 210-534-8833.

The park preserves a chain of Spanish missions built in the 18th century along the San Antonio River.

Excursions

Hill Country

Fredericksburg Convention and Visitors Bureau; 106 North Adams Street; Fredericksburg, TX 78624; tel: 830-997-6523.

German immigrants were the first white settlers in this region of gentle hills, rocky soil, and bountiful wildflowers north of San Antonio. Their influence is still evident in the architecture of Fredericksburg, where the Pioneer Museum illustrates frontier life. The Lyndon B. Johnson National Historical Site preserves the birthplace and boyhood home of the 36th president as well as a working historical farm and a collection of buildings from the 19th and early 20th centuries. Enchanted Rock, a dome of pink granite held sacred by the Comanche, is a popular camping and hiking area. Jack Hays, a famous Texas Ranger, battled Comanches at the summit in 1841. The little town of Bandera, about 35 miles from San Antonio, is known for its dude ranches.

Oklahoma City

Oklahoma City Convention and Visitors Bureau; 123 Park Avenue; Oklahoma City, OK 73102; tel: 800-447-2698 or 405-297-8912.

Aficionados of cowboy culture shouldn't miss the superb National Cowboy Hall of Fame, a thorough exploration of America's most beloved folk hero. Elsewhere in town, you can buy a Stetson and other cowboy gear at Stockyard City, the historic cattle-trading district, or get a taste of pioneer life at the 10-acre Harn Homestead and 1889er Museum. The Oklahoma Territorial Museum in nearby Guthrie, an 1889 land-rush settlement, chronicles the town's brief stint as the territorial capital.

Tulsa

Tulsa Convention and Visitors Bureau, 616 South Boston Street; Tulsa, OK 74119; tel: 800-558-3311 or 918-585-1201.

Tulsa's Gilcrease Museum houses one of the premier collections of Western art and artifacts in the country. About three miles northeast is Oologah, birthplace of Will Rogers, the famed American humorist and homespun philosopher. Rogers grew up in ranching country shared with the Cherokee Nation and was himself part Cherokee. He kept cattle at the Dog Iron Ranch, a 60,000-acre spread that's now a state historic site, and is buried at the Will Rogers Memorial in nearby Claremore.

West Texas

CHAPTER **9**

The centuries-old path to the **Rio Grande** is well worn, but there's no one else walking it this morning in late autumn. Around a corner, the river comes into view, a lone boatman waiting on the other side. With a few strong strokes, he is across the water, ready to accept his passenger and a few dollars for his trouble. A minute later, they're back on the landing at the Chihuahuan village of **Santa Elena** – one short row for this Mexican entrepreneur, a giant leap for a traveler eager to leave the pack behind. ◆ At most places along the U.S.–Mexico border, traffic is tightly controlled through official crossings. But here in the backcountry of and around **Big Bend National Park**, where the nearest formal border crossing is more than 50 miles west at Presidio, Texas, residents and visitors simply ford the Rio Grande at the small Mexican villages of **Paso Lajitas, Boquillas del Carmen**, and **Santa Elena**. Here, there is a sense that you're neither in the United States nor in Mexico, but in a thinly populated *frontera* that's really – as Texas tourism slogans of a few years back used to insist – a whole 'nother country. In many ways, this border vibe extends clear across the West Texas outback, from the Rio Grande up the Pecos and into the panhandle. ◆ When the 16th-century Spaniards passed through this area en route to establishing missions farther west, they called it "El Despoblado," the place without people. The name is still apt today; there are fewer than 9,000 people in Brewster County, Texas, an area larger than Maryland and Delaware put together. It's never been an easy place to live. Scattered cultures have existed near the river or in the Chisos Mountains, and the Comanches used the area as a route into

> **"The place without people" has one of the Lone Star State's best-preserved frontier forts and is the birthplace of rodeo.**

The Rio Grande flows through Santa Elena Canyon in Texas' Big Bend National Park, which protects 1,200 square miles of desert terrain on the U.S.–Mexico border.

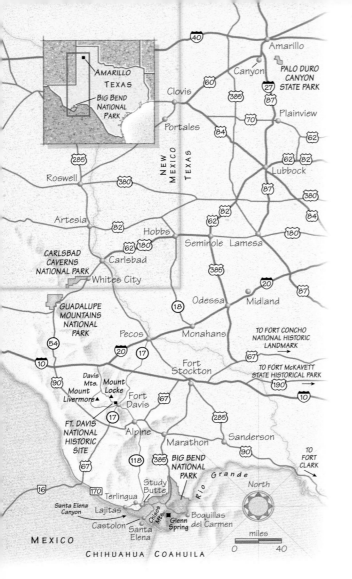

spring, **Terlingua** and its neighbors **Study Butte** and **Lajitas** come alive as the base camps for Big Bend adventure. (Summer, with its blazing heat, draws far fewer visitors.) Outfitters guide trips and rent gear for horseback riding into the **High Chisos**, mountain biking across the **Chihuahuan Desert**, and river excursions down the **Rio Grande** – the highlight for most visitors. Don't leave without spending at least a day floating through **Santa Elena Canyon**, where light and shadow do their subtle *pas de deu.* before hushed boaters, or **Colorado Canyon** where thrilling rapids are the rule.

Big Bend National Park itself has about 150 miles of hiking trails, including several short paths that focus on the past. The two-mile round-trip **Hot Springs Historic Walk** is a good choice, leading to the homestead and health resort pioneered by J. O. Langford in 1909. Modern hikers can still see what's left of the community and soak in the same hot springs Langford touted as "the fountain that Ponce de Leon failed to find." Other short walks may be taken at the all-but-abandoned communities of **Castolon** and **Glenn Spring**, both of which saw action as cavalry encampments during the days of Pancho Villa's border raids around 1916.

From the Big Bend area, all roads lead to history and adventure. Farm-to-Market (FM) Road 170, the River Road west of Terlingua, often turns up on lists of the most scenic drives in the United States. U.S. Highway 38. heads north for **Marathon** and the **Gage Hotel**, built in 1927 and still going strong as one of Texas's finest historical lodgings. An Highway 118 travels north from **Study Butte** through **Alpine** on to **Fort Davis**, a major outpost in Texas frontier history.

Fortified Outpost

On the grounds of **Fort Davis National Historic Site**, bugle calls sound across the parade grounds, echoing off the slopes of **Sleeping Lion Mountain**. The fort went into business in 1854 among the first of the line of garrisons placed along the San Antonio–El Paso Road. For the

Mexico, but the harsh environment dissuaded other settlers until the late 19th century and the cinnabar boom. Cinnabar, favored by Indians for face paint and rock art, is the principal ore for mercury. The cinnabar mining camps at **Terlingua** and **Study Butte** were among the world's most productive during their early 20th-century heyday. But when the boom ended, prospectors found little other reason to stick around. The area's population, once about 2,000, dwindled into the dozens; some maps even call Terlingua a ghost town.

Don't believe it. Fall, winter, and

rst decade, troops stationed at 'ort Davis waged a mostly uphill attle against the Indian depreda- ions they'd been dispatched to nd. The Civil War compounded ifficulties; although Confederate roops occupied the post for about year in 1861–62, they were evac- ated following a failed campaign nto New Mexico. The Apaches acked the fort, which sat empty for five ears. But in 1867, Lt. Col. Wesley Merritt, a Civil War cavalry commander, returned to eclaim the fort site. With him, he brought our units of the 9th U.S. Cavalry, the famous buffalo soldiers" comprised of newly freed African-American slaves. They rebuilt Fort Davis and fought numerous hard battles in he Apache wars of the 1880s, including the inal campaign against Geronimo.

The fort is equally notable as a launch ad into one of the most beautiful regions n Texas, the **Davis Mountains**. First-time isitors who think of West Texas as uninter- upted desert are stunned to see this soaring ange. Fort Davis itself sits at 5,050 feet bove sea level; from here, the elevation limbs more than 1,700 feet to **Mount Locke**, ome of the University of Texas' famed

An artist (left) works from his palette in Terlingua, Texas.

Desert scorpion (opposite, bottom): Folks in West Texas say that everything in Big Bend "sticks, stings, or bites."

Fort Davis (below) was established in 1854 to protect travelers from hostile Indians; it's one of the best-preserved forts in Texas.

McDonald Observatory and the highest point on any Texas highway, and on to 8,378 feet at **Mount Livermore**.

From Fort Davis, Highway 17 winds a scenic 39 miles to Interstate 10. From here, fans of frontier military history may want to drive east to **Fort Stockton** (though the preservation there isn't nearly as extensive as that at Fort Davis); others will probably opt to continue – after a brief jog eastward on the interstate – up Highway 17 to **Pecos**. If ever a town's name conjured up thoughts of the Wild West, Pecos is the place. Although it's hardly a tourist hotbed, Pecos has plenty to offer travelers interested in western lore. It was here, for example, that the sport of rodeo probably got its start back in 1883, and where it's still going strong today. The town also is home to the terrific

West of the Pecos Museum, a former saloon and hotel that now houses more than 50 rooms of exhibits, plus several outbuildings, including a replica of Judge Roy Bean's Jersey Lily Saloon. (The real thing is down in Langtry, Texas, on the Rio Grande.) Bean, who declared himself "the Law West of the Pecos," was among the most colorful characters Texas has ever seen. His saloon was his courthouse, his six-shooter his gavel. "I'm fining you $45 and a round of drinks for the jury, and that's my ruling!" was a typical Bean sentence.

From Pecos, it's a long way – more than 200 miles – to the next major attraction, but that's West Texas for you; the region covers two time zones, seven degrees of longitude, and eight degrees of latitude. East of Pecos, the **Odessa-Midland** area is worth a stop for quick looks at the **Presidential Museum** and the **Permian Basin Petroleum Museum**. The former has interesting exhibits on every U.S. presidential campaign; the latter offers a comprehensive look at West Texas's most important industry. Then it's north to the South Plains of Texas and Lubbock.

Texas' Grand Canyon

Lubbock is best known as the hometown of rock 'n' roll legend Buddy Holly and of Texas Tech University, one of the state's biggest colleges. The Tech campus has many high points, including the **Ranching Heritage Center**, an indoor-outdoor museum dedicated to exploring everyday ranch life on the frontier. More than 30 ranch buildings, most at least a century old and from many architectural styles, have been preserved here, along with other Old West artifacts.

Another outstanding West Texas institution, the **Panhandle–Plains Historical Museum**, can be found in **Canyon**, a small college town south of **Amarillo**. Plenty of people think this is the best history museum in all of Texas; its scope and depth make it a Texas counterpart to the Buffalo Bill Historical Center in Cody, Wyoming. The Panhandle-Plains facility has all the goodies you might expect in a Texas museum, including thorough exhibits on petroleum, paleontology, geology and western heritage. But it also harbors many unexpected treasures, particularly in its art collection, which features everything from Chinese antiquities to works by Georgia O'Keeffe, who once was on the faculty at

Buffalo Soldiers

Cactus (opposite, top) blooms in spring in the Chihuahuan Desert.

Windmills (opposite, bottom), used to pump groundwater to the surface, are a common sight on the treeless plains of northwest Texas.

Black soldiers, like these members of the 10th Cavalry (below), were assigned to some of the toughest posts in the West.

African-Americans made their mark on the West in many ways: as cowboys, as homesteaders, and as miners. But no chapter in black frontier history seems quite as compelling as the story of the troops sent West in the 1870s.

After the Civil War, the military needed all the help it could get preserving order in the West. So Congress created six new regiments – two cavalry units and four infantry corps – to get the job done. Although commanded by white officers, these regiments were filled by black men, many of them newly freed slaves. The Comanches admired their new adversaries. The soldiers' black hair, dark skin, and sheer fortitude reminded the Indians of bison, and they called them "buffalo soldiers." The black troops accepted the nickname as a badge of honor, even adding the animal's likeness to their regimental coat of arms.

Historians frequently note the irony that long-oppressed blacks were used to help subdue Native Americans, another marginalized population. By most accounts, the buffalo soldiers had the worst assignments in the West, but they served without complaint. Frederic Remington, who spent time on patrol with one black unit, wrote: "They may be tired and they may be hungry, but they do not see fit to augment their misery by finding fault with everybody or everything. In the particular, they are charming men with whom to serve."

The buffalo soldiers' story is well told throughout West Texas. Fort Davis, Fort Concho, Fort McKavett, Fort Stockton, and Fort Clark all include interpretation on the black troops' contributions. The most poignant tale may well belong to 2nd Lt. Henry Ossian Flipper, the first African-American graduate of West Point. Flipper was sent to Fort Davis to serve as acting commissary of subsistence, only to be accused of embezzling government funds and court-martialed. The Army found Flipper innocent, but he was still booted out of the military with a dishonorable discharge. Nearly 100 years later – and 36 years after his death in 1940 – the Army reviewed the trial transcripts and changed Flipper's discharge status to honorable.

From Canyon, head east to **Palo Duro Canyon State Park**, one of the best-known and most popular parks in Texas. Palo Duro is the second-largest chasm in the United States, 120 miles long by five miles wide, its dimensions bested only by the Grand Canyon. Historically, too, Palo Duro looms large: Coronado probably traveled through the area in 1541; the park was the site of fierce battles between Comanche and Kiowa warriors and the U.S. Army in 1874; and pioneer rancher Charles Goodnight started running cattle here in 1876. Modern visitors are drawn to Palo Duro Canyon by a gala outdoor musical, *Texas*, held nightly except Sunday in the summer.

There's no question that the best way to wind down a West Texas sojourn is at sunset, either from astride a horse or around an old-time cowboy campfire. The Goodnight Stables at Palo Duro Canyon State Park can saddle you up for the former; for the latter, try Cowboy Evening, which features a horse-drawn wagon ride to a more remote part of the canyon rim, followed by a rib-sticking frontier repast. Either way, take time to memorize the sky as the sun layers the horizon in hues of red, orange, gold, and purple. Linger a while to see those famous stars, big and bright, deep in the heart of Texas. Listen to the coyotes' cries and the breeze rustling through the mesquite and sagebrush, then promise yourself that you will return.

TRAVEL TIPS

DETAILS

When to Go

Searing summer heat makes fall, winter, and spring the best times to visit West Texas. Summer temperatures soar over 100°F at lower elevations. Winter temperatures range from 30° to 65°F, with occasional snowfall.

How to Get There

Commercial airlines serve El Paso International, Midland International, Lubbock International, and Amarillo International Airports.

Getting Around

You'll need a car to traverse the region's vast, lonely distances. Services are few and far between in some areas, so pack extra food, water, clothing, and other supplies.

INFORMATION

Texas Tourism

P.O. Box 12728; Austin, TX 78711; tel: 800-888-8839.

Texas Parks

4200 Smith School Road; Austin, TX 78744; tel: 800-792-1112 or 512-389-4800.

LODGING

PRICE GUIDE – double occupancy

$ = up to $49	$$ = $50–$99
$$$ = $100–$149	$$$$ = $150+

Chisos Mountain Lodge

Basin Rural Station; Big Bend National Park, TX 79834; tel: 915-477-2291.

Big Bend National Park's only accommodations, situated in the Chisos Basin, offers 72 basic rooms, including six popular stone cottages. A restaurant offers not only the lone dining experience in the park, but spectacular views. Reservations are a must. $$

Gage Hotel

P.O. Box 46; Marathon, TX 79842; tel: 800-884-4243 or 915-386-4205.

This historic hotel's public areas are decorated with cowboy gear and Southwestern art and artifacts. Built in 1928 by a successful rancher, the hotel offers rooms furnished with handcrafted wood-and-leather antiques; some rooms have shared baths. $$–$$$

Hotel Limpia

P.O. Box 1341; Fort Davis, TX 79734; tel: 800-662-5517 or 915-426-3237.

This classic small-town Texas hotel is set on the town square and offers rustic comfort at moderate prices. The hotel dining room and saloon offer a lively contrast to the quiet guest quarters. $$–$$$$

Indian Lodge

P.O. Box 1458: Fort Davis, TX 79734; tel: 915-426-3254.

This adobe lodge in Davis Mountains State Park is a popular Texas getaway. The Civilian Conservation Corps built the main lodge and much of the furniture in the 1930s. Reservations are essential. $$

Lajitas on the Rio Grande Resort

HC 70, Box 400; Terlingua, TX 79852; tel: 800-944-9907 or 915-424-3471.

About 40 miles west of Big Bend National Park, this resort offers a variety of accommodations, all with private baths. Hotel rooms, condominiums, and two- to three-bedroom houses are available. A restaurant, saloon, golf course, trading post, and several shops are on the premises. $$

Prude Guest Ranch

P.O. Box 1431; Fort Davis, TX 79734; tel: 800-458-6232 or 915-426-3202.

Guests stay in batten-and-board cottages, family cabins, and bunkhouses at this large, 19th-century cattle ranch, six miles from Fort Davis. Cafeteria-style food and chuck-wagon fare are available, as are tours to nearby parks. $$

Sharpshine Bed and Breakfast

Route 1, Box 386; Canyon, TX 79015; tel: 806-655-5746.

This working ranch features comfortable, private accommodations in a converted bunkhouse. Quarter horses and Texas longhorns roam the grounds, along with a wide array of wildlife. $$

TOURS & OUTFITTERS

Big Bend River Tours

P.O. Box 317; Terlingua, TX 79852; tel: 800-545-4240 or 915-424-3219.

Rafting, horseback riding, hiking, and combination trips in and around the national park.

Cowboy Evening

Route 1, Box 69; Claude, TX 79019-9712; tel: 800-658-2613 or 806-944-5562.

Wagon rides and cowboy cooking at Palo Duro Canyon.

Texas River Expeditions

P.O. Box 583; Terlingua, TX 79852; tel: 800-839-7238 or 915-371-2633.

Rafting trips on the Rio Grande through the Big Bend region.

MUSEUMS

Panhandle-Plains Historical Museum

West Texas A&M University, 2401 4th Avenue, Box 60967; Canyon, TX 79016; tel: 806-656-2244.

The Texas counterpart to Wyoming's Buffalo Bill Historical Center has exhibits on paleontology, geology, and Old West heritage, as well as an art collection featuring works by Georgia O'Keeffe, who once taught at the university.

Ranching Heritage Center

3121 4th Street, Box 43200; Lubbock, TX 79409-3200; tel: 806-742-0498.

This indoor/outdoor Old West museum explores ranch life on the frontier and preserves more than 30 old ranch buildings, corrals, a 1923 steam locomotive, an 1830 cotton gin, and a collection of bits and spurs.

West of the Pecos Museum

1st and Cedar Streets; Pecos, TX 79772; tel: 915-445-5076.

A former saloon and hotel that now houses more than 50 rooms of themed exhibits, plus several outbuildings, including a replica of Judge Roy Bean's Jersey Lily Saloon.

PARKS

Big Bend National Park

P.O. Box 129; Big Bend National Park, TX 79834; tel: 915-477-2251.

The park protects a diverse section of the Chihuahuan Desert, encompassing desert scenery, mountains, canyons, and ghost towns on the U.S.–Mexican border.

Fort Davis National Historic Site

P.O. Box 1456; Fort Davis, TX 79734; tel: 915-426-3224.

The best-preserved frontier fort in the Southwest has 25 restored structures and a number of other buildings used by the U.S. Army to protect settlers from Apache incursions between 1854 and 1891.

Palo Duro Canyon State Park

Route 2, Box 285; Canyon, TX 79015; tel: 806-488-2227.

The nation's second largest chasm has seen the Spanish incursion, fierce battles between the U.S. Army and both Comanche and Kiowa warriors, and pioneer rancher Charles Goodnight's cattle operation in 1876. The main draw now is the summer outdoor musical *Texas*.

Excursions

El Paso

El Paso Civic, Convention and Visitors Bureau; 1 Civic Center Plaza; El Paso, TX 79901; tel: 800-351-6024 or 915-534-0696.

Metropolitan they may be, but El Paso and its Mexican sister city, Juarez, abound with Texas history. The state's first permanent settlement, the Mission Trail, located southeast of El Paso, today is home to the communities of Ysleta, Socorro, and San Elizario. Mid-19th-century life at Fort Bliss, now the largest air-defense training center in the Western world, is recreated in the fort's museum. John Wesley Hardin and other legendary westerners are buried in Concordia Cemetery.

Langtry

Del Rio Chamber of Commerce; 1915 Avenue F; Del Rio, TX 78840; tel: 830-775-3551.

It's worth the long trip to Langtry to see the original Jersey Lily, the courtroom and saloon ruled by Judge Roy Bean, a frontier justice of the peace. A new visitor center here interprets his life. Bean is buried in the Whitehead Memorial Museum in Del Rio. While in the area, visit Seminole Canyon State Park, site of fascinating ancient rock paintings near Comstock. Also visit Bracketville's Alamo Village, used as a film set for Westerns and commercials.

Turkey

Turkey City Hall; Box 415; Turkey, TX 79261; tel: 806-423-1033.

The main attraction of this delightful small town, about two hours northeast of Lubbock, is the Bob Wills Museum, honoring native son Bob Wills, "King of Western Swing." Nearby, Caprock Canyons State Park has topography similar to Palo Duro Canyon and serves as the centerpiece of a 90-mile trail system built on an abandoned railroad bed. The park also has its own bison herd, descendants of the herd begun by legendary rancher Charles Goodnight in 1876.

Lincoln County
and Southern New Mexico

CHAPTER **10**

He is said to have been born Henry McCarty in a grim New York ghetto late in 1859 and to have grown up in Kansas. The first evidence of his presence in New Mexico came in March 1873, when he witnessed the marriage of his 43-year-old mother to her longtime companion, Bill Antrim, 30, in Santa Fe. The family moved south to Silver City, a boom-town near the Santa Rita Mine, where his schoolteacher described the quiet adolescent as "a scrawny little fellow with delicate hands and an artistic nature." Believe it or not, he loved music and books. ◆ Then his mother, whom a neighbor called "a jolly Irish lady, full of life and mischief," died of tuberculosis. His stepfather abandoned him. Suddenly, at age 15, Henry McCarty was on his own. Searching desperately for an identity, the lonely teenager adopted his runaway step-father's last name. Then his first. Then the name William H. Bonney. He was eventually called Billy the Kid. ◆ The Kid's first

His life was short and tragic, but Billy the Kid still casts a long shadow across southeastern New Mexico.

recorded crime was the theft of several pounds of butter from a Silver City ranch. But soon Billy had blood on his hands, murder on his conscience, and a habit of sneaking out of jails. By the age of 22, he was dead, a complex hero-villain destined to inspire thousands of other lost youths who came after him. In large part, he remains a mystery. ◆ No place in New Mexico has stronger links to Billy the Kid than **Lincoln**. This dusty, one-horse town (population now under 100), in the heart of southeastern New Mexico's vast ranch lands, was the scene of the Kid's greatest escapades. The entire town is preserved as a state monument honoring the Lincoln County War and Billy the Kid, and it has become one of New Mexico's leading tourist destinations.

Mogollon ghost town in the Gila Mountains is typical of the hardscrabble mining camps that went bust after the silver boom of the late 1800s.

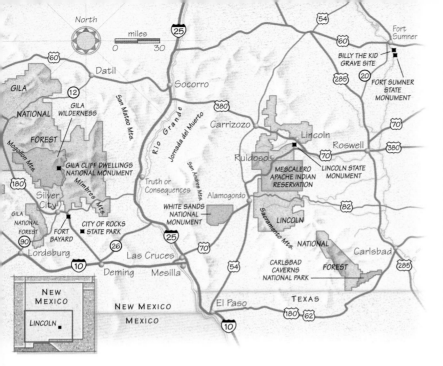

McSween. Rifle shots exploded from the corral. Brady dropped dead. His murderers vanished.

The final showdown in the vendetta came on the night of July 14, 1878. The Kid and McSween rode back into town with 45 gunmen. Some took up positions in the Montaño store, across from the fortified tower known as the *torreón*. The Kid, McSween, and others settled into McSween's house. The rest of Lincoln's 400 inhabitants, mostly Hispanic, fled or hid in their homes.

During what came to be known as the Five Day Battle, the two sides emptied their guns at each other. Then soldiers arrived, aiming a mountain howitzer and a Gatling gun at the Montaño store. Soon the only Tunstall partisans still fighting were those holed up with the Kid in McSween's house. Deputies torched it.

Inside the burning building, Billy the Kid, McSween, and their henchmen waited for night to come. The fire moved from room to room until it burned so brightly that it lit the entire town and the surrounding hills. The Kid bolted first. He darted through the shower of lead, remained unscathed, then vanished. With the timbers of his house collapsing around him, McSween finally fled. He died full of bullets in his own backyard. That day more than 2,000 shots echoed through the streets of Lincoln.

Lincoln's Landmarks

Other towns of Billy the Kid's era died as quickly and predictably as the outlaws who gave the Wild West its name. But Lincoln hung on. Today, you can still walk into Tunstall's store and see the sort of merchandise Tunstall himself might have arranged on the shelves in the days before he died – buttons, shoes, garments, coffee grinders, spittin' tobacco, and more. The store and a

How did such a small town accidentally find itself the center of so much attention? The story is vintage Wild West.

It was February 18, 1878. In the mountainous countryside south of Lincoln, English-born John Henry Tunstall – store owner, financier, and cattleman – was gunned down in cold blood. There were no witnesses. The official cause of death: shot while resisting arrest. Billy the Kid, Tunstall's employee and friend, retorted through clenched teeth, "On trumped-up charges," and vowed revenge. The most famous range war of them all – the Lincoln County War – had begun and, with it, the legend of Billy the Kid.

Six weeks later, the Kid and four other gunslingers slipped into Lincoln and concealed themselves in an adobe corral next to Tunstall's store. The next morning, Sheriff Brady and four deputies strode through the streets, carrying a warrant for the arrest of Tunstall's partner, attorney Alexander A.

Rattlesnakes (right), inhabitants of southern New Mexico's rugged Jornada del Muerto region, keep cool under rocks during the day and become active at dusk.

Billy the Kid (opposite, right), guns blazing, makes one of his miraculous escapes in this Lincoln mural.

dozen other structures have turned Lincoln into a fascinating historic destination where you can walk in the footsteps of one of the West's most notorious outlaws.

Start your walking tour at the Montaño store, then stroll past the eye-catching *torreón*, a circular stone fort built by early Hispanic settlers as a haven against Apache attack, long before the infamous Five Days Battle. Just past Tunstall's store is the old **Wortley Hotel** (now closed), rumored to be haunted.

The most famous spot on the street is the **Old Lincoln County Courthouse**, the site of the Kid's dramatic escape after being sentenced to death for the murder of Sheriff Brady. Immobilized by handcuffs, leg irons, and chains, Billy was able nonetheless, on the evening of April 28, 1881, to slip his slender hands from the handcuffs and blast his way out of jail, killing his guards (bullet holes can still be seen in the wall). Still wearing ankle manacles, he severed the chain between his legs with a pickax and looped the remnants around his belt. He proceeded to chat a while with unnerved townspeople

outside the Wortley Hotel before commandeering a horse and heading west, the dangling chains slapping rhythmically against his legs and thighs.

If the ghost of the Kid wanders today, it seems unlikely that he recognizes the version of his life celebrated in such tourist extravaganzas as Lincoln's three-day Last Escape of Billy the Kid Pageant, which features a reenactment of bloody moments from the Lincoln County War, a fiddling contest, Apache dancing, can-can girls, and handicraft items. But other sites in New Mexico have a legitimate claim on Billy's ghost, too.

On the Trail of Billy the Kid

Southwest of Lincoln is **Silver City**, built in 1800 by Spanish copper miners, the Kid's first home in New Mexico. Like Bisbee in neighboring Arizona, Silver City boomed and then bust. And like Bisbee, this historic community of 12,000, with gingerbread Victorian inns and boutiques, has recently experienced a renaissance. It was discovered by artists and travelers looking for the perfect

Range Wars

The Lincoln County War was only one of dozens of so-called range wars that flared up across the West between 1850 and 1910. Skirmishes, not true wars, they pitted those who had gained power and wealth against those who wanted it. Like some savage rite of dominance, they often boiled down to a futile test of courage against men who held this belief: "If I say I'm right, I am. And I'll shoot you to prove it."

Cattle raids like the one depicted in this 1874 *Harper's Weekly* illustration (below) often ignited a bloody cycle of violence and revenge between ranchers, sheepmen, and suspected rustlers.

An Apache mountain spirit dancer (opposite) dons a traditional headdress and black hood. The Apache were fierce fighters and held back Spanish and American settlement for decades.

Some, like Arizona's Pleasant Valley War in the 1880s, were a conflict between cattlemen and sheepmen. Others involved ranchers who saw rustlers in every face they encountered. In Montana's Horse Thief War of 1884, for example, a band of vigilantes hanged more than a dozen alleged rustlers without benefit of trial. Eight years later, in Wyoming's Johnson County War, a party of cattlemen and hired gunmen known as the Invaders set out to execute 70 suspected rustlers, including the county sheriff and deputies. The Invaders were arrested after a week of bloodshed, but Johnson County was so poor it couldn't afford to jail them, and they eventually were set free. Typical of every range war, no one agreed on how many people were killed and wounded. Some said a handful. Others said dozens. Sporadic gunfights between rich and poor continued for two decades.

Violence over rangeland has simmered down now, but old animosities persist, and a war of words is still being waged in the press, the courts, and Congress. Museums occasionally feature exhibits on range wars, and the Jim Gatchell Memorial Museum of the West in Buffalo, Wyoming, has ongoing exhibits depicting the tragedies, complexities, and ironies of the Johnson County War.

base from which to explore the area.

The site of the Kid's boyhood home is a parking lot now, but you can experience the feeling and mood of the countryside as it was in Billy's day by visiting the nearby **City of Rocks State Park**, whose stark, boulder-strewn landscape evokes visions of outlaws shooting it out against a barren and beautiful Wild West backdrop. Also close to Silver City is **Gila Cliff Dwellings National Monument**, where the artistically gifted Mogollon people built cliffside apartment homes 700 years ago. The adjoining **Gila Wilderness** (the first in the nation) and **Gila National Forest** offer some of the region's best backcountry hiking and wildlife watching.

Picturesque **Fort Bayard**, adjoining a state elk refuge, was built in 1866 and housed a regiment of "buffalo soldiers" from the Ninth Cavalry. Today it's a state hospital, but visitors may drive around the grounds. At the **Chino Mine**, the Southwest's oldest active mine, workers still pull copper ore from a vast open pit.

Mesilla, southeast of Silver City on the southern edge of Las Cruces, holds dramatic memories of Billy. The buildings lining the plaza give the illusion that no time has passed since April 13, 1881. On that day Billy, not yet 22, stood in **Mesilla Courthouse** and listened as the judge sentenced him to "hang by the neck until his body be dead" for the murder of Sheriff Brady. Heavily armed guards escorted him back to Lincoln. By then the only artistic bent left in Billy was a talent for escape – which he did, as soon as possible.

Final Resting Place

Some say the Kid kept on running for decades. But historians believe that on the night of July 14, 1881, while hiding in a home in **Fort Sumner**, north of Lincoln, the Kid saw a figure crouched in a darkened room and called, *"Quién es?"* Who is it? The figure, Sheriff Pat Garrett, shot in the direction of the voice. Billy the Kid fell dead and was buried in this lonely spot, a long way from the New York of his birth.

Like Lincoln, Fort Sumner (population about 1,500) bursts with reminders of Billy the Kid's day, and thousands of visitors arrive each year to honor his memory. For many the pilgrimage begins at Billy's grave, outside town. The **Old Fort Sumner Museum** showcases letters from both Pat Garrett and the Kid. Garrett became something of a celebrity after gunning down the famous outlaw and even went on to write a book celebrating the fact. In town, the **Billy the Kid Museum** houses a jail cell from Carrizozo, west of Lincoln, said to have caged the Kid himself for a time.

It is ironic that the injustices done to and by one man, Billy the Kid, should be the main draw at Fort Sumner today, rather than the injustices suffered by thousands of Navajos and Apaches imprisoned here in the 1860s. The story of the roundup of the Navajos and the subsequent Long Walk, a forced 300-mile march from Fort Wingate to Bosque Redondo, is full of such brutality and evil that those who died, and survived, deserve a significant memorial. Instead, travelers make do with the modest visitor center at **Fort Sumner State Monument**. Stones carried from the Navajo Reservation have been piled into a simple commemorative shrine. Such modest shrines exist all around the West. Mostly unnoticed by non-Indians, they are a reminder of a complex and layered past.

So is Lincoln. There are other, splashier attractions nearby: the spectacular scenery of the **Mescalero Apache reservation**, the sensuous dunes of slithering gypsum at **White Sands National Monument**, the eerie underground chambers at **Carlsbad Caverns**. But nowhere are the nuance-filled contradictions of the Wild West more obvious than on the streets of Lincoln.

Maybe, on those streets or in the quiet miles between Silver City and Fort Sumner, you'll find yourself wondering whether the West's quintessential hero-villain ever would have existed if Henry McCarty's mother hadn't died, or he'd grown up in different circumstances. Or was there something in Billy himself that destined him to become what he became and die as he died? Regardless of all that, the core truth is that Billy the Kid remains both a legend and a symbol of the Wild West, a place that exists as much in imagination as in fact.

TRAVEL TIPS

DETAILS

When to Go

Spring and fall are the most pleasant times to visit, but New Mexico is sunny year-round. Temperatures at low elevations top 100°F in summer, when 10,000-foot-plus mountains offer cool alternatives. Thunderstorms are common in July and August.

How to Get There

Airlines serve Albuquerque International Airport and Las Cruces Municipal Airports.

Getting Around

A car is by far the most convenient means of travel; rentals are available at the airports.

INFORMATION

Las Cruces Convention and Visitors Bureau

211 North Water; Las Cruces, NM 88001; tel: 800-343-7827 or 505-541-2444.

Ruidoso Valley Chamber of Commerce and Visitors Center

P.O. Box 698; Ruidoso, NM 88355; tel: 800-253-2255 or 505-257-7395.

Silver City Chamber of Commerce

201 North Hudson; Silver City, NM 88061; tel: 800-548-9378 or 505-538-3785.

LODGING

PRICE GUIDE – double occupancy

$ = up to $49 $$ = $50–$99
$$$ = $100–$149 $$$$ = $150+

Bear Mountain Guest Ranch

Box 1163; Silver City, NM 88062; tel: 800-880-2538 or 505-538-2538.

This two-story ranch house, built in 1928, sits on 160 acres adjacent to Gila National Forest. Basic accommodations include 11 double rooms with baths, two suites, and two cottages. Birding, archaeological tours, hiking, and family-style meals are available. $$$

Black Range Lodge

Route 2, Box 119; Kingston, NM 88042; tel: 888-252-5652 or 505-895-5652.

This rustic mountain lodge is situated in the old mining community of Kingston in Gila National Forest. The lodge has three suites and four double rooms with private baths; two rooms have balconies. $–$$

Casa del Patrón

Box 27; Lincoln, NM 88338; tel: 800-524-5202 or 505-653-4676.

This adobe, once the home of Lincoln County Clerk Juan Patrón, was used in 1878 to confine Billy the Kid. Three guest suites have wood floors and both contemporary and antique furnishings. One- and two-bedroom casitas are also available. $$

Ellis Store and Country Inn

Highway 380, MM 98, Box 15; Lincoln, NM 88338; tel: 800-653-6460 or 505-653-4609.

McSween loyalists once stayed in this 1850 adobe inn during the Lincoln County War, and Billy the Kid was kept here prior to his trial. Two of the four guest rooms have private baths and a fireplace or wood-burning stove. An adjoining mill house has four rooms, a bath, and den. $$

Lodge at Cloudcroft

1 Corona Place, Box 497; Cloudcroft, NM 88317; tel: 800-395-6343 or 505-682-2566.

Built in 1899, this ornate hunting lodge in the Sacramento Mountains offers 47 hotel rooms, 11 guest suites, and a four-bedroom cottage with kitchenette. A pool, spa, golf course, skiing, and hiking are available. $–$$$$

Mesón de Mesilla

1803 Avenida de Mesilla; Mesilla, NM 88046; tel: 800-732-6025 or 505-525-9212.

About 10 minutes from historic Mesilla Plaza, this 1983 pueblo-style inn has an award-winning restaurant, nine rooms with baths, and four suites with kiva fireplaces. Free shuttle service from Las Cruces Airport, gourmet breakfasts, and picnic baskets are available. $–$$

TOURS & OUTFITTERS

Lincoln State Monument Walking Tours

P.O. Box 36; Lincoln, NM 88338; tel: 505-653-4372.

Tours of Billy the Kid territory for 10 or more people are available by reservation.

Silver City Museum Downtown Walking Tours

312 West Broadway; Silver City, NM 88061; tel: 505-538-5921.

The museum accepts reservations for tours of historic downtown Silver City.

MUSEUMS

Billy the Kid Museum

1601 East Sumner Avenue; Fort Sumner, NM 88119; tel: 505-355-2380.

Exhibits include a jail cell from Carrizozo, west of Lincoln, said to have held Billy the Kid.

Lincoln County Courthouse Museum

P.O. Box 36; Lincoln, NM 88338; tel: 505-653-4372.

The center of Billy the Kid lore in Lincoln, this was the site of the Kid's greatest jailbreak.

Old Fort Sumner Museum

Route 11; Fort Sumner, NM 88119; tel: 505-355-2573.

This museum showcases letters from Pat Garrett and Billy the Kid, as well as other mementos of the young outlaw.

Tunstall Store Museum
P.O. Box 36; Lincoln, NM 88338; tel: 505-653-4372.

This store was owned by the English businessman whose murder triggered the Lincoln County War.

PARKS

City of Rocks State Park
P.O. Box 50; Faywood, NM 88034; tel: 505-536-2800.

These strange formations were formed by volcanic fallout from the Kneeling Nun region 17 miles away.

Fort Selden State Monument
P.O. Box 58; Radium Springs, NM 88054; tel: 505-526-8911.

This 1865 fort protected settlers from Apache incursions.

Fort Sumner State Monument
Route 11, P.O. Box 356; Fort Sumner, NM 88119; tel: 505-355-2573.

The site where Pat Garrett shot Billy the Kid is now a state monument, with the Kid's grave and two museums.

Gila Cliff Dwellings National Monument
HC 68, Box 100; Silver City, NM 88061; tel: 505-536-9344.

Protected here are the remains of 13th-century cliff dwellings in caves above the Gila River.

Lincoln State Monument
P.O. Box 36; Lincoln, NM 88338; tel: 505-653-4372.

The "town that time forgot" is a state monument with a number of historical buildings.

Excursions

Carlsbad Caverns National Park
3225 National Parks Highway; Carlsbad, NM 88220; tel: 505-785-2232.

This park preserves eerie stalactites and stalagmites in some of the world's largest limestone caves. Walk three miles down or take an elevator to the 750-foot-high Big Room, site of the Twin Giants and other fantastical sculptures shaped by acidic groundwater. Don't miss Carlsbad's 300,000 Mexican long-tailed bats, which make their spectacular exit from the caves at dusk, May through October.

Salinas Pueblo Missions National Monument
P.O. Box 517; Mountainair, NM 87036; tel: 505-847-2585.

Three extremely well-preserved Spanish missions are protected in this park along the Salt Trail (or "salinas"), which gave the monument its name. Lovely sandstone Abó and Quarai Missions can be visited near Mountainair, east of Interstate 25. Gran Quivira, in remote country off Highway 55, was the southernmost trading hub of the Plains and Pueblo Indians who once thrived at all three sites.

White Sands National Monument
P.O. Box 1086; Holloman Air Force Base, NM 88330; tel: 505-479-6124.

The largest gypsum desert in the world undulates across the Tularosa Basin, the result of sediment washed down from the San Andres and Sacramento Mountains. White lizards and mice have adapted to this harsh place, along with kit foxes, coyotes, and other desert creatures. Summer full-moon hikes are unforgettable, as is a monthly ranger-led tour of Lake Lucero near the site of the White Sands Missile Range, where the first atomic bomb was exploded in 1945.

Santa Fe and Taos
New Mexico

CHAPTER **11**

The natives sometimes call it "Fanta Se," twisting the name of the United States' oldest state capital city into a wry commentary on what it appears to be today. A fantasy city, too expensive for real people to live in, too exotic for a more or less homogenized America. Fanta Se, an elaborate illusion staged for the tourist dollar. ◆ Or is it? History and tradition run close to the surface here. You find them in the alleylike streets of an old *barrio* as the sun huddles with the horizon and amber light picks out the straws of a 200-year-old adobe; or in a *ristra* of dried red chiles hanging by a turquoise window sash in the most flamboyant display of architectural color you've ever seen; or there, in a tiny courtyard with a private shrine to Santa Fe's patron, St. Francis. Suddenly you know this is the most real city in the country, maybe the only one. And you understand why for nearly four centuries, people have been coming here and then finding ways to stay, whatever the cost. ◆ "It was New Mexico that liberated me from the present era

Many generations and cultures, from ancient pueblo dwellers to Spanish colonists to artistic pioneers, have left their mark on the Land of Enchantment.

of civilization," D. H. Lawrence wrote three-quarters of a century ago. That altogether *real* liberating power is undiminished today. ◆ History doesn't merely permeate Santa Fe; it drives the place – physically, culturally, sensually. It's most obvious in the architecture, protected by some of the toughest historic-preservation laws in the country. There are four historic districts with some 3,500 historically significant buildings, and all new con- struction has to be compatible in style and scale. (This causes occasional silliness, as in the case of the homeowner who wanted to demolish his

Taos Pueblo, one of northern New Mexico's most popular destinations, is thought to be the oldest inhabited village in North America.

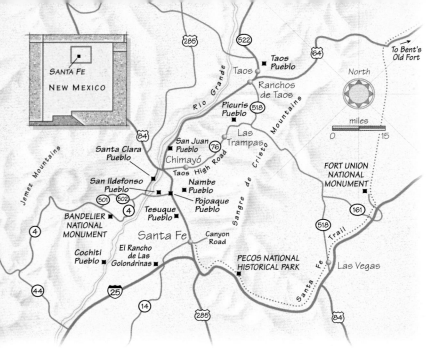

and spiritual heart. People go there to eat, sleep, argue, flirt, dance, or just while away the day reading on a park bench. The traditional Spanish Market (every July) and Indian Market (every August) are fairs with vast offerings of arts and crafts, and both center on the Plaza.

On the Plaza's north side is the **Palace of the Governors**, begun in 1610. It served as home and office for two centuries of Spanish governors. In 1680, an army of several hundred Pueblo Indian warriors camped in the Plaza, laying siege to a thousand Spanish settlers squeezed into the palace. After nine terrifying (and smelly) days, a ragtag caravan of Spanish refugees fled the capital for El Paso. When, a dozen years later, the Spanish finally retook Santa Fe, they discovered that the Indians had remodeled it into a pueblo, which included a ceremonial kiva. After New Mexico became an American territory in 1848, its governor, Lew Wallace, completed work on his blockbuster novel Ben Hur while residing in the palace. No other government building in the United States has seen such a colorful history.

The palace now serves as the **Museum of New Mexico**'s historical center, focusing on colonial life in New Spain. Some docents can draw on 300 years of personal family history in the region. An equally fascinating attraction for visitors is the several dozen Indian artisans who sell their jewelry on blankets spread out daily in the palace portal.

Just passing through the rest of Santa Fe's dozen museums could consume days, so here's a connoisseur's list of the best: The **Museum of Fine Arts** concentrates on New Mexico's 20th-century art, which has been endowed by the collision of Anglo, Hispanic, and Indian cultures and illuminated by sensuous and probing sunlight. The

chicken coop, and found that the city determined it to be a historic structure.) Maybe less obvious, but perhaps more important, is the way in which Santa Fe's Indian and Hispanic past merges with its trendy present to create a city entirely different from other tourist meccas such as Aspen or Santa Barbara. There is a soft Hispanic edge to its life, something called *duende* in Spanish, which can be felt more easily than it can be translated. Call it "magic" for starters.

Santa Fe is a walker's city, never meant to be cursed with the car, and most of her historic treasures radiate no more than a few blocks in any direction from downtown's center – which, is, of course, the **Plaza**.

La villa de Santa Fée, established by order of New Spain's viceroy Luis de Velasco in 1609, was a fortified compound in a dangerous neighborhood. The Plaza was the *agora*, safe within the village walls, that served as marketplace, parade ground, and entertainment center – public floggings took place there, and later bullfights. Today the plaza is half its original size but still very much Santa Fe's physical

Institute of American Indian Art Museum exhibits powerful and sometimes combative contemporary Indian art – the opposite pole of the romantic work found in the galleries. **The Museum of Indian Arts and Culture** has a stunning collection of southwestern pottery spanning nearly two millennia. And the **Georgia O'Keeffe Museum**, opened in 1997, finally offers homage to New Mexico's most famous artist, who, long before her death in 1986 a year short of her hundredth birthday, had liberated nature from mere interpretation and turned it into an exploration of the human soul. One of the city's best tourist deals is the Museum of New Mexico's $10 four-day pass to all four of its branches plus the O'Keeffe Museum.

Controversies and Legends

Virtually every historic building in Santa Fe holds a story, usually one bristling with controversy. Among the most dramatic is **St. Francis Cathedral**, as startling a presence as a docked starship in the otherwise low-rise, mud-brown town. Jean Baptiste Lamy, the first non-Spanish bishop of New Mexico, arrived in Santa Fe in 1851 and found a church that embraced pagan imagery and tolerated priests who kept live-in girlfriends. Lamy went to war with his own Spanish-speaking priests and commissioned this striking Romanesque

cathedral, believing that its sheer architectural authority would startle the desultory natives into line with strict Catholic doctrine. Willa Cather later transformed Lamy into a saintly hero in her historical novel *Death Comes for the Archbishop*, although some Hispanic New Mexicans still prickle at the Frenchman's arrogance. The cathedral is a perfect metaphor for the outside world's efforts to wrench New Mexico into the mainstream, which typically fail.

At least two other Santa Fe churches are worth a visit. **Loretto Chapel**, a storybook Gothic confection, has a "miraculous staircase" that spirals to the choir loft like a Slinky toy, unaided by a central support. A

Decorative details (opposite) brighten the textured, earth-colored walls of a Santa Fe adobe.

A tired tourist (right) finds a restful spot in the Plaza.

mysterious carpenter who plodded into town on a donkey designed and built it; after he disappeared a legend arose that it was St. Joseph himself. The **Chapel of San Miguel** is squat and inelegant by comparison, but the play of light and shadow on its uneven adobe walls and buttresses, formed by hand in 1710, is wonderful. Archaeological investigation has shown that the Spanish built the church atop a prehistoric Pueblo site dating to the early 14th century – the symbolic snub of a conqueror raising a temple over the ruins of the conquered.

History also lives on **Canyon Road**, although the street stretching east from downtown is more famous for its 80-odd art galleries. Some of Santa Fe's rambling historic

Strings of red chiles (left), or *ristras*, are hung up to dry after the August harvest.

Indian Market (below) is one of Santa Fe's most popular annual events, with artisans and their wares filling up the Plaza and nearby streets.

haciendas, such as **El Zaguán** (now a private apartment house) line the road. Most visitors try to drive, which is a mistake. Parking is scarce, and only pedestrians can appreciate the intimate details of the architecture – let alone the galleries' offerings, which range from prehistoric Pueblo pottery to gay erotic cowboy paintings. Think of Canyon Road as a mile-long museum of art and

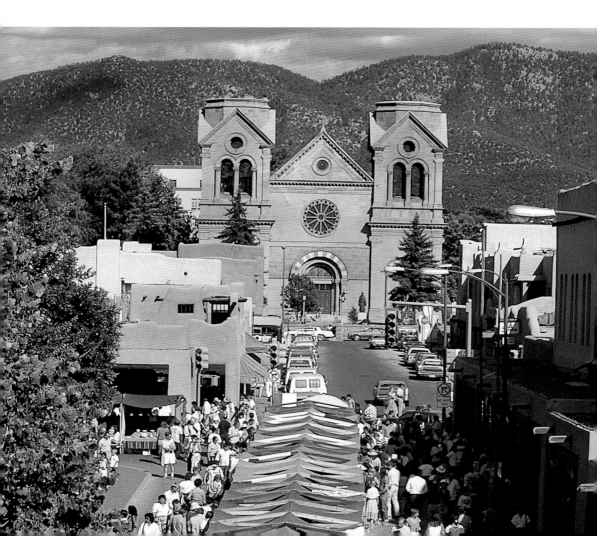

architecture, and budget time accordingly.

It pays, in fact, to think of all northern New Mexico as a vast museum, a delta of history where three cultural rivers – Indian, Spanish, and Anglo-American – collide and diffuse, creating some new channels and stubbornly forcing old ones ahead.

Fifteen miles southwest of Santa Fe is **El Rancho de Las Golondrinas**, which began life as a working ranch around 1710 alongside El Camino Real – the famous Royal Road – from Santa Fe to Mexico City. The old ranch reopened as a "living history" museum in 1972 with restored and reconstructed buildings evoking Spanish Colonial life – something like an adobe Williamsburg. Blacksmithing, baking, weaving, arts and crafts, and folkloric dance and music are just some of the activities that take place on the grounds and in the buildings. There is a hacienda, a defensive tower, a water wheel, a mill, a frontier-era schoolhouse, and even a *morada*, a Penitente-era chapel.

Heading north, two possible routes meander the 70-odd miles to Taos, each offering so many side trips that a modern trip by car could well take longer than a Spaniard's trip in a rattling wagon two centuries ago.

The route up the **Rio Grande Valley**, the deep rift between the **Sangre de Cristo** and **Jemez Mountains**, is a juxtaposition of sun-burnt high desert, an extravagant riparian ribbon of cottonwood forest, and northwest of Taos, the nightmare black gash of the river gorge. The **Taos High Road** winds into the Sangre de Cristos themselves and offers views of the softer rolling valleys and hills east of the mountains, where background mountains tower higher than 13,000 feet.

Windows on the Ancient Past

New Mexico's famous eight northern pueblos (there are 19 throughout the state) form a constellation from Santa Fe to Taos: **Tesuque**, **Pojoaque**, **San Ildefonso**, **Santa Clara**, **Nambe**, **San Juan**, **Picurís**, and **Taos**. Visitors are welcome – up to a point. Don't seek answers to questions about ceremonies and spiritual matters. As for photography, video-taping, and sketching, they are generally

forbidden or taxed within the pueblos, as at Taos Pueblo. But these are contemporary considerations. The pueblos are most important for their modern link to an ancient past.

One place that narrowly missed being part of that link is the abandoned **Tyuonyi Pueblo** at **Bandelier National Monument**, nestled in Frijoles Canyon in the foothills of the Jemez Mountains, northwest of Santa Fe. Coronado's foray into New Mexico in 1540 probably passed within a few miles of the spectacular 400-room pueblo, which was constructed from

A mural of a *santero* (above), a wood-carver who specializes in figures of saints, adorns a Taos building.

A sombrero (right) is part of the traditional finery worn for a fiesta at El Rancho de Las Golondrinas.

forced a migratory tide of people into the Rio Grande Valley, mingling and skirmishing with others already there.

Except for Taos, the modern villages are not physically enchanting, and visitors with romantic images in mind may be disappointed (as were the 16th-century Spaniards). But several of the pueblos produce exquisite crafts, most notably pottery, and some willingly place their culture on public view during annual celebrations. On "feast days" visitors may even be invited into homes to share family meals – a custom lingering from the more peaceful contacts with the early Europeans. (An indispensable free guide and calendar of pueblo events is available from the Santa Fe Convention & Visitors Bureau.)

Taos Pueblo is a special case, a monument of ancient architecture and even more ancient culture that has been astounding visitors for centuries. "Never shall I forget the Christmas dances at Taos," wrote D. H. Lawrence, "twilight, snow, the darkness coming over the great wintry mountains and the lonely pueblo, then suddenly again, like dark calling to dark, the deep Indian cluster-singing around the drum ...." The buildings themselves, great cellular piles of adobe cubes standing five stories high, seem to echo the massing of the mountains behind them. They date from shortly after the Pueblo Revolt of 1680, but the site may have been occupied for a thousand years.

Heading up to Taos via the **Taos High Road** (New Mexico Highways 518 and 76), you pass through an area steeped in Spanish history and culture. The old farming village of **Las Trampas** has a beautifully restored, broad-shouldered mission church dating from the late 18th century. **Chimayó** has the famous **Santuario de Chimayó**, built as a

volcanic tuff. The pueblo was abandoned around 1550, probably because the population had grown too large for the natural resources – game, firewood, and arable land – but the people of modern **Cochiti Pueblo**, just to the southeast, trace a direct link to the site.

The history of the Rio Grande pueblos is murky, but it is probably safe to say that modern Puebloans are direct descendants of people once known as the Anasazi, among other cultures. The prehistoric southwestern world was churning between AD 1150 and 1400, with entire cultures moving, merging, fighting, and fading. A great drought that lasted from 1276 to 1299 probably

private family chapel in 1816 and still believed to have miraculous healing powers. On Holy Week each year, more than 10,000 Christians make a pilgrimage to the santuario to pray for healing or to make amends for misdeeds. The *Penitente* culture, in which members endured flogging to atone for Christ's suffering, still resonates in these villages.

Visitors also make secular pilgrimages to Chimayó, some to buy brilliantly colored wool rugs that have been handwoven here by Spanish families for centuries; others to sample its homegrown chile. Connoisseurs regard Chimayó as New Mexico's finest chile, fresh and piquant with a subtle undercurrent of sweetness. All along the High Road are unadvertised and unexpected gastronomic adventures: a crock full of grandmother's

Covered wagons (right), dubbed "prairie schooners," served as temporary homes for travelers along the Santa Fe Trail.

Bent's Old Fort, Colorado (below), on the Santa Fe Trail, was a rendezvous point for mountain men, traders, and Indians.

Santa Fe Trail

History still lies close to the surface in this part of the country, and a stop at any of the remnants of the **Santa Fe Trail** offers an immersion into a time that required vigilance, courage, endurance, and arrogance hardly imaginable today.

In November 1821, Indian fighter and entrepreneur William Becknell plodded a pack train 800 miles from Franklin, Missouri, to Santa Fe, where the residents swarmed it like children mobbing Santa Claus. Becknell's timing was perfect: three months earlier, Mexico had finally broken off the Spanish yoke, which included a ban on trade with the United States. Wagon trains followed, sometimes scoring incredible successes: one 1824 Becknell caravan stuffed with $30,000 in merchandise brought back $180,000 in gold and silver and $10,000 in furs.

The risks, modern investors would say, justified the profits. Blizzards swept the Kansas prairies in winter; summer brought grass fires that could outrun a horse. Grizzlies and rattlesnakes authoritatively defended their turf. And Indians, particularly the Comanches, were a constant threat. But at their destination, traders and trappers found relaxation in forms unimaginable in

Deer dances (opposite, top) such as this one at Santa Clara Pueblo are traditionally held in winter, a time for hunting and preserving meat.

Traditional Pueblo pottery (opposite, bottom) like this piece from Santa Clara is shaped by hand and painted with a yucca brush.

contemporary America. Santa Fe welcomed them to all-night fandangos and gambling. Women walked around with arms, shoulders, and feet scandalously bared, and enjoyed liberated sex lives.

The trail's epic ended in 1879, when the first locomotive wheezed into northern New Mexico, but landmarks along the trail remain. **Bent's Old Fort** "exactly fills my idea of an ancient castle," wrote pioneer Susan Magoffin in 1846. The reconstructed Colorado fort raises the same impression today, with its ingenious adobe cylindrical towers, battlements, and massive walls.

Travelers could breathe easy when they reached the safety of **Fort Union**, a large military installation north of Las Vegas, New Mexico. It is now a national monument preserving the remains of the second and third forts; wagon ruts are clearly visible nearby. To the west is **Pecos National Historical Park**, site of an Indian pueblo established about AD 1300 and later colonized by the Spanish. Ruins of the pueblo, a ceremonial kiva, and an adobe church remain.

A young dancer (left) takes a break at a San Juan Pueblo Comanche Dance.

San Francisco de Asís (opposite, top), built by Franciscans in the late 1700s, was a favorite subject of painter Georgia O'Keeffe.

killed in the fighting or hanged after a trial.

Taos became an artists' mecca literally by accident – in 1898, a wagon carrying two New York artists broke down nearby and they decided to stay. The pueblo, the polychrome desert, and 11,819-foot Taos Mountain were irresistible attractions. Today Taos has some 80 galleries, nine museums, and a plague of T-shirt shops. It is much smaller, scruffier, and less self-conscious than Santa Fe. Its ongoing struggle, exposed in John Nichols' brilliant satirical novel *The Milagro Beanfield War*, is the squeeze on old Hispanic families, which are having to leave because of inflating property values and taxes.

Like Santa Fe, Taos is a walker's town, presenting history, art, or a quirk of culture at every random turn of a corner. One sobering place to ponder the region's history is the **Kit Carson Home and Museum**, just a minute's walk east of the Plaza. Carson presents a fascinating contradiction. He zestfully killed Apache warriors and spearheaded the brutal "long walk" that expelled the Navajos from a vast homeland that spread from modern northern Arizona to northern New Mexico; and yet, he adopted an Apache orphan and

steaming tamales at a gas station, a ramshackle stand selling fresh tortillas and hot burritos. Tourist traffic swarms the High Road in summer, but so far it has failed to spoil the experience.

Artists' Mecca

The town of **Taos** began humbly as a far-flung mission in 1598, and over the next two centuries it grew into a modest trading outpost. This was a matter of politics, not geography: it was far enough from Santa Fe that the governor's bureaucrats couldn't enforce the Spanish ban on trade with foreigners. In the first half of the 19th century, white trappers made the town a staging area for their assault on the beaver of the southern Rockies. Like Santa Fe, Taos' history is awash in blood and turmoil. In 1847, a year after the United States' peaceful seizure of New Mexico, Mexican loyalists in Taos joined Pueblo Indians in a revolt, killing Gov. Charles Bent and any other Americans they could find. The uprising lasted only three weeks, and as usual, the Indians took the greatest losses – more than 150

Indian elders like this Santa Domingo Pueblo man (left) are honored members of tribal society and keepers of traditional ways.

Santuario de Chimayo (right) on the High Road to Taos was built about 1814 and is believed to be the site of miraculous cures.

ultimately argued for the Navajos' repatriation.

Also essential are the **Harwood Foundation Museum**, which features Taos artists; the **Millicent Rogers Museum**, with its stunning collection of Pueblo and Navajo art and craft; and the **Hacienda Martinez**, a perfectly restored 1804 ranch that offers a dramatic picture of Spanish colonial life. One exhibit provocatively observes, "For the Spanish conquistadores and their followers, the non-existent gold and silver was replaced by the bodies and labor of the Native Americans."

Taos' most astounding work of art is a modest adobe church at **Ranchos de Taos**, four miles south of town, designed by an anonymous priest around 1815. **San Francisco de Asís** rises from the land like a force of nature, the line between earth and architecture almost indistinguishable. Its unadorned, abstract forms greet the daybreak like an empty canvas, waiting for the New Mexican light to brush it not only with color but also mood. Velvet serenity today, maybe angry fire tomorrow. O'Keeffe

said that artists who spend any time in Taos have to paint it, "just as they have to paint a self-portrait." Nearly every evening, photographers and artists flit around it like moths circling a lantern.

The nightly ritual around this church explains why people come to northern New Mexico, whether they're shopping for trinkets or art, savoring the paper-bag luminarias lining Santa Fe's streets at Christmas, or investigating the 17th century: they are discovering something outside conventional experience, or perhaps deep within. The words of D. H. Lawrence resonate today: "In the magnificent fierce morning of New Mexico one sprang awake, a new part of the soul woke up suddenly, and the old world gave way to a new."

TRAVEL TIPS

DETAILS

When to Go

Santa Fe is lovely year-round – sunny and warm in summer, cold and clear in winter. October may be the best time to visit. It falls between the summer tourist and winter ski seasons and offers glorious autumn color, pinyon-scented air, and a quiet experience. Expect cool evenings, even in summer.

How to Get There

Commercial airlines serve Albuquerque International Airport. Commuter flights are available to Santa Fe and Taos.

Getting Around

Car rentals are available at the airport in Albuquerque. Shuttle Jack, 505-243-3244, offers transportation from the airport to Santa Fe.

INFORMATION

Santa Fe Convention and Visitors Bureau

201 West Marcy Street; Santa Fe, NM 87504-0909; tel: 800-777-2489 or 505-984-6760.

Taos Chamber of Commerce

1139 Paseo del Pueblo Sur; Taos, NM 87571; tel: 800-732-8267 or 505-758-3873.

LODGING

PRICE GUIDE – double occupancy

$ = up to $49 $$ = $50–$99
$$$ = $100–$149 $$$$ = $150+

Bishop's Lodge

Bishop's Lodge Road, P.O. Box 2367; Santa Fe, NM 87504; tel: 800-732-2240 or 505-983-6377.

Once the mountain retreat of Bishop Lamy, who paid $80 for the property in the 1860s, this elegant stopping place has been a luxury resort since 1918. The lodge offers fine dining, horseback riding, tennis, and a daily summer kid's program in quiet, forested surroundings. $$$$

Historic Taos Inn

125 Paseo del Pueblo Norte; Taos, NM 87571; tel: 800-826-7466 or 505-758-2233.

This famous 1936 downtown hotel has massive viga-and-latilla ceilings and plenty of historic Taos atmosphere. Rooms, most with kiva fireplaces, are decorated in modern Southwestern style. $$$$

Hotel Santa Fe

1501 Paseo de Peralta; Santa Fe, NM 87501; tel: 505-982-1200.

Owned by Picurís Pueblo, this attractive Pueblo Revival hotel combines Native American aesthetics with good value, six blocks from the Plaza. Its 129 rooms, mostly suites, have modern Santa Fe-style decor, balconies, and views. $$$–$$$$

Inn of the Anasazi

113 Washington Avenue; Santa Fe, NM 87501; tel: 505-988-3030.

This new luxury hotel, situated near the Plaza, has Pueblo Indian and Hispanic details, including massive hand-carved doors and sculpted stairways. Each of the inn's 59 rooms has a kiva fireplace and four-poster bed. $$$$

Mabel Dodge Luhan House

240 Morada Lane; Taos, NM 87571; tel: 800-846-2235 or 505-758-9456.

New Mexico's most famous salon hostess built this rambling adobe early in the century and entertained such prominent artists and writers as D. H. Lawrence, Willa Cather, and Georgia O'Keeffe. Today it's an 11-room bed and breakfast. $$$$

TOURS & OUTFITTERS

Aboot About Santa Fe

Tel: 505-988-2774.

Two-hour walking tours of downtown Santa Fe.

Outback Tours of Santa Fe

Tel: 800-800-5337

Jeep tours throughout Northern New Mexico focus on wilderness areas, Indian ruins, ghost towns, and Pueblo Indian culture.

MUSEUMS

El Rancho de Las Golondrinas

334 Los Pinos Road; Santa Fe, NM 87505; tel: 505-471-2261.

A 1710 hacienda with Spanish Colonial structures and living-history demonstrations.

Georgia O'Keeffe Museum

217 Johnson Street; Santa Fe, NM 87501; tel: 505-995-0785.

A new museum celebrating O'Keeffe and her artistic vision.

Governor Bent Home and Museum

117A Bent Street; Taos, NM 87571; tel: 505-758-2376.

Frontier memorabilia and period furnishings are displayed in the former home of Charles Bent, the first governor of New Mexico Territory.

Kit Carson Home and Museum

113 East Kit Carson Road; Taos, NM 87571; tel: 505-758-4741.

The life of frontiersman Kit Carson is chronicled in the home he shared with his Mexican wife, Josefa Jaramillo.

Martinez Hacienda

708 Ranchitos Road; Taos, NM 87571; tel: 505-758-0505.

This restored 1804 ranch highlights Spanish Colonial life.

Millicent Rogers Museum

1504 Millicent Rogers Road, P.O. Box A; Taos, NM 87571; tel: 505-758-2462.

An impressive collection of Pueblo and Navajo art.

Museum of Fine Arts
107 West Palace Avenue; Santa Fe, NM 87501; tel: 505-827-4455.
A collection of 20th-century New Mexican art.

Museum of Indian Arts and Culture
710 Camino Lejo; Santa Fe, NM 87504; tel: 505-827-6344.
Indian art from ancient cultures to the present.

Palace of the Governors
105 West Palace Avenue; Santa Fe, NM 87501; tel: 505-827-6483.
The oldest building on the Plaza features exhibits on state history.

PARKS & HISTORIC PLACES

Bandelier National Monument
HCR Box 1, Suite 15; Los Alamos, NM 87544; tel: 505-672-3861, ext 517 or 505-672-0343.
The ruins of a 250-room, pre-Columbian pueblo.

Bent's Old Fort
35110 Highway 194; La Junta, CO 81050; tel: 719-383-5010.
The fort was a vital trading center on the Santa Fe Trail. The present structure is a reconstruction of the original, which was built in 1833.

Fort Union National Monument
P.O. Box 127; Watrous, NM 87753; tel: 505-425-8025.
This fort, built in 1851, was a way station on the Santa Fe Trail.

Pecos National Historical Park
P.O. Box 418; Pecos, NM 87552; tel: 505-757-6032.
The park protects the ruins of 17th- and 18th-century Spanish churches and an Indian pueblo.

Excursions

Albuquerque
Albuquerque Convention and Visitors Bureau, P.O. Box 26866; Albuquerque, NM 87125; tel: 800-284-2282 or 505-243-3696.

Founded in 1706, the "Duke City" lies in the Rio Grande Valley, with the Sandia Mountains to the east and the fabled Rio Grande to the west. The Indian Pueblo Cultural Center offers the best introduction to the state's 19 pueblos, with exhibits, dancing on weekends, and Indian foods. Old New Mexico still lives at the lovely Old Town Plaza, where the Church of San Felipe de Neri, built in 1793, stands next to gift shops and restaurants.

Chaco Canyon
Chaco Culture National Historical Park, P.O. Box 220; Nageezi, NM 87037; tel: 505-786-7014.

It's a long drive over rough roads to Chaco Canyon, but don't miss this premier archaeological site – mecca for people of the Chaco culture from AD 900 to 1130. An eight-mile loop road passes seven of the 11 great houses in the canyon, clearly intended to impress those traveling here to pay tribute, celebrate, and trade. Pueblo Bonito, with numerous kivas and five-story walls of tightly laid sandstone, remains imposing, as does the view enjoyed by hikers above the canyon.

Turquoise Trail
Santa Fe Convention and Visitors Bureau, 201 West Marcy Street, P.O. Box 909; Santa Fe, NM 87504-0909; tel: 800-777-2489 or 505-984-6760.

Scenic Highway 14 northeast of Albuquerque passes through ghost towns and Hispanic villages. The route takes its name from turquoise mines used for centuries by ancient Pueblo Indians. Artists and entrepreneurs have given the old mining towns of Cerillos, Golden, and Madrid a new lease on life. Abandoned shacks and saloons now serve as shops and galleries and, in Madrid, an old-fashioned melodrama theater.

Tombstone
and Southern Arizona

CHAPTER 12

The taunting and the threats are over. Snarls curl the lips of hardened faces. Eyes squint with hatred. The gunslingers face one another, guns drawn. In the distance a dog barks. Heat comes off the roofs in waves. Suddenly, the street explodes in a volley of gunfire. Bodies drop to the ground, twitch, and lie still. Guns are reholstered and their owners race away, leaving the fallen to the flies and the creeping silence. ◆ Time freezes. The spectators are silent. Then the actors jump up and take a bow, the crowd cheers, and the spell is broken. Dozens of video cameras click off, and the hordes return to the boardwalk to be captured by souvenir shops, costumed cowboys, and the many other tourist traps laid for the unsuspecting. ◆ Just over a century ago, the guns in **Tombstone, Arizona**, fired live bullets, not blanks, and their owners – some of the most infamous gunslingers in the West – walked the mean streets of this ambitious little mining town. Gunfights were infrequent but memorable events –

Ghost towns, Spanish missions, old mining towns, and breathtaking borderlands surround the place made famous by the shootout at the O.K. Corral.

and the most memorable of them all was the Gunfight at the O.K. Corral, a 30-second showdown that became Tombstone's Day of Infamy. ◆ The shootout at the O.K. Corral was the culmination of a feud that had been brewing for months. Wearing the black hats were brothers Ike and Billy Clanton and Tom and Frank McLaury – all known or suspected cattle rustlers – and their friend Billy Claibourne. Wearing the white hats (as every kid who's ever played Cowboys and Indians can tell you) were U.S. Marshal Virgil Earp and his brothers Morgan and Wyatt. With them was John "Doc" Holliday – less a hero than a ruthless killer emboldened by terminal tuberculosis.

Saguaro cactus, the many-armed sentinels of the Sonoran Desert, can take 75 years or longer to begin sprouting their appendages and can live for two centuries.

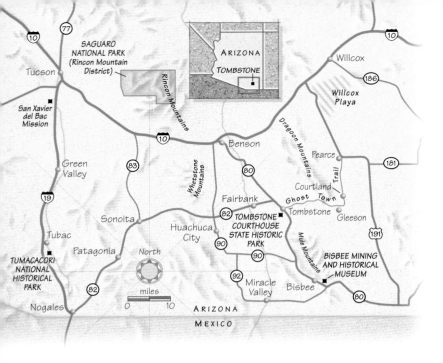

it turned out, Schieffelin both survived and found silver ore.

In dark tribute, he filed two mining claims he called the Graveyard and the Tombstone, and by the 1880s the camp had grown into one of the largest, wealthiest, and liveliest towns in the West. American settlers worked their claims, brawled and brotheled, and occasionally settled their differences with shootouts like the one at the O.K. Corral. All claims to the contrary, hard living and disease trumped murder most years. "A man will go to the devil pretty fast in Tombstone," George Parsons wrote in his 1880 diary. "Faro, whiskey, and bad women will beat anyone."

Discovering Authentic Tombstone

Today, Parsons might well lament: "Overpriced jewelry, bad art, and credit cards will beat anyone." There's quality and value in this touristy little town, but you'll have to dig for it. More than 200,000 tourists invade Tombstone Territory annually, corraling their herds of Winnebagos into crowded parking lots and seemingly buying everything. At its worst, Tombstone features tacky mementos, staged gunfights, and stagecoach rides around cobbled streets. At its best, it showcases the American West as few other towns can.

The best begins with a visit to the elegant 1882 red-brick **Tombstone Courthouse State Historic Park**. The first floor has an exhibit about the Gunfight at the O.K. Corral, including rare documents, varied accounts, even diagrams of the action. The second floor features an authentic 1880s courtroom. From here, you can look down into the courtyard, where you'll see justice's final weapon – a gallows reconstructed from the original.

One spot seldom visited by gunfighters or gallows birds is **St. Paul's Episcopal Church**, built in 1882. The oldest Protestant church in

On the afternoon of October 26, 1881, both sides met near (but not at) the O.K. Corral. Doc Holliday and Morgan Earp probably fired the first shots. Ike Clanton and Billy Claibourne fled. When the smoke cleared, Tom and Frank McLaury and Billy Clanton lay dead, Virgil and Morgan Earp were wounded, and Wyatt Earp and Doc Holliday beat a hasty retreat from what came to be called "the town too tough to die."

Tombstone, surrounded by the fiercely beautiful **Sonoran Desert**, was no tougher than any settlement had to be to survive. Mining gave the scrappy little town its start. In 1877, prospector Ed Schieffelin arrived at **Camp** (later **Fort**) **Huachuca**, built to protect stage lines and supply trains from Apache depredations, and quickly saw the promise in the colorful hills to the northeast. "All you'll find in those hills is your tombstone," warned one soldier weary from fighting Apache raiders. As

A grave marker in Boothill Cemetery (left) stands at the final resting place of Tombstone's infamous gunmen.

Latter-day gunslingers (right) reenact the O.K. Corral shoot-out with blanks and blather on the now-paved mean streets of Tombstone.

Arizona, it is made of local adobe brick and features handsome hand-hewn rafters and graceful lighting fixtures that came from a 19th-century whaling ship.

On the opposite end of town, both geographically and morally, is the **Bird Cage Theater**, once known as the most wicked place between New Orleans and San Francisco. A self-guided tour of the Bird Cage takes you to the seamier side of the Old West, where "soiled doves" plied their trade in 14 individual "cages" or "cribs" suspended from the ceiling above the dance hall. In the basement are more cribs, including one for "Sadie Jo," actually Sarah Josephine Marcus, who carried out a dalliance with Wyatt Earp. On the wall next to her crib is a copy of her prostitute's license (which cost $7.50), signed by Earp himself.

Boothill Cemetery, on the northern end of town, is filled with many of Tombstone's famous dead, including Billy Clanton and Frank and Tom McLaury of the O.K. Corral gunfight. Nowadays the place has been so gussied up that many visitors think it's phony. It's not, but the gift shop at the entry to the cemetery and the piped-in music gives the place an air of unreality. Add freshly painted wooden markers, some with overly clever epitaphs ("Here lies Lester Moore. Four slugs from a .44; No Les, No More") and you may wish to either avoid the cemetery or make your own hasty exit.

Should you venture into the O.K. Corral? It's a genuinely historic place, so if you want to see a blacksmith's forge, horse stalls, and the studio-gallery of C. S. Fly (an important early Arizona photographer), go on in. The setting for today's rehashed gunfight isn't at all inspiring, though. An audiotape dramatizes the battle, whose visual drama is poorly conveyed by the none-too-realistic models of the principal players posing stiffly within the adobe corral. It doesn't seem to matter to anyone that the gunfight didn't take place here. In fact, to stand in Wyatt Earp's shoes, you'll have to head north of the corral to the middle of what is now the main highway through town.

Bisbee and the Ghost Town Trail

That same highway (Arizona 80) connects Tombstone with other lesser-known but equally important places in southern Arizona's history, where you leave behind the gunfire and glitz and enter a world of historic understatement. Like old-time prospectors who sought only gold and silver, too many visitors seek the glitter of Tombstone and overlook many of the lasting treasures

that give Arizona its unique character.

One of the most charming of these treasures is **Bisbee**, which lies southeast of Tombstone in the russet-tinted **Mule Mountains**. A copper mining town of faded grandeur dating from the late 1870s, Bisbee has dozens of architecturally interesting historic buildings that have been revived as crafts shops, restaurants, and pleasant inns.

In downtown Bisbee, visit the gracious 1902 **Copper Queen Hotel**, the grande dame of all southern Arizona hostelries, named for Bisbee's most successful mine. John Wayne stayed here during location filming. Another must-see is the **Bisbee Mining and Historical Museum**, located in the 1897 Copper Queen

Consolidated Mining Company Headquarters a good stop before heading over for the Queen Mine Tour, one of the better underground mine tours in the West.

To the northeast of Tombstone is the **Ghost Town Trail**, which passes through several old mining camps. First stop is **Gleeson** an early-20th-century copper town, with the ruins of a jail, school, and hospital. Farther up the road, in the barren hills of the **Dragoon Mountains** (the stronghold of Apache warrior Cochise), all that's left of **Courtland** is its jail, but before World War I the town had its own automobile dealership and a population of 2,000. Neighboring **Pearce**, the site of an 1894 gold rush, has also been spirited away

Peacemakers

The gun. It was a necessary tool for most western pioneers, providing game for the table and protection from predators of both the two-legged and four-legged variety. If you knew how to handle them, six-shooters conveyed power, respect, freedom, even a fearsome reputation. They could also bring you to an early grave.

The West's most famous revolvers were the Peacemakers, descendants of Samuel Colt's 1836 Patersons, the first really practical revolver. They first showed their worth in June 1844, when Captain Jack Hays and his greatly outnumbered company of Texas Rangers used Patersons against fearless Comanche Indians, who had not expected the Rangers to fire again and again without reloading.

For so-called "gunfighters," who operated on both sides of the law, guns were more than tools; they were a way of life. A gunfighter's piece had to be reliable and easy to handle, but a little style never hurt. Nattily dressed Wild Bill Hickock, one of the West's flashiest gunfighters, favored a pair of Colt 1851 Navy revolvers fitted with carved ivory grips. When Sheriff Pat Garrett shot Billy the Kid in 1881, he used a regular .44-caliber Single Action Army Colt Peacemaker. Twenty years later, though, Garrett carried out his role as customs collector with a far different gun: a double-action .41-caliber Colt Thunderer that was plated with gold and had grips fashioned of sterling silver.

Revolvers were as common in the West as sunsets, but long arms were even more important. Breechloading, single-shot rifles had superior range and included such durable, accurate rifles as the .45-caliber Springfield used by the U.S. Army from 1874 to 1893. The most famous gun of them all was the Winchester .44-caliber, 15-shot Model 1873. None other than Buffalo Bill pronounced it the best for "general hunting or Indian fighting." At a time when violence resolved all disputes, this was "the gun that won the West." – *Gregory Lalire*

Revolvers such as these Colts (left and below) went by many names – six-shooters, hog legs, peacemakers, equalizers – and were regarded as essential equipment for frontier life. As the saying went, "God made some men big and some small, but Colonel Sam Colt made them equal all."

Mission San Xavier del Bac (opposite) was founded by Jesuit missionary Eusebio Kino in 1700; the present church was completed in 1797.

Located in the flat Sulphur Springs valley, the sole reminder of the past here is the **Old Store**, a large two-story adobe with an impressive tin facade.

The Spanish Influence

A very different piece of Arizona history unfolds as you drive west from Tombstone, through **Fairbank**, once a rail stop for Tombstone and the site of an ambitious attempted train robbery. Beyond Fairbank the highway leaves mining country, and desert cactus gradually gives way to the grasslands and ranches near **Sonoita** and **Patagonia**. This area is such quintessential cattle country that it was used to film the classic *Oklahoma!* Southwest of Patagonia, the border town of **Nogales** displays the strong influence of the Spanish and Mexican cultures and is the Arizona entry point of the Santa Cruz ("Holy Cross") River, which gave rise to settlements as far as Tucson. Several Indian cultures – Papago (now known as Tohono O'Odham), Apache, and Pima Indians vied with Spanish, Mexican, and American newcomers for sites along the precious river.

Spanish missionary efforts sought to exert both religious and political holds on Arizona, with mixed results. North of Nogales is **Tumacácori National Historic Park**, which preserves a partly ruined, white-domed adobe Spanish mission. Founded in 1691 by Father Eusebio Kino, a Jesuit who made the first missionary efforts among the Pima, the present mission was begun by the Franciscans in 1800, completed in 1820, then abandoned after repeated Apache attacks in 1848. A few miles north of the mission is **Tubac**, founded by the Spanish in 1752 and Arizona's oldest European settlement. The town was originally a presidio, or garrison, protecting Spaniards following the Pima Revolt. Today,

it's a pleasant artists' colony with a state park museum recounting the human history of the Santa Cruz River.

Just north, on the banks of the Santa Cruz, is one of Arizona's most beloved landmarks. The beautiful 1778 Spanish **Mission of San Xavier del Bac**, known affectionately as the "White Dove of the Desert," sheltered Spaniards and Pimas fleeing Apache incursions at Tumacácori Mission in 1848. Highly photogenic, San Xavier is considered the finest example of mission architecture in the United States. Situated just southwest of Tucson, on the **Tohono O'Odham Reservation**, it is both an historic landmark and an active parish church, and with its quiet elegance and dignity serves as an appropriate contrast with the bustle and ballyhoo of Tombstone.

TRAVEL TIPS

DETAILS

When to Go

Spring, fall, and winter are all good times to visit the Sonoran Desert. Head for the high country in summer, when temperatures at lower elevations often exceed 100°F. Be prepared for thunderstorms. Temperatures are typically in the 60s and 70s from October to May. Nighttime temperatures, however, can fall below freezing.

How to Get There

Commercial airlines serve Tucson International and Phoenix Sky Harbor International Airports.

Getting Around

You'll need a car to explore the desert. Car rentals are available at the airports. Roads are generally passable, but watch for flooding around Willcox and other low-lying areas from July to September.

INFORMATION

Bisbee Chamber of Commerce

P.O. Box BA; Bisbee, AZ 85603; tel: 520-432-5421.

Tombstone Chamber of Commerce

P.O. Box 995; Tombstone, AZ 85638; tel: 520-457-9317.

LODGING

PRICE GUIDE – double occupancy

$ = up to $49 $$ = $50–$99
$$$ = $100–$149 $$$$ = $150+

Circle Z Ranch

P.O. Box 194; Patagonia, AZ 85624; tel: 520-394-2525.

Guests stay in seven adobe cottages about 60 miles south of Tucson, at the foot of the Patagonia and Santa Rita Mountains. The ranch, which has 27 guest rooms, offers horseback riding, pack trips, and bird watching at the adjoining Nature Conservancy preserve. A three-day minimum stay is required. $$

Cochise Hotel

P.O. Box 27; Cochise, AZ 85606; tel: 520-384-3156 or 520-384-3414.

The one-story Cochise Hotel, built in 1882 to serve railroad workers, is still going strong, though a bit faded. The hotel has five guest rooms with private baths and period furniture, and maintains a studied austerity. Reservations must be made at least one week in advance. $–$$

Copper Queen Hotel

11 Howell Avenue; Bisbee, AZ 85603; tel: 800-247-5829 or 520-432-2216.

An elegant turn-of-the-century landmark built during the heyday of the Copper Queen Mine. Past guests include John Wayne and Teddy Roosevelt. A dining room, saloon, and swimming pool are on the premises. $$$

Lazy K Bar Guest Ranch

8401 North Scenic Drive; Tucson, AZ 85743; tel: 800-321-7018 or 520-744-3050.

Lazy K's nine adobe cottages are set in the Tucson Mountains, overlooking the Santa Cruz Valley, about 16 miles northwest of Tucson. Horseback riding, a swimming pool, spa, and ranch store are available. A three-night minimum stay is required. $$

Schoolhouse Inn

P.O. Box 32; Bisbee, AZ 85603; tel: 800-537-4333 or 520-432-2996.

Guests stay in a 1918 brick schoolhouse at the west end of Tombstone Canyon. Themed suites, which have 12-foot-high ceilings, include the Principal's Office and Art, Reading, and Writing Rooms. $$

Vineyard Bed and Breakfast

92 South Los Encinos Road; Sonoita, AZ 85637; tel: 520-455-4749.

Located in the rolling border country, the 1910 Hacienda Los Encinos ("House of the Oaks") has been updated to include three suites in the main house and a charming Southwest-style guest house. $$

TOURS & OUTFITTERS

Goldfield Ghost Town and Mine Tours

4650 East Mammoth Mine Road; Apache Junction, AZ 85219; tel: 602-983-0333.

Tour a reconstructed gold camp along the Apache Trail east of Phoenix.

Old Tucson Studios

201 South Kinney Road; Tucson, AZ 85735; tel: 520-883-0100.

Staged gunfights, Native American storytelling, games, and rides on the rebuilt set of *Rio Lobo* and other western films.

Queen Mine Tour

118 Arizona Street; Bisbee, AZ 85603; tel: 520-432-2071.

Tour a large copper mine in Bisbee.

MUSEUMS

Bisbee Mining and Historical Museum

5 Copper Queen Plaza; Bisbee, AZ 85603; tel: 520-432-7071.

This superb little museum has interactive exhibits that bring Bisbee's human history to life – a must before taking one of the mine tours.

Heard Museum

22 East Monte Vista Road; Phoenix, AZ 85044; tel: 602-252-8848.

One of the Southwest's premier

cultural institutions presents the region's Indian tribes, superb collections of Indian arts and crafts (including the late Barry Goldwater's historic kachina doll collection), and special exhibitions and related programs.

Mission San Xavier del Bac
1950 West San Xavier; Tucson, AZ 85706; tel: 520-294-2624.

This beautiful mission church, still used by the Tohono O'Odham tribe, was established by Father Eusebio Kino in 1629.

PARKS

Organ Pipe Cactus National Monument
Route 1, Box 100; Ajo, AZ 85321; tel: 520-387-5849.

Organ Pipe protects its namesake, a many-armed cactus, on the U.S.–Mexican border of the Sonoran Desert.

Saguaro National Park
3693 South Old Spanish Trail; Tucson, AZ 85730; tel: 520-733-5153 (east unit); or 2700 North Kinney Road; Tucson, AZ 85743; tel: 520-733-5158 (west unit).

Protects stands of saguaro cactus in two separate units close to Tucson, and several prehistoric Indian rock-art sites.

Tombstone Courthouse State Historic Park
219 East Toughnut Street; Tombstone, AZ 85638; tel: 520-457-3311.

The park includes an authentic 1880 courtroom, displays about the shootout at the O.K. Corral, and a gallows.

Tumacácori National Historical Park
P.O. Box 67; Tumacacori, AZ 85640; tel: 520-398-2341.

Preserves a partly ruined, white-domed adobe Spanish mission built by the Franciscans in 1820.

Excursions

The Apache Trail
Greater Phoenix Convention and Visitors Bureau; 400 East Van Buren, #600; Phoenix, AZ 85004; tel: 877-225-5749 or 602-254-6500.

The Apache Trail, east of Phoenix, was created during construction of the Theodore Roosevelt Lake and Dam. Enjoy views of the ruggedly beautiful Superstition Mountains, site of the legendary Lost Dutchman Gold Mine, and of Goldfield Ghost Town, a reconstructed mining camp. Remains of the Salado culture are on view at Tonto National Monument, which preserves a 12th-century cliff dwelling, and at Besh-Ba-Gowah, a 200-room pueblo in the mining town of Globe, bordering the San Carlos Apache Reservation.

Chiricahua National Monument
Dos Cabezas, HCR 2, Box 6500; Willcox, AZ 85643; tel: 520-824-3560.

A godsend in summer, the lush 5,000- to 7,000-foot-high Chiricahua Mountains, 36 miles southeast of Willcox, preserve the Land of Standing-Up Rocks, the Apache name for the eerie volcanic formations found here. Trails offer close-ups of odd rock columns, or hoodoos, and Sonoran and Chihuahuan Desert wildlife from both sides of the international border. A trail in Bonita Canyon leads to the Faraway Ranch, built by the Erickson family, who ran cattle here for nearly 90 years.

Tucson
Tucson Convention and Visitors Bureau; 130 South Scott Avenue; Tucson, AZ 85701; tel: 800-638-8350 or 520-624-1817.

Hispanic and pioneer influences dominate the "Old Pueblo" of Tucson. Walk to Presidio Park, site of the 1776 Spanish garrison; to the 1848 Casa Cordova, a Mexican-era adobe; and to the 1928 tile-domed Pima County Courthouse. Fourteen miles west of town, eyeball a chuckwalla or coatimundi at the world-famous Arizona–Sonora Desert Museum, where desert flora and fauna are exhibited in natural settings. Nearby, Saguaro National Park preserves the state's most recognizable symbol: the saguaro cactus, which can grow as high as 60 feet. Tucson Studios gives visitors a chance to "shoot 'em up" where *Rio Lobo* and other Westerns were filmed.

Grand Canyon
Arizona

CHAPTER **13**

S tick 'em up! Or I'll stick 'em up for you." The mood of the bandanna'd bandito with the twirled moustache, worn boots, and long duster is black – as black as his garb. The passengers aboard the train don't know whether to laugh or scream, hand over their cameras or steal a shot. Two youngsters giggle nervously. ◆ It's been a day straight out of *Family Vacation*: sing-alongs, lame jokes, name the 10 natural wonders of the world, be the first to spot an antelope, a fictitious Woolly Woopsie, and finally the canyon itself. Like time travelers, the passengers climbed aboard this old steam train at **Williams, Arizona**, to journey across pale grasslands, through timeless ponderosa forest, past silent buttes, to the Big Ditch itself. There, they swooned over the views, then it was off for lunch, a hike, a ranger chat, a museum visit, and perhaps a purchase before the train whistle sounded for departure. ◆ The holdup by the Cataract Creek Gang is soon over. The lanky sheriff bursts through the door, guns blazing, and

Natives and newcomers, explorers and prospectors, dreamers and schemers – all have been drawn to this wonder of nature.

chases the gang off the train onto waiting horses. The carriages jolt into life and move slowly toward the old rail depot, where passengers are serenaded by the local brass band and greeted by the sheriff, who poses for photos before sending them on their way. It's been a lot of fun. ◆ The holdups and shootouts may be fake, but the historic Grand Canyon train is an authentic delight. Built by the Santa Fe Railroad in 1901, the line was an immediate success. Visitors, tired of bumpy stagecoaches, reveled in the railroad's powerful steam engines, gracious carriages, fine hotels, and gourmet restaurants.

Havasu Canyon, in the western Grand Canyon, is the home of the Havasupai Indians, known as the People of the Blue-Green Water.

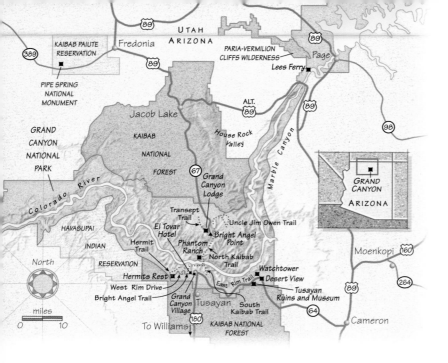

ex-miners like Civil War veteran Capt. John Hance who, along with fellow prospectors, began mining zinc, copper, lead, and asbestos in the Grand Canyon in 1883, then parlayed his love of the canyon into a successful guide and lodging business. Hance sold his hotel to the Santa Fe, then stayed on to charm visitors with such tall tales that one exclaimed: "To see the canyon only, and not to see Capt. John Hance, is to miss half the show."

The genteel El Tovar, named for Spanish explorer Don Pedro de Tovar, who first reported the canyon's existence in 1540, is the ideal place to start a tour of **Grand Canyon Village**. The hotel's relaxing veranda, authentic southwestern atmosphere, elegant dining room, and unbeatable views make El Tovar a place to linger. Nearby is **Hopi House**, the canyon's oldest retail establishment. A Pueblo-style building designed in 1904 by Mary Colter, it incorporates features like vigas, latillas, and roof ladders and sells superb Indian crafts. West of El Tovar, Colter's 1935 **Bright Angel Lodge** is built in pioneer-cabin style and houses a hotel and restaurant and a small museum that tells the Fred Harvey story. Another Colter gem, the 1914 **Lookout Studio**, merges with its Kaibab Limestone surroundings so successfully you hardly know it's there. Also overlooking the canyon is the refurbished 1904 **Kolb Studio**, built by Emory and Ellsworth Kolb, who were the first to film a Grand Canyon river run and sold souvenirs to tourists using the adjoining Bright Angel Trail.

Bright Angel Trail and **South Kaibab Trail** are the park's only maintained trails and have heavy hiker and mule traffic. Following an old Indian route, Bright Angel Trail was operated by miners Pete Berry and Ralph Cameron as a toll trail from 1891 until the

Early Tourism

In partnership with the Santa Fe Railroad was concessionaire Fred Harvey, an English immigrant with business savvy whose dapper Harvey Girls were celebrated for their beauty, brains, and dedication to service. They worked at landmarks like the 1905 log-and-stone **El Tovar Hotel**, designed by architect Charles Whittlesey to emulate a European hunting lodge. Most remarkable, though, were the creations of architect-designer Mary Elizabeth Jane Colter, who used the Southwest's indigenous materials and cultures as inspiration for her many buildings at the South Rim. It was a far cry from the tent camps and early hotels built by

Grand Canyon Railway (left) runs vintage locomotives from Williams to the South Rim.

Mules (opposite, top) have been transporting visitors into the canyon for more than a century, although not always willingly.

A mule wrangler treats visitors to a breathtaking canyon view (opposite, bottom).

federal government took over the canyon. Mule rides, popular for more than a century, remain so today. Dude wranglers lead mule strings down to verdant **Indian Creek** onto the broad **Tonto Platform**, then descend into the Inner Canyon to Phantom Ranch, a 1922 rustic hideaway designed by Mary Colter and located on Bright Angel Creek.

Nature's Sculpture

What can you say about the 1,904-square-mile Grand Canyon? British writer J. B. Priestley thought it looked like "Beethoven's Ninth Symphony in stone and magic light." But everyone has his or her own opinion. From any viewpoint along the pleasant **Rim Trail**, the 277-mile-long, 18-mile-wide, mile-deep Grand Canyon transmutes with the seasons and shifting light: magical in fog after a heavy winter rain; brilliant with cactus blooms in April below the rim while the plateau sleeps under snow; heat-blurred in summer, when temperatures at the river top 100 degrees.

"Nature takes cinders, ashes, sediments, and makes all divine in fineness and

beauty," said John Muir, eloquently summing up the volcanism, sediment deposition, and erosion that created the world's most spectacular chasm. From rim to river, 1.7 billion years of earth's history – four geologic eras and 12 different formations – are on display here. The **Colorado River** was the genie that opened this geologic Sesame, cutting down through the **Colorado Plateau** uplift just a few million years ago. As it descends through 160 major rapids from Lees Ferry to Diamond Creek, this master sculptor is often lost from view, but the apprentices – tributary streams, rain, ice, wind, and gravity – work in plain sight, widening and carving this great labyrinth of buttes, temples, and sheer cliffs.

To appreciate the artistry, take a walk or drive at sunset. Several overlooks along the eight-mile **West Rim Drive** offer excellent

sunset views. The road (closed to private vehicles in summer) ends at **Hermits Rest**, although the canyon continues for another 180 miles through the **Havasupai and Hualapai Reservations** to **Lake Mead**. The country-cottage feel of the 1914 Hermits Rest makes it Colter's quaintest folly. Just beyond is the delightful **Hermit Trail**, a beautiful side canyon that leads to French-Canadian prospector Louis Boucher's old camp. The rocky path descends from fossiliferous Kaibab Limestone to the red-and-gray Toroweap Formation, through pinyon, juniper, and netleaf hackberry. On quiet days, listen for tuneful canyon wrens singing among the rocks. Natural quiet is a scarce commodity at the South Rim but still available at the North Rim on the **Kaibab Plateau**, 215 car miles away.

Sacred Places

Take your time driving out the East Rim Drive to Highway 89, and stop at **Tusayan Pueblo**, a 12th-century village built by the ancestors of today's Hopi people, who live on the Hopi Mesas to the east and consider the canyon their place of origin and final destination. The canyon is also sacred to the Hualapai and Havasupai, who live in the west canyon, and the Navajo, whose large reservation begins east and north of here. Panoramic views of the Navajo and Hopi Reservations, the Painted Desert, and volcanic peaks can be had from the 70-foot-high **Desert View Watchtower**, a 1932 Colter reconstruction of an Ancestral Pueblo tower structure. The Puebloan theme is also evoked in Hopi artist Fred Kabotie's striking mural found inside the building.

Just north of the junction with Highway 89 is **Cameron**, at the Little Colorado River crossing. Ralph Cameron and other miners successfully blocked national-park status for Grand Canyon until 1919, but there's little trace of him at Cameron, which preserves a bustling trading post built to serve the Navajo community nearly a century ago. Gas, food, and lodging are available here, and inside the post you can buy Indian crafts or sample Navajo tacos and other fare in the tin-ceilinged dining room.

You leave the Navajo Reservation at **Marble Canyon**, where, in 1929, the 467-foot-high Navajo Bridge made history as the highest steel structure in the world and the only bridge over the Colorado River for 600 miles. Rubberneckers no longer take their lives in their hands: A wider bridge was opened in 1997, and you can walk across the old structure. A handsome interpretive center offers books and information on nearby Lake Powell and Glen Canyon Dam. Behind the 2,000-foot Vermilion Cliffs is **Lees Ferry**, once a ferry crossing operated by Mormon John D. Lee. Today, it's the put-in for Grand Canyon river trips, and Lee's old homestead, **Lonely Dell**, is a historic site.

Into "the Great Unknown"

Indian art (opposite, top) is sold at Hopi House, a historic Pueblo-style building on the South Rim.

Desert View Watchtower (opposite, bottom) was architect Mary Colter's last – and most complex – building at Grand Canyon.

John Wesley Powell (right) confers with his Kaibab Paiute guide Chuarrumpeak.

A wooden dory (below), similar to those used by Powell, narrowly avoids swamping in Lava Falls.

A mile upstream, boaters strain to hear the faint roar of **Lava Falls**. They want to allow plenty of time to pull in to scout the rapid. With boats securely tied on shore, guides and passengers scramble up a well-worn trail to a high rock. Below, they witness a foaming mass of whitewater spanning the width of the **Colorado River**. Lava Falls plummets 37 feet in a quarter mile, one of the infamous "big drops" of the river-running world. A Class 10 (they don't go any higher), three-buckle, white-knuckle rapid if ever there was one.

Lava Falls is neither the first nor the last rambunctious whitewater on the Colorado River through the Grand Canyon, but it is one of the most legendary. It adds mystique to a trip on the West's great river as it flows wild and free for 277 miles through Grand Canyon National Park. More than 15,000 people a year boat the "Grand," as it's affectionately known, most of them on commercial trips in oar- or motor-powered rafts.

Modern expeditioners on the Colorado River follow in the footsteps of one individual – Major John Wesley Powell. With nine other men, the Powell expedition became the first to successfully navigate the Colorado River. In May 1869 the major and his crew launched in four wooden, oar-powered boats from Green River, Wyoming. Although river-savvy by the time they reached Grand Canyon, Powell knew they were entering "the Great Unknown." Despite the ensuing travails, the one-armed major scaled the canyon's sheer cliffs and ran the river's rapids while tied to a chair in his boat. To him, all this was "the music of waters." – Rose Houk

Mormon Settlements

Highway 89A continues to the base of the **Kaibab Plateau**, through a route used by Spaniards Dominguez and Escalante, passing **House Rock Valley**, a grassy break in the cliffs long used by Kaibab Paiutes and, later, Mormon ranchers. Today it abuts the BLM-administered **Paria-Vermilion Cliffs Wilderness**, and you may glimpse a soaring condor, one of about 20 released in the area as part of a rescue program, or the buffalo herd introduced by "Uncle" Jim Owen, warden of the 1906 Grand Canyon Game Reserve.

The road winds onto the 8,000-foot plateau and turns south to the North Rim at **Jacob Lake**, named for Mormon missionary Jacob Hamblin, who came through in the 1860s. Starting in 1866, Franklin Woolley,

followed by his brother Edwin "Dee" Woolley, explored the plateau's potential for lumber, grazing, and Mormon settlement. "Dee" Woolley, a church elder from nearby Kanab, Utah, is said to have seen the Grand Canyon and remarked: "People would pay a lot to look at that."

It took a while. Mormons from the Kanab area built a sawmill and cabins, and they grazed cattle here in summer, but the plateau's remoteness, hard winters, and lack of surface water impeded development. In 1892, Woolley tried to interest English noblemen in game hunting and ranching (even hiring Buffalo Bill as escort), then tried, also unsuccessfully, to get the railroad to build a link to the South Rim. Then, in 1893, much of the North Kaibab was withdrawn as the new Grand Canyon Forest Reserve. In 1901, Woolley and brothers-in-law Henry Bowman and David Rust began the long, tedious work of improving the steep trail to Bright Angel Creek and constructed a short-lived cable car over the river at present-day Phantom Ranch (it is no longer visible).

Roosevelt to the Rescue

One of the cable car's first passengers was President Teddy Roosevelt, a man after Woolley's heart with his love of the West, thrill of the hunt, and political acumen. In 1903, Roosevelt took the train to the South Rim and cabled across to the North Rim on a hunting expedition. He had such a bully time that he had a portion of Grand Canyon Forest Reserve converted to a 612,736-acre game reserve in 1906. Thus began a complicated process that eventually split the plateau into a national forest and a national park.

A visit here starts at turn-of-the-century **Jacob Lake Inn**, operated by descendants

Antelope Canyon near Page, Arizona, was shaped by centuries of flowing water.

Utah agave (opposite) is found in warm, dry environments below the canyon rim.

Canyon view (below): Teddy Roosevelt described Grand Canyon as "the one great sight which every American should see."

of Edwin Woolley and Henry Bowman, and the only services open year-round. The little log inn is a cozy place. Enjoy the family atmosphere, gas up, try one of the famous milkshakes and pies, and pass up the tiny, duplex-style log cabins – unless you like hearing your neighbor snore. A second option in summer is the 1926 **Kaibab Lodge**, five miles from the park entrance and also modest but friendly. At **Jacob Lake**, a small Forest Service visitor center has exhibits and information on visiting the rough backcountry of the North Kaibab Ranger District. There's

olitude and hiking aplenty here, including a hike to **Snake Gulch**, a remarkable site for rock art. A campground and concession-aire-run horseback rides are also available near the inn.

The scenic highway winds 44 miles from Jacob Lake to the North Rim, through forests of ponderosa, aspen, and fir interspersed with meadows dotted with Indian paintbrush, lupine, and other wildflowers in summer. Look for the tassel-eared Kaibab squirrels, the white-tailed cousins of the Coconino Plateau's darker Abert squirrels, which are separated by the Grand Canyon. At the park, make your first stop historic **Grand Canyon Lodge**, a soaring stone-and-rock structure perched on the rim. Walk the few yards out to **Bright Angel Point**, where the 4,000-foot dropoff is dramatic and the views awe-inspiring. Many visitors are surprised to learn that they're not actually viewing the Grand Canyon proper but a tributary called **Bright Angel Canyon**. It's hard to believe that such a vast space is merely a side branch. To reach the main canyon, follow **Cape Royal Road** to **Cape Royal**. The drive is only about 23 miles but can take at least half a day, with stops at **Point Imperial** and

other stunning view-points along the way.

Hiking into the canyon is only for the initiated here, but there are a number of enjoy-able rim hikes. The lodge and campground are linked by the 3½-mile round-trip **Transept Trail**, which offers glimpses of a major tributary canyon of Bright Angel Creek. The four-mile **Uncle Jim Owen Trail** follows part of the maintained **North Kaibab Trail** and commemorates game warden "Uncle" Jim Owen, a former member of the Jesse James gang and the favorite guide of Teddy Roosevelt and Zane Grey. It was said that Owen never met a mountain lion he couldn't kill – 532, by his count, a number that radically altered the balance of lions and deer.

If you get to the North Rim late in the day, you may have trouble finding a bed for the night or a campsite. One option is to continue to nearby **Fredonia**, Arizona, or Kanab, Utah. As Highway 89A drops into the lonely **Arizona Strip**, views of the **Grand Staircase**, a series of colorful geological ascending "steps," dominate the horizon, with the Navajo Sandstone of **Zion National Park** forming one of the steps. It's hard to believe now but the eroded grasslands of the Arizona Strip were once tallgrass prairie splashed with sunflowers and other plants used by the more than 5,000 Kaibab Paiutes who lived here until Spanish raiding, Navajo and Ute incursions, and Mormon settlers virtually wiped out the tribe.

For a look at both historic and modern Kaibab Paiute lifeways, western ranching history, Mormon settlement, and public land development of the Arizona Strip, finish your trip at **Pipe Spring National Monument**, an 1872 fortified Mormon ranch surrounded by the tiny **Kaibab Paiute Reservation**, a few miles west of Fredonia, where you can tour the fort, visit tribal headquarters, and hike a nature trail.

TRAVEL TIPS

DETAILS

When to Go

The South Rim is open year-round; the North Rim is closed from November to May, except for snowshoeing, skiing, and winter camping. Spring and fall are pleasant. Summer is crowded, hot, dry, and prone to spectacular thunderstorms and sudden temperature drops. Winters are bitterly cold but marked by beautiful snowfalls and quiet.

How to Get There

Major airlines fly to Phoenix Sky Harbor International and McCarran International in Las Vegas. Commuter airlines serve Pulliam Field in Flagstaff and Grand Canyon National Airport in Tusayan. The Grand Canyon Railway runs a vintage steam engine 65 miles from Williams to the South Rim (see "Tours & Outfitters").

Getting Around

Free shuttle buses run from Tusayan to the South Rim and along the West Rim and East Rim Drives in summer. Shuttle service also connects the North and South Rims, but you'll want a car to explore the surrounding area. Car rentals are available at airports in Phoenix, Las Vegas, and Flagstaff.

Backcountry Travel

Overnight trips are restricted in the national park. Reserve permits up to a year in advance.

Handicapped Access

The South Rim visitor center and some shuttle buses are accessible.

INFORMATION

Grand Canyon National Park

P.O. Box 129; Grand Canyon, AZ 86023; tel: 520-638-7888 (general information) or 520-638-7875 (backcountry information).

CAMPING

The South Rim has two campgrounds with more than 350 sites; the North Rim has 82 campsites. There are about 60 backcountry campsites as well. To reserve a site, write to DESTINET, National Park Service, P.O. Box 85705; San Diego, CA 92186-5705; or call 800-365-2267.

LODGING

PRICE GUIDE – double occupancy

$ = up to $49 $$ = $50–$99

$$$ = $100–$149 $$$$ = $150+

Bright Angel Lodge

Grand Canyon National Park, P.O. Box 129; Grand Canyon, AZ 86023; tel: 303-297-2757.

This 1935 log-and-stone lodge, on the site of the old Bright Angel Camp, has been called architect Mary Colter's finest achievement. The rustic lodge, surrounded by 50 historic cabins, has 37 rooms, some with private baths and views of the canyon. $$–$$$$.

El Tovar Hotel

Grand Canyon National Park, P.O. Box 129; Grand Canyon, AZ 86023; tel: 303-297-2757.

Completed in 1905, the 76-room El Tovar once boasted its own dairy, greenhouse, and fine furniture, china, and linens. Food and lodging are still top-notch, and Christmas is particularly memorable. $$$–$$$$

Fray Marcos Hotel

1201 West Route 66, Suite 200; Flagstaff, AZ 86001; tel: 800-843-8724.

A reconstruction of the original 1908 Fray Marcos, this new 89-room hotel at the historic depot mixes turn-of-the-century ambiance with convenience. The Western-style lobby celebrates the art of Frederic Remington; a saloon features a player piano and a beautifully carved bar from a London pub. $$–$$$$

Grand Canyon Lodge

Grand Canyon National Park, P.O. Box 129; Grand Canyon, AZ 86023; tel: 303-297-2757.

Designed in the 1920s by Gilbert Stanley Underwood, this limestone-and-timber lodge offers breathtaking views from the edge of the North Rim. The main structure has 40 rooms; 160 historic cottages also are available. $$–$$$

Horseshoe Ranch

HCR 34, Box 5005, Mayer, AZ 86333; tel: 520-632-8813.

One of Arizona's oldest and most hospitable working ranches, the 100-square-mile Horseshoe is located at 3,200 feet on the Agua Fria River, 42 miles from Prescott. Guests rise early to help hired hands with the ranch's 1,700 cattle. The Horseshoe has eight large, tastefully decorated rooms. A three-day minimum stay is required. $$$$

Jacob Lake Inn

Jacob Lake, AZ 86022; tel: 520-643-7232.

A turn-of-the-century trading post run by the descendants of Mormon pioneers, this modest inn has motel-style rooms and duplex cabins. $$

TOURS & OUTFITTERS

Arizona Raft Adventures

4050 East Huntington Drive; Flagstaff, AZ 86004; tel: 520-526-8200.

Whitewater excursions on the Colorado River last six to 16 days

Grand Canyon Field Institute

P.O. Box 399; Grand Canyon, AZ 86023; tel: 520-638-2485.

Educational programs combine

hiking and other travel in the canyon with examinations of canyon geology, archaeology, and history.

Grand Canyon Lodges – Amfac Parks and Resorts

14001 East Iliff; Aurora, CO 80014; tel: 303-297-2757 or 520-638-2631.

Mule rides, bus tours, and other Grand Canyon activities.

Grand Canyon Railway

1201 West Route 66, Suite 200; Flagstaff, AZ 86001; tel: 800-843-8724.

A turn-of-the-century steam engine runs between Williams and the South Rim.

MUSEUMS

Museum of Northern Arizona

3101 North Fort Valley Road; Flagstaff, AZ 86001; tel: 520-774-5213 or 520-774-5211.

The region's premier museum interprets the geological, natural, and cultural history of the Colorado Plateau.

Sharlot Hall Museum

415 West Gurley; Prescott, AZ 86301; tel: 520-445-3122.

The personal collection of Sharlot Hall, an early Arizona pioneer and writer, is displayed here in several early buildings.

Tusayan Museum and Ruins

Grand Canyon National Park, P.O. Box 129; Grand Canyon, AZ 86023; tel: 520-638-7888.

About 23 miles east of Grand Canyon Village, this museum interprets a 12th-century pueblo, its ancient inhabitants, and their descendants, the Hopi.

PARKS

Pipe Spring National Monument

HC 65, Box 5; Fredonia, AZ 86022; tel: 520-643-7105.

A fortified Mormon ranch built in 1870.

Excursions

Flagstaff

Flagstaff Visitor Center, 1 East Route 66; Flagstaff, AZ 86001; tel: 800-842-7293 or 520-774-9541.

Nestled beneath the glorious San Francisco Peaks, the mountain town of Flagstaff sits within the country's largest ponderosa pine forest. Logging, ranching, and the railroad have been eclipsed by cultural institutions like Northern Arizona University, Lowell Observatory, and the fine Museum of Northern Arizona, but tourism is the mainstay. Travelers wanting to get their "kicks" on Route 66 should two-step over to the historic Museum Club, a bizarre log roadhouse where Willie Nelson got his start.

Jerome

Cottonwood Chamber of Commerce, 1010 South Main Street; Cottonwood, AZ 86326; tel: 520-634-7593.

The old copper mining community of Jerome, perched high above the culturally rich Verde Valley, was a place of numerous saloons, gambling dens, and brothels. In fact, Jerome was dubbed "the wickedest town in the West" in the 1880s. In recent years, Jerome, lovingly restored by artists, has sprung delightful galleries, boutiques, and three museums that celebrate its mining history. Winding streets offer remarkable views of Sedona's redrock country and the San Francisco Peaks to the north.

Wickenburg

Wickenburg Chamber of Commerce, 216 North Frontier Street; Wickenburg, AZ 85390; tel: 520-684-5479.

"Guest Ranch Capital of the World," Wickenburg is in prime cowboy country, 58 miles from Phoenix. Henry Wickenburg's 1863 Vulture gold mine is gone, but the Desert Caballeros Museum tells its story, and galleries display Indian artifacts and the paintings of Remington, Russell, and others. When you're not riding the range, check out Wickenburg's Old Jail Tree, where prisoners were shackled for lack of a prison, and the shady trails along Hassayampa River Preserve, a nature sanctuary.

Indian Country
Arizona

CHAPTER 14

onument Valley. It's one of the most famous, yet one of the most remote, regions in the United States – 30,000 acres of high desert straddling the Arizona-Utah border, a tiny parcel amid the sprawling Navajo Nation. This valley is a raw, bare land worked by wind and water into fantastic shapes and forms, a place of contrasts and extremes: rippled sand dunes sashed with delicate evening primrose; dry washes brimming with turbid water in flood. It is the home of the Wild West in the imagination, and literally the home of the Navajo, who have lived here for centuries.   ◆   In 1939, trading-post owner Harry Goulding introduced Hollywood filmmaker John Ford to Monument Valley, and between 1939 and 1964, Ford used the valley as backdrop for many of his Westerns, including such classics as *Stagecoach*. The result is a strange sense of familiarity as you drive into the area, as if memory were stronger than reality. But there is more to Monument Valley than remembered images, and a visit here takes

At home in remote and sacred valleys and mesas, the Navajos and Hopis walk a path between centuries-old rituals and modern lifeways.

you into another way of living, among a people who really do live the Old Ways.   ◆   To the Navajo, or the Diné, as they call themselves, Monument Valley is *Tse' Bii' Ndzisgaii*, "space between the rocks." It's interesting that their name for this place evokes more of what is absent than what is present. To Navajos, the individual stone monuments are associated with their holy people, and only medicine men may utter the names of the most sacred ones. Soft-spoken, private people, Navajos offer gentle handshakes and avert their eyes upon first meeting. Yet they've become accustomed to the swell of visitors who pour through their famous valley each year, speaking a variety

Navajo sheepherders at Ear of the Wind in Monument Valley continue a centuries-old way of life.

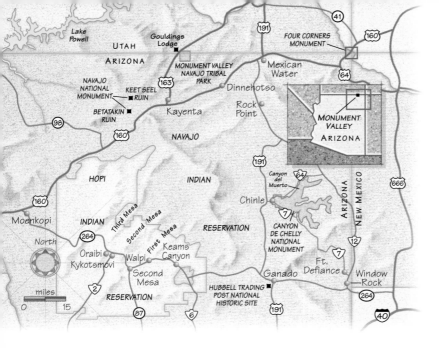

where your hostess is seated on a sheepskin on the dirt floor in front of her loom, dressed in a long tiered skirt and velveteen blouse, and adorned with a silver squash-blossom necklace. Her slender fingers are like the roots of the yucca plant from a lifetime of weaving, and her hair is tied back in a traditional bun fastened with cord. If you are lucky, perhaps she will demonstrate the technique, combing a visitor's long hair with a grass brush and then arranging it to her satisfaction. After answering a few questions, translated by the woman's daughter, you may be offered lunch – possibly mutton stew or "Navajo hoagies," made of bread dough fried in a skillet on a wood stove and stuffed with delicious fillings. In such a place, it's easy to savor the absolute silence of Monument Valley and to begin to imagine what it would be like to grow up in this bewitching, empty land.

Just across the road from Monument Valley, tucked up against Big Rock Door Mesa, is **Goulding's Lodge**. Harry Goulding and his wife "Mike" started a trading post here in 1924 and ran it until the 1960s. Harry, a persuasive man, did much to promote Monument Valley, both through his Hollywood connections and eventually in getting the valley set aside as a tribal park. Now, as

of languages and staring in awe at this wilderness of mesas, buttes, and arches.

Monument Valley is now a tribal park, with a campground, visitor center, museum, and attached restaurant. Diners enjoy picture-window views of the valley and shouldn't be too surprised when the odd stray dog saunters through looking for a handout. Part of the valley can be viewed along the 17-mile, mostly one-way road that heads down from the visitor center. You can drive it yourself (though the road is sandy and difficult to negotiate in places), passing formations such as **The Mittens** and **Rain God Mesa**. Or you can hire a local guide and see more. It's a lively competition out in the parking lot of the visitor center, where enterprising Navajos hawk their services, offering tours for an hour or a day, in vehicles of all sizes and descriptions. Some lead horseback rides, while others conduct hikes into the hidden parts of the valley.

If you're lucky, you may be invited to meet a Navajo grandmother in a hogan, the octagonal, one-room, mud-and-log dwelling still used by traditional Navajos. Such a visit is a special privilege. Upon your arrival, you will be shown into the hogan,

A **"princess"** at the Navajo Nation Fair (left): Navajo children retain strong ties to their homeland but live an increasingly modern life.

Navajo pottery (top, right) has received less attention than Pueblo pottery yet still possesses a unique beauty.

Navajo weaver Susie Yazzie (bottom right), a well-known resident of Monument Valley, spins wool in front of her traditional upright loom.

hen, Goulding's modern motel, dining room, gift shop, and campground are a spot of civilization in the Four Corners country. The original post is now a museum filled with early Monument Valley photographs and mementos.

Canyons of Sorrow and Refuge

Southeast of the nearby town of Kayenta, **Canyon de Chelly** (pronounced de-SHAY) and its major tributary, **Canyon del Muerto**, have been carved into the flanks of the **Defiance Plateau**. Though preserved by the National Park Service as **Canyon de Chelly National Monument**, Canyon de Chelly is still Navajo land, and Navajos control nearly all access to its 130 square miles.

At their highest points, the burnished copper sandstone walls of the canyons rise more than a thousand feet. Drives along the rims of De Chelly and Del Muerto offer stunning views into the inner canyons. The 1.5-mile **White House Trail** is the only trail accessible without a Navajo guide. It descends into **Chinle Wash** and up to the base of the multilevel pueblo cliff dwelling called **White House**. Nearly a thousand years before the Navajos arrived, the Ancestral Pueblo people, whom they call the Anasazi or "enemy ancestors," built this and other protected dwellings. White House Trail provides a wonderful introduction to the heart of the canyons. White-throated swifts and violet-green swallows slash across the blue sky. Black ravens glide beside the meandering slickrock cliffs. It's not unusual to see a Navajo elder in tennis shoes and full skirt on her way to the rim for supplies.

Visitors can also join a tour at **Thunderbird Lodge**, from where Navajo guides, many of them born and raised in the area, take people up the canyons in big, jostling, open-air vehicles they jokingly call "shake and bakes." Passengers ooh and aah as the drivers skillfully dodge quicksand that can swallow a vehicle up to its door latches. Guides stop

to point out **First Ruin**, **Junction Ruin**, **Antelope House**, and other beautiful pueblos preserved under canyon overhangs, some of which appear impossible to reach.

Rock art on the walls reveals a millennium of occupation and intrusion in the canyons. Depictions range from early Ancestral Puebloan and Navajo historical scenes and star paintings to accounts of the Spanish invasion. At a site called **Standing Cow**, one painted scene records musket-bearing Spanish cavalry on horseback. Led by Lt. Antonio Narbona, Spaniards came into the canyons in the winter of 1804–05 and killed nearly a hundred Navajo men, women, and children who had taken refuge in a cave high on a cliff. Narbona's troops suffered heavy casualties as well.

Warfare has been replaced today with the sweet tinkling sounds of sheep bells. Visitors

will see the summer camps of Navajo residents alongside the washes – hogans, corrals, and shade ramadas, with fields green with corn, squash, watermelons, beans, alfalfa, and fruit trees. In autumn, families drive out of the canyons, their pickups loaded with peaches or corn still in the husk. They spend winters on the rims where firewood is plentiful and schools are closer.

The Long Walk

By about 1700, Navajos were farming and herding sheep in Canyon de Chelly. But their lives changed dramatically when the U.S. Army arrived in 1864, charged with making the area accessible to European settlers. Under the command of General James Carleton, famed scout Kit Carson destroyed homes and orchards in Canyon de Chelly and surrounding lands, then force-marched nearly 8,500 Navajos for 300 miles to Bosque Redondo on the Pecos River in eastern New Mexico. Many Navajos died during what came to be known as the Long Walk. At Bosque Redondo, the Navajos built Fort Sumner, the

place they called *Hweeldi*, and for four years suffered through illness, starvation, and hopelessness brought on by separation from their homeland. In 1868, the Diné signed a treaty with the United States, freeing them to return to their land, safe within the circle of the sacred mountains Blanca Peak, Hesperus Peak, Mount Taylor, San Francisco Peaks, Huerfano Mountain, and Gobernador Knob.

Back at Canyon de Chelly the Navajos resumed their pastoral lives and prospered. But they have never forgotten the Long Walk. When the 1868 treaty was brought

rom the National Archives in Washington,).C., and placed on temporary exhibit in Flagstaff, Arizona, one of the signers' descendants said that to him the treaty is "like a constitution so I can live peacefully and enjoy he freedom I am entitled to." This poignant history has endowed Canyon de Chelly with a great spiritual importance to the Diné.

Trading Post Life

From 1868 until well into the 20th century, he trading post was the center of the reservation economy. Traditional trading posts re rapidly disappearing, but one has been saved as a national historic site. **Hubbell Trading Post** reposes under stout, spreading cottonwoods beside Pueblo Colorado Wash at Ganado, Arizona, not far from the Navajo Nation capital of **Window Rock**. John Lorenzo Hubbell bought the post in 1878 and built his home there. Today rangers take visitors through the house, the dark interior filled with woven baskets, Navajo rugs, and artwork. Inside the trading post itself, skeins of colorful yarn hang from the rafters, bolts of velvet line the walls, and flour, coffee, canned goods, and tools fill the shelves. Visitors can watch as the modern-day trader conducts subtle negotiations with a weaver over the price of her work, and they can also purchase one of

The Rug Room at historic Hubbell Trading Post (opposite, top) is filled with antique and contemporary Navajo weavings.

The Totem Pole (left) is one of many eroded sandstone formations in Monument Valley Tribal Park.

Silver and turquoise concha belt (above, right): Navajos learned silversmithing from Mexican craftsmen in the mid-19th century.

the fine rugs stacked in the inner room. Everything is so well preserved at Hubbell it takes only a little effort to imagine the smell of bread baking in the large outside oven, the ring of the blacksmith's hammer at the forge, or the soft voices swapping news in the store.

John Hubbell, known as "Old Mexican" or "Double Glasses" among local Navajos, was much more than a merchant. He influenced and promoted Navajo weavers and silversmiths to the outside world and helped them adjust to reservation life. He and other traders assisted Navajos in personal and medical matters. Hubbell himself believed that the foremost job of a trader was to look after the welfare of his neighbors. His Navajo friends grieved when John Lorenzo Hubbell died in 1930. He is buried on the hill overlooking his trading post.

Hopi Mesas

While the Navajos live dispersed across the 16 million acres of their reservation, another group of southwestern Native Americans, the Hopi, reside in close-knit villages. Surrounded by the Navajo Nation, the much smaller **Hopi Reservation** sits on three high, windswept sandstone mesas in northeastern Arizona. The *Hopitu*, the "peaceful people," are the recognized descendants of the Ancestral Puebloans, whom they call the *Hisatsinom*. A sense of timelessness pervades the Hopi Mesas. To visit means an opportunity to see things seen nowhere else in modern America.

The village of **Old Oraibi** on **Third Mesa** dates at least to A.D. 1125, one of the oldest continuously inhabited towns in North America. There are 11 other autonomous villages, all located on the three mesas except for **Moenkopi**, several miles to the west. On

The Ancient Ones

The ancient pueblo of **Betatakin** is almost perfectly hidden in the sweeping sandstone alcove where it so elegantly reposes. After walking the half-mile along the **Sandal Trail**, visitors to **Navajo National Monument** look down into the canyon for some time before they spot the golden stone walls that blend so perfectly with their surroundings. Once sighted, the pueblo's true size soaks in – 135 rooms that conform to the shape of the 450-foot-high alcove.

The builders of Betatakin arrived in the **Tsegi Canyon** system around AD 1250. With a nearby flowing spring and the protection of the overhang, it looked like a good place to build a home. Word went out that there was plenty of land for their crops of corn, beans, and squash, and so more families arrived and expanded the structure. Yet despite the effort required to construct the village, the people lived here only about 30 years, departing for good by the year 1300.

They were the Ancestral Puebloans, once dubbed the Anasazi, whose central homeland was the **Four Corners**, where the states of Arizona, Utah, New Mexico, and Colorado come together. Within the Four Corners region are the stunning archaeological reserves of **Mesa Verde**, **Canyon de Chelly**, and **Chaco Canyon**, which showcase the most spectacular cliff dwellings and pueblos left by these early people.

Although best known for the remnants of their culture on display in these famous parks, the Ancestral Puebloans lived all over the Four Corners for nearly 1,500 years. More typical than the cliff dwellings are pithouses and open pueblos of stone and mud mortar and wooden beams. They made clay pottery, some of it plain, others beautifully painted black-on-whites, redwares, and polychromes that required far more skill and patience than mere utility would require. These agricultural people also left signs of a rich ceremonial life – exquisite turquoise jewelry, clay figurines, mysterious towers, and underground rooms called kivas.

The earliest group, known as the Basketmakers, dates to 200 BC. They were named for their handsome, well-crafted basketry goods woven of willow, sumac, and yucca and lived in simple but secure pithouses dug into the ground. Around AD 500, the Ancestral Puebloans took a big leap, figuratively, and started building above ground. They shaped slabs and boulders, joined them with mud mortar, and laid up high walls. As time went on, walls became stouter, the construction finer. They were resourceful corn farmers, relying on rains to bring a good harvest so they would have food for the winter. In bad times, they knew how to gather, hunt, and prepare wild plants and animals too.

But by the year 1300, nearly all the Ancestral Puebloans had left the Four Corners. Driven out by drought, depleted resources, social unrest, or a combination of these factors, they moved south and east to better-watered places such as the Rio Grande, the Hopi Mesas, and Zuni. Their descendants are still there, alive and well, and continuing the ways of their ancestors.

Pueblo del Arroyo in remote Chaco Canyon (above) feature the tightly laid stones favored by skilled Chacoan masons.

Ancient potsherds and corn cobs (left) were found at Keet Seel, a 13th-century cliff dwelling with more than 150 rooms, now encompassed by Navajo National Monument.

Unmarried Hopi girls (opposite), like these in Walpi in the early 1900s, wore "squash-blossom" hairstyles to indicate their status.

White House Ruin (below), occupied by Puebloans from the 11th to 13th centuries, is sheltered by an alcove in the sheer rock face of Canyon de Chelly.

First Mesa sits the venerable village of **Walpi**, "place of the notch." There, a guide will take visitors along winding dirt paths, past flat-roofed, mud-and-stone homes clinging to the edge of the cliffs above a sweeping valley. Steps lead down off the mesa into the fields, where Hopi farmers still go each day to tend the corn, squash, and melons. Potters still use plant pigments and yucca brushes to paint designs on their pots.

Hopis steadfastly guard their sacred sites, oral traditions, and ceremonies, which mark important events throughout the year. In July the Niman, or Home Dances, mark the sendoff of the spirit beings, called katsinas, from the physical world of the villages back to their spiritual world on the San Francisco Peaks, the mountains that rise on the western horizon. The katsinas, residing in the villages since winter solstice, blessing the crops and bringing rain, will spend the rest of the year on the sacred Peaks, which the Hopi call *Nuvatukya'ovi*.

At sunrise, the katsina dancers come out into the village plaza wearing elaborate masks, moccasins, white kilts, and red woven sashes, singing and moving to the hypnotic sounds of turtle-shell rattles, bells, and drumbeats, and carrying melons and stalks of fresh corn. Afternoon clouds billow up, a promise that the prayers for rain will be answered.

Visitors may be welcome at some dances – if they remain unobtrusively in the background and refrain from recording ceremonies in any form. But it should never be assumed that a dance is open; visitors should always ask permission locally, and if asked to leave, should do so. Religious dances, held in the underground chambers called kivas, are almost always closed to non-Indians. Hopis are kind and generous, but outsiders have sometimes taken advantage of them and not accorded the proper respect for their privacy.

Hopis are well known for their expert arts and crafts. Throughout the reservation visitors will find galleries and shops where they can meet artists and purchase authentic pieces directly. Each mesa is known for its specialties – Third Mesa for wicker-style baskets and silver overlay jewelry, Second Mesa for coiled baskets and intricately carved katsina dolls, First Mesa for fine pottery, weaving, and katsina dolls.

Everywhere on the "Rez" these days change is afoot – a poster for a reggae concert beside an announcement for a rodeo, video stores and satellite dishes as prevalent as chants and old jewelry. Still, the dry, windy land spirals skyward in plumes of dust devils. Pink-bellied cumulus clouds reflect the colorful rockscape below. Ravens and hawks fly among the sagebrush and pinyon pine. And the native people nurture their histories, clan ties, and the old, deep knowledge of the land: the rocks, plants, animals, water, and guiding landmarks.

TRAVEL TIPS

DETAILS

When to go

Weather is unpredictable on the mile-high Colorado Plateau, so dress in layers year-round. Late spring and early fall are the best times to visit. Winter temperatures drop into the 20s and 30s; summer is dry and scorching, with daytime temperatures in the 90s.

How to Get There

Commercial airlines serve Phoenix Sky Harbor International Airport. Commuter airlines fly into Pulliam Field in Flagstaff and Grand Canyon National Airport in Tusayan.

Getting Around

Distances are great and roads sometimes poor on the Navajo Nation; lodging and services are few and far between. Car rentals are available at the Phoenix and Flagstaff airports. Drive a reliable vehicle, preferably with four-wheel-drive on poorly maintained back roads, and pack extra water, food, clothes, and a good map.

INFORMATION

Hopi Cultural Center
P.O. Box 67; Second Mesa, AZ 86043; tel: 520-734-2401.

Navajo Nation Tourism Office
P.O. Box 663; Window Rock, AZ 86515; tel: 520-871-6436 or 520-871-7371.

Kayenta Visitor Center
P.O. Box 545; Kayenta, AZ 86033; tel: 520-697-3572.

LODGING

PRICE GUIDE – double occupancy

$ = up to $49 $$ = $50–$99
$$$ = $100–$149 $$$$ = $150+

Cameron Motel
P.O. Box 339; Cameron, AZ 86020; tel: 800-338-7385 or 520-679-2231.

The motel adjoins a trading post built in the early 20th century to serve the Navajo Reservation. $$–$$$$

Coyote Pass Hospitality
Route 12, P.O. Box 91-B; Tsaile, AZ 86556; tel: 520-724-3383.

A genuine Navajo experience is had at Coyote Pass near Canyon de Chelly. Anywhere from one to 15 guests sleep in a dirt-floor hogan and are served a traditional Navajo breakfast. Guided hikes, nature programs, and tours of Navajo sites are also available. $$

El Rancho Hotel
1000 East 66 Avenue; Gallup, NM 87301; tel: 800-543-6351 or 505-863-9311.

This landmark hotel was built in 1937 by the brother of legendary Hollywood director D. W. Griffith. Ronald Reagan, Jane Wyman, Alan Ladd, and other actors have stayed here during nearby film productions. The two-story lobby has a huge fireplace, classic Navajo rugs, and Western furniture. Some guest rooms have wagon-wheel fixtures and cowboy curtains; others offer standard motel accommodations. $–$$

Goulding's Lodge
P.O. Box 1; Monument Valley, UT 84536; tel: 435-727-3231.

This former trading post has more than 60 motel-style rooms, a pool, and an adjoining restaurant with a fine view of Monument Valley. Horseback riding and a gift shop are available. $$–$$$

Hopi Cultural Center Motel
P.O. Box 67; Second Mesa, AZ 86043; tel: 520-734-2401.

This motel, next to the Hopi information center and museum, has about 30 standard rooms. An adjacent restaurant serves Hopi blue-corn specialties. $$

Navajo Nation Inn
Box 2340; Window Rock, AZ 86515; tel: 800-237-7506 or 520-871-4108.

A modern motel with more than 50 guest rooms in the capital of the Navajo Nation. Navajo tacos and other local fare are served in the dining room. $$

Thunderbird Lodge
P.O. Box 548; Chinle, AZ 86503; tel: 800-679-2473 or 520-674-5841.

This classic lodge, built in 1902, retains its trading post origins and ambience, sporting rustic wood furniture and colorful Navajo rugs. There are 71 motel rooms and one suite, all with private bath. A restaurant serves local fare. Jeep tours of Canyon de Chelly are available. $$

TOURS & OUTFITTERS

Crawley's Monument Valley Tours
P.O. Box 187; Kayenta, AZ 86033; tel: 520-697-3734.

Jeep and van tours of Monument Valley's backcountry.

De Chelly Tours
P.O. Box 2539, Chinle, AZ 86503; tel: 520-674-3772.

Jeep tours of Canyon de Chelly.

Goulding's Monument Valley Tours
P.O. Box 360001; Monument Valley, UT 84536; tel: 800-874-0902 or 435-727-3231.

Jeep and horseback tours run from an hour to a full day.

Nava-Hopi Tours
P.O. Box 339; Flagstaff, AZ 86002; tel: 520-774-5003.

Motor coach tours of the Navajo and Hopi Reservations and the Grand Canyon area.

MUSEUMS

Navajo Nation Museum

Highway 264 and Loop Road, P.O. Box 4950; Window Rock, AZ 86515; tel: 520-871-6675.

A hogan-style building with exhibits on Navajo history.

PARKS

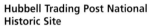

Canyon de Chelly National Monument

P.O. Box 588; Chinle, AZ 86503; tel: 520-674-5500.

Spiritual home of the Navajo, this beautiful gorge rivals the Grand Canyon for beauty.

Hubbell Trading Post National Historic Site

P.O. Box 150; Ganado, AZ 86505; tel: 520-755-3475.

The historic home and trading post of Lorenzo Hubbell is set on the Navajo Reservation near Window Rock.

Monument Valley Tribal Park

P.O. Box 360289; Monument Valley, UT 84536; tel: 801-727-3353.

The park protects spectacular sandstone buttes and columns made famous in countless John Ford Westerns. Tours emphasize the traditional way of life of Navajo residents.

Excursions

Homolovi Ruins State Park

HCR 63, Box 5; Winslow, AZ 86047; tel: 520-289-4106.

This park, site of several large 13th- and 14th-century pueblos, grants sweeping views of the Painted Desert and the Little Colorado River. Homolovi ("place of the little hills") is considered a sacred ancestral home by the Hopi, who live 67 miles north. Two sites are open to the public.

Navajo National Monument

HC 71, Box 3; Tonalea, AZ 86044-9704; tel: 520-672-2366.

Nestled in spectacular slickrock country near Monument Valley, this often-overlooked park protects several Kayenta culture pueblo ruins – some of the most beautiful and well preserved in America. The 135-room Betatakin ruin harmonizes with the canyon alcove in which it sits, and may be viewed from the rim-top Sandal Trail or on a daily ranger-led tour in summer. Other sites, such as the 160-room Keet Seel ruin, the largest in Arizona, may be visited by special request.

Walnut Canyon National Monument

Walnut Canyon Road; Flagstaff, AZ 86004-9705; tel: 520-526-3367.

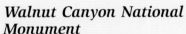

Warm southern exposures, reliable water, and abundant plants and animals attracted farmers known as the Sinagua ("without water") to this picturesque canyon in the 12th and 13th centuries. A steep trail leads past some of the 300 cliff dwellings built snugly into limestone overhangs throughout the canyon. A visitor center perched on the rim exhibits Sinagua pottery and other artifacts, and has gorgeous canyon views.

Wupatki National Monument

HC 33, Box 444A; Flagstaff, AZ 86004; tel: 520-556-7040.

Fifty miles north of Flagstaff, Wupatki National Monument preserves the ruins of more than 2,000 Indian structures built between A.D. 500 and 1400. Indians were attracted to the area largely on the strength of its soil, made fertile by the extensive San Francisco Volcanic Field. The main pueblo, Wupatki, displays an unusual Hohokam-style ballcourt, a Mesoamerican feature linked with prehistoric trading centers farther south. Trails lead to other sandstone ruins off the 18-mile scenic route.

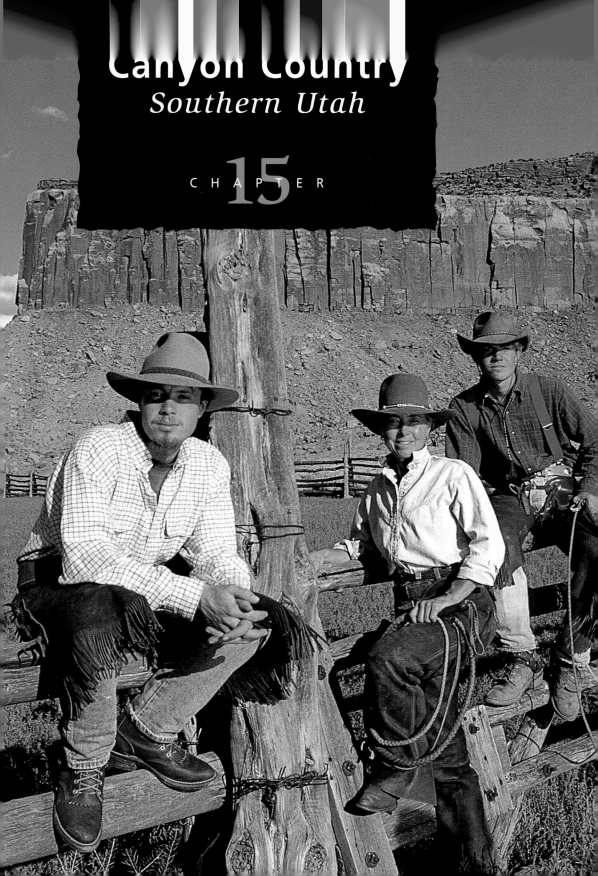

Canyon Country
Southern Utah

High in southeastern Utah's La Sal Mountains, in the shadow of 12,721-foot Mount Peale, rancher Hardy Redd stops the truck at a rocky overlook, gets out, and stretches out the kinks from the rough road. Tipping back his hat, he places one dusty, booted foot on a granite boulder, the other on smooth slickrock, and points out the landmarks in the Redd backyard. ◆ To the south, about a thousand feet below, electric-green hayfields butt up against the tidy Redd Ranch, a cluster of refurbished pioneer log cabins and stuccoed houses surrounding a low-slung ranch house, sheds, and corrals. An expanse of sagebrush and pale grass undulates past the tackle of a uranium mine to the Abajo Mountains near Monticello and beyond to the San Juan River. To the east the snaggle-toothed Rockies wall the horizon, rearing above the reddish earth of pinto bean fields near the Four Corners. ◆ But it's the land immediately to the west and north that boggles the eye. Stacked

Amid breathtaking canyons, expansive deserts, and stunning mountains are vestiges of pueblos, rock art, uranium mines, and Butch Cassidy's hideout.

sandstone planes, plateaus, and plunging abysses tilt and fall away into the convoluted canyons of the Green and Colorado Rivers, then climb out the other side into fantastically sculpted rock gardens and glowing orange cliffs. In the distance are the Henry Mountains and the San Rafael Swell; farther still lie Capitol Reef and Grand Staircase–Escalante National Monument. This is Canyon Country, and stretched before us is 527-square-mile Canyonlands National Park, one of America's most magnificent desert parks. ◆ Yup. Quite a backyard!

Rancher Heidi Redd and her sons Matt and Adam run cattle at the historic Dugout Ranch in the spectacular red-rock country of southern Utah.

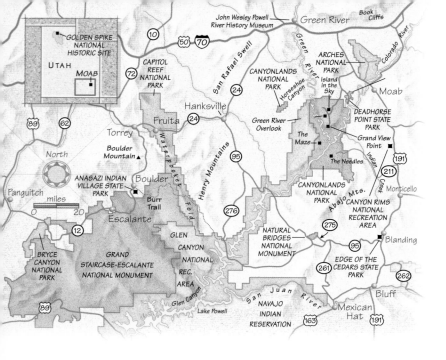

where they grew beans, squash, and other staples. In time, hamlets became larger pueblos with more inhabitants, cultural interaction, and trade.

The remains of six pueblos can be seen at Blanding's excellent **Edge of the Cedars State Park**. Only one of the pueblos has been excavated, but there is a rare great kiva here, and the museum has an impressive pottery collection and exhibits that explore the links among the area's Ancestral Puebloan, Navajo, Ute, and modern white residents. Blanding was the scene of the Old West's last gun battle, in 1923, when a couple of Indian rustlers broke out of jail with the help of a Ute chief named Old Posey. A posse chased them for two days before Posey was fatally wounded.

Canyonlands Backcountry

From Monticello, a little-used but spectacular high-country route through the Blues makes an unusual back road into the **Needles District** of **Canyonlands**, through cool coniferous forest that contrasts dramatically with the desert vistas unfurling below. You can also follow Highway 191 north to the main Needles entry point or turn off at the next road and drive the **Canyon Rims Recreation Area**, which offers a wealth of hiking and camping possibilities. Paved and graded roads lead to overlooks like **Hatch Point**, which has splendid views of **Lockhart Basin** and the canyons below the rim that have been used for grazing cattle since the heyday of the great Texan cattle drives. The Redds' herd of red Angus-Hereford cross cattle winter on the rim, then are rounded up in spring and gradually drifted up to summer pastures in the La Sals. A fall roundup returns the cattle to the home ranch, where the calves are weaned before being shipped to Kansas to

Pueblos and Pioneers

Hardy Redd's great-grandfather Lemuel arrived with southeastern Utah's earliest Mormon pioneers in 1880 and helped found **Bluff City**, on the San Juan River. It wasn't an easy mission. The party crossed 180 miles of dangerous, unexplored canyon country, blasting a wagon route through rocks above the Colorado River now known as the **Hole in the Rock**. Today, the Bluff historic loop runs past the old pioneer cemetery and several original houses, some restored and occupied by artists.

The Redds and a number of Hole in the Rockers farmed and ranched here for 30 years. Others moved north to found **Monticello** in 1887. When **Blanding** was founded in 1910, Bluff was abandoned. The Mormons weren't the first residents in the area. Archaic hunter-gatherers wandered remote canyons for millennia, leaving behind only their haunting rock art. When agriculture arrived, extended family groups began building hamlets beside streams and rivers,

be readied for market and the mamas returned to Hatch Mesa.

The Needles road passes through **Indian Creek**, where ramparts of soaring sandstone frame willowy bottomlands. The roadside **Inscription Rock State Park** preserves a panel of rock art, where ancient hands used the patinated surface as blackboard, carving bighorn sheep, anthropomorphs, horseback riders, spirals, and other representations that still look fresh today.

Just ahead is historic **Dugout Ranch**, one of the West's oldest ranches. Originally part of the SS Cattle Company owned by Al Scorup, it was once a 1.5-million-acre cattle operation reaching from the La Sals to the San Juan River. Scorup's heirs sold the Dugout to the Redds in 1965. In 1998, the Nature Conservancy purchased the property to preserve it as an example of historic ranching in the West. Look carefully as you pass and you may glimpse one of the Redds baling hay or astride a horse going out to check herds in Beef Basin or on summer range in the Blues.

The best way to see the **Needles**, one of Canyonlands' three large districts, is to hike or rent a Jeep. The scenic drive is just the appetizer; for the full meal you'll need to hike the backcountry. Remarkably preserved Ancestral Pueblo ruins and rock art, elegant arches, and other landmarks lie secreted in sandy-bottomed side canyons like **Horse Canyon**

and **Salt Creek**. One easy hike, though, is **Cave Spring Loop**, near the entrance to Salt Creek, which preserves a historic cowboy camp, complete with rough-hewn furniture, barrel stove, rusted tins, even cupboards.

The Uranium Boom

To the north of the Needles, near Moab, off Highway 191, is 6,000-foot-high **Island in the Sky**, a headland carved by the conjoining Green and Colorado Rivers. The views up here are to die for – you won't ever forget your first look at the looping meanders of the Colorado River 2,000 feet below, from **Deadhorse Point State Park**, nor the glimpses of river moving through bare rock from **Green River Overlook**, and certainly not the 100-mile eyeful from Grand View Point.

Molar Rock (left) stands near Salt Creek in the Needles District of Canyonlands National Park.

The Sundial towers above Dugout Ranch (right) in Canyon Rims Recreation Area.

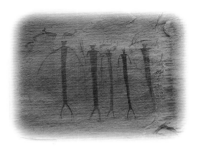

One of the places to benefit from a uranium boom here in the 1950s was the little town of **Moab**, just to the east, on the Colorado River. Originally used by Spanish travelers as a river crossing, Moab was home to Utes who drove away the first Mormon missionaries in 1851, before finally giving in to settlement in the 1870s. A rowdy, largely non-Mormon community from the get-go, Moab burst at the seams during the uranium years, died down for a while, and boomed again after being discovered by outdoors enthusiasts. If you can stand the Kokopelli T-shirts, spandexed mountain bikers, microbrew and espresso culture, and furnace heat radiating off the surrounding red rock in summer, Moab makes a good base. There are lots of hotel rooms and services, campsites among the tamarisk on the riverbanks, cool hikes in places like **Negro Bill Canyon** (named for an early Black settler), and stunning Indian petroglyphs along the **Potash Road** en route to **Behind the Rocks Recreation Area**. The **Dan O. Laurie Museum** has exhibits on local geology, archaeology, and history, but most useful is the **Multiagency Information Center** (MIC), a must-stop for information on visiting adjoining public lands, hiring Jeeps, horseback riding, river trips, historic walking tours, movie locations, and other attractions.

Rio Bravo and several other John Wayne movies were shot in the area, with **Arches National Park**, just five miles north of town, among the most popular locations. Famous for its more than 2,000 sandstone arches, this 114-square-mile park can be visited in a half day – a blessing and a curse, since it tends to be mobbed in summer (and undeservedly neglected in winter). A hike out to the world's most photogenic rock sculpture, 45-feet-tall Delicate Arch, is de rigueur, but don't miss

Ancient pictographs (opposite, top) in the Barrier Canyon style are more than 3,000 years old.

Horses (opposite, bottom) are still used on roundups and cattle drives in the rugged terrain of canyon country, though many ranchers use four-wheel-drive trucks for daily monitoring of stock.

Cow Canyon (right) in Bluff is a traditional trading post with an artsy twist, offering supplies, food, and poetry gatherings.

A wrangler at Pack Creek Ranch near Moab (below, right).

The **John Wesley Wolfe cabin** at the trailhead. In 1888, it housed a crusty Civil War veteran and his son trying to make a new start in ranching. One of Arches' most remote and historic sections is **Klondike Bluffs**, an old mining claim belonging to a German prospector named Ringhoffer who tried, unsuccessfully, to interest the railroad in making the area a tourist stop. Today, it offers hours of quiet hiking and the chance of spotting a cougar or coyote track or two.

Road to Robber's Roost

If it's quiet time you crave, you'll have lots of it after picking up Interstate 70, west of Highway 191. To the north are the imposing **Book Cliffs**; to the south, the **Maze District of Canyonlands**. If you pass through **Green River** in late summer, be sure to purchase one of the town's famous melons and picnic at the fascinating **John Wesley Powell River History Museum** on the riverbank. Major Powell made the first explorations of the Green and Colorado Rivers and surrounding country in 1869, and again in 1871, mapping the area and naming landmarks like the Henry Mountains, the dark peaks on the southern horizon.

The Henrys loom ahead as you turn south on Highway 95 toward sleepy **Hanksville**, skirting the lonely grasslands of the Maze District of Canyonlands. The Maze leads deep into **Robber's Roost Country**, Butch Cassidy's old hideout in the 1880s. A Mormon rancher's son from Circleville, Utah, Butch was desperate to swap a hardscrabble existence for a more exciting life. His celebrated exploits as peripatetic gentleman bandit, admired trail boss and ranch hand, and elegant ladies' man are proof that there are always those who make their own rules, even in the most hard-working and God-fearing communities. Butch and his Wild Bunch were feared, tolerated, even liked, in local towns, as much by youngsters, for whom Butch was a kindly figure, as by the local barkeeps, who were as sure of getting paid for shot-out fixtures as they were that shoot-outs would happen in the first place.

One popular Wild Bunch stop was **Fruita**, now headquarters of **Capitol Reef National Park**, where the boys purchased locally grown apples and other fruit. Nowadays, you can pay a fee and pick your own fruit at harvest time, visit the 1896 schoolhouse and pioneer Behunin Cabin, and view Butch Cassidy's carved signature among the historic inscriptions in the narrow **Capitol Gorge Trail**, which functioned as a highway from 1884 to 1962. This huge geological park preserves the unearthly-looking **Waterpocket Fold**, a 100-mile-long, eroded bulge in the earth's crust, and the distinctive rock art and other remains of the Fremont culture, named

Bound By Iron

Today **Promontory, Utah**, is high windswept country filled with sagebrush and a few ranches. But in late spring and summer, it comes alive with history.

At Golden Spike National Historic Site on the north side of the Great Salt Lake, visitors gather to view two gleaming steam engines, replicas of the *Jupiter* and the *119*, facing each other on the track. The mustachioed engineer crows that people can now travel from the Atlantic to the Pacific in so little time "they won't even have to take a bath."

The scene recreates the event that took place here on May 10, 1869, when the last spike was driven in the nation's first transcontinental railroad.

In the midst of the Civil War, the country's power brokers developed a scheme to build a railroad across the country. In 1862 President Abraham Lincoln signed the Pacific Railroad Act, and in 1863 the job began. The Central Pacific started in California, crawling eastward across the Sierra Nevada. Meanwhile, the rival Union Pacific worked westward from Omaha, Nebraska, moving rapidly across the Great Plains.

Tens of thousands of men – Chinese, Irish, Mormon – graded, blasted, tunneled, and spiked, racing to the rhythm of the "Grand Anvil Chorus." Approaching Promontory Summit in late April, the two companies had still not received word of the precise place where the tracks were to meet. So the surveyors simply continued past each other, creating some 200 miles of parallel rights-of-way. At long last the meeting place was decided, and with all the dignitaries assembled, the last spike ceremony was held on May 10, joining 1,776 miles of track. Leland Stanford, president of the Central Pacific, raised his hammer to nail in the final spike, swung – and missed. The toasts were made anyway, a photographer snapped the shutter, and a telegraph message – "Dot... Dot... Dot... Done" – ignited a wild celebration across the nation.

A journey that had taken six months in a jostling covered wagon would now take six days by rail. A nation torn asunder by civil war was united by iron. – *Rose Houk*

A replica of the Central Pacific's *Jupiter* (left) operates in summer at Golden Spike National Historic Site.

The *Jupiter* and *No. 119* meet at Promontory Summit on May 10, 1869, for the last spike ceremony (below).

A sign marks a record-breaking day of track laying (left). "Four rails go down to the minute!" a journalist reported. "It is a grand Anvil Chorus playing across the plains."

Inspiration Point (opposite) in Bryce Canyon National Park overlooks a maze of eroded pinnacles known as hoodoos.

for the Fremont River, which parallels Route 24, the main east-west highway. Stay on Route 24 as it traverses the Fold to Torrey, then take Highway 12 south over 10,000-foot **Boulder Mountain**, where there are more mesmerizing views of the Fold and the glorious wilderness of the country's newest park – **Grand Staircase–Escalante National Monument**.

One of the most popular destinations in the new park is the **Burr Trail**, an unpaved ranch trail over the Fold with breathtaking dropoffs; it offers hikes through narrow, water-carved slot canyons as far as Lake Powell. As recently as the 1940s, Boulder was still receiving its mail by mule from Escalante over nerve-tingling Hell's Backbone Road. Today, you can either drive to Escalante via the back road or continue on Highway 12 through multihued desert scenery that will leave you lost for words.

Leave room for one more scenic dessert before you go. Stop at **Bryce Canyon** and drive the 18-mile scenic road paralleling the edge of the 8,000-foot **Paunsaugunt Plateau**. Water pouring down across the exposed cliff edge has carved a series of strange amphitheaters, populated by a menagerie of weirdly sculpted rock hoodoos. Thirteen overlooks and hikes such as the **Queen's Garden Trail** offer views of the formations, which look just as bizarre close up. Before leaving, rest up at historic **Bryce Canyon Lodge**, built in 1923 by the Utah Pacific Railroad. Its log frame and green, wavy-shingled roof were designed by architect Gilbert Stanley Underwood to harmonize with the park's natural features.

Bryce Canyon is one of the most popular parks in Canyon Country, but the area didn't seem so remarkable to pioneer Mormon ranchers like Ebenezer Bryce for whom the canyon was named. Never one to mince words, Bryce is said to have shrugged and said: "It's a hell of a place to lose a cow." Hardy Redd would surely have agreed.

TRAVEL TIPS

DETAILS

When to Go

Spring and fall are the most pleasant seasons, though you may want to avoid the hordes of mountain bikers who swarm Moab and other small towns during spring break. Summer temperatures top 100°F at lower elevations, and thunderstorms occur regularly from July to September. Winter brings heavy snowfall and freezing temperatures.

How to Get There

Major airlines serve Salt Lake City, about four hours northwest of Moab. Commuter airlines serve Moab and Grand Junction, Colorado.

Getting Around

A car is essential in canyon country. Car rentals are available at airports. Four-wheel-drive vehicles are often necessary on unpaved backcountry roads.

INFORMATION

Moab Information Center

Center and Main Streets, P.O. Box 550; Moab, UT 84532; tel: 800-635-6622 or 435-259-8825.

LODGING

PRICE GUIDE – double occupancy

$ = up to $49 $$ = $50–$99
$$$ = $100–$149 $$$$ = $150+

Boulder Mountain Lodge

P.O. Box 1397; Boulder, UT 84716; tel: 435-335-7460.

This beautifully detailed lodge, housed in several unusual stucco-and-tin-roof buildings, was designed to reflect the dramatic setting adjacent to the Burr Trail and Grand Staircase-Escalante National Monument. The lodge has a great room, Southwest-style furnishings, and quiet guest rooms, some with balconies overlooking a waterfowl sanctuary. $$$

Bryce Canyon Lodge

Amfac Parks and Resorts, 14001 East Iliff; Aurora, CO 80014; tel: 303-297-2757.

This 1924 lodge, situated off the scenic drive in Bryce Canyon National Park, was designed by architect Gilbert Stanley Underwood to harmonize with the natural landscape. The lodge has 114 rooms, including 40 cabins. Reservations should be made a year in advance. Open April to October. $$–$$$

Coral Canyons Ranch

P.O. Box 50; Orderville, UT 84758; tel: 800-469-3789 or 702-358-5553.

Set in beautiful Orderville Canyon near Zion National Park, this working ranch and retreat offers cattle drives, horseback riding, wagon rides, and other activities. $$–$$$$

La Sal Mountain Guest Ranch

P.O. Box 247; La Sal, UT 84530; tel: 888-870-1088 or 435-686-2223.

Guests enjoy bed-and-breakfast comfort on a family's working ranch in the La Sal foothills. Eleven historic buildings, including a 19th-century log cabin and old miners' homes, accommodate up to 70 people. $$

Pack Creek Ranch

P.O. Box 1270, Moab, UT 84532; tel: 435-259-5505.

A sophisticated yet rustic retreat on the La Sal Loop Road, the ranch has 12 guest rooms and offers fine dining, massage, and horseback riding. $$$

Zion Ponderosa Ranch Resort

P.O. Box 5547; Mount Carmel, UT 84755; tel: 800-293-5444 or 435-648-2700.

Set on the east rim of Zion National Park, this new resort offers cozy log cabins, campsites, and excellent food. Activities include hiking, horseback riding, wagon rides, and climbing. $$–$$$

TOURS & OUTFITTERS

Canyon Trail Rides

P.O. Box 128; Tropic, UT 84776; tel: 435-679-8665.

Horseback rides in Bryce Canyon, Zion, and Grand Canyon National Parks.

Dalton Gang Adventures

P.O. Box 8; Monticello, UT 84535; tel: 435-587-2416.

Seasonal cattle drives, roundups, and ranch activities in the Canyon Rims area.

Outlaw Trails, Inc.

P.O. Box 129; Hanksville, UT 84734; tel: 435-542-3421 or 435-542-3221.

Overnight horseback rides through Robber's Roost country in spring and fall.

MUSEUMS

Dan O. Laurie Museum

118 East Center Street; Moab, UT 84532; tel: 435-259-7985.

Exhibits on geology, archaeology, and history of southeast Utah.

John Wesley Powell River History Museum

885 East Main Street; Green River, UT 84525; tel: 435-564-3427.

The museum showcases two historic expeditions led by Powell on the Green and Colorado Rivers.

PARKS

Arches National Park

P.O. Box 907; Moab, UT 84532; tel: 435-259-8161.

The park made famous by Ed Abbey in *Desert Solitaire* protects more than 1,700 sandstone arches; archaeological remains range from ancient Indian sites to pioneer artifacts.

Bryce Canyon National Park

P.O. Box 170001; Bryce Canyon, UT 84717; tel: 435-834-5322.

Named for an early pioneer, this park protects geological hoodoos carved into the edge of the 9,000-foot-high Paunsaugunt Plateau.

Canyonlands National Park

2282 Southwest Resource Boulevard; Moab, UT 84532-3000; tel: 435-259-7164.

Preserved in this 527-square-mile park are deep desert canyons, prehistoric dwellings and rock art, and the remains of historic ranches and mines.

Capitol Reef National Park

HC 70, Box 15; Torrey, UT 84775; tel: 435-425-3791.

The highlights of this park are the desert scenery, the highly eroded, 100-mile-long Waterpocket Fold, and the remnants of Fremont Indian and early Mormon pioneer cultures.

Deadhorse Point State Park

P.O. Box 609; Moab, UT 84532; tel: 435-259-2614.

The park, which has a celebrated view of the Colorado River meandering through the canyon, is a good place for campers in search of developed facilities in the Island in the Sky area.

Edge of the Cedars State Park

660 West 400 North Street; Blanding, UT 84511; tel: 435-578-2238.

Preserved here is an Ancestral Pueblo site occupied between A.D. 770 and 1200. The museum has innovative displays and a superior pottery collection.

Grand Staircase–Escalante National Monument

755 West Main Street, Box 225; Escalante, UT 84726; tel: 435-826-5499 or 435-865-5100.

The park protects 1.7 million acres of wilderness and early Indian and pioneer artifacts.

Excursions

Kanab

Kane County Office of Tourism; 78 South 100 East; Kanab, UT 84741; tel: 800-753-5263 or 435-644-5033.

The 1870 Mormon town of Kanab, at the crossroads to Bryce Canyon, Zion, Grand Canyon, and Lake Powell, claims to have the "Greatest Earth on Show." Countless movies and TV series have been filmed amid these stunning red rocks, including *Gunsmoke* and *The Outlaw Josie Wales*. Worth visiting is Pahrea, east of town, which preserves buildings constructed for *Sergeants Three* on the site of an 1873 Mormon town.

St. George

St. George Area Chamber of Commerce; 97 East St. George Boulevard; St. George, UT 84770; tel: 435-628-1658.

St. George, the largest of the Mormon Cotton Mission towns, was founded in 1861. A downtown walking tour passes the 1876 St. George Temple, an 1863 tabernacle, Brigham Young's winter home, and other historic structures on and around Ancestor Square. A scenic drive west, through Santa Clara, takes in Jacob Hamblin's house and the poignant site of the Mountain Meadows Massacre, where Mormons and Indians waylaid a party of California emigrants in 1851.

Zion National Park

Springdale, UT 84767; tel: 435-772-3256.

The park preserves some of the most dramatic geologic formations in Utah. At its heart, the North Fork of the Virgin River knifes through Zion Canyon, which soars 2,000 feet high and, in some places, is only 20 feet wide. One Mormon settler was so taken by the landscape that he likened it to the "man-made temples of Zion." The name caught on with his religious brethren, although Brigham Young is said to have taken a dimmer view. After a particularly trying visit, he remarked grumpily that it was definitely "not Zion."

Durango
and Southwestern Colorado

CHAPTER 16

A legend told in Colorado's San Juan Mountains goes like this: Spanish prospectors looking for gold rode across the high deserts of New Mexico in the 1700s, maybe earlier, and found what they sought. They built *arrastras* – simple horse-powered mills used for concentrating ore – took the precious concentrate, abandoned the mills for later miners to find, and disappeared into history. ◆ It's an appealing legend, conjuring images of gleaming helmets and cuirasses, but it is, alas, only a legend. The *arrastras* were actually built by Anglo miners in the 1870s and were used only until a steam-powered mill could be acquired. But Spanish phantoms die hard. Unresolved reports remain of European-style tools (made, strangely, of copper) found in a cave north of Silverton, and of a Spanish coin, dated 1775, uncovered in the same general area by a man digging a foundation around 1900. The coin and tools have disappeared like the *arrastra* builders, yet it seems likely

High-country settlements tell the story of early cliff dwellers, the lure of gold, and the coming of the railroad.

that Spanish adventurers explored the area. After all, they were good miners and would have recognized promising ground when they saw it. Even if they did vanish like ghosts. ◆ Ghosts are appropriate in this land where human roots run deep, and it seems that mysteries emerge every time you kick the dirt. If you count the legendary Spanish miners, the history of San Juan gold goes back about 250 years. But it's a puff of dust compared to the far older cultures whose relics lie scattered across the region. Some of the more famous relics occupy a green mountain called Mesa Verde, where silent cities of stone were built and later abandoned by Ancestral Puebloan people who also left architectural mysteries at Chaco Canyon, Aztec,

A backcountry road meanders past weathered ranch buildings in the San Juan Mountains (left) of southwestern Colorado.

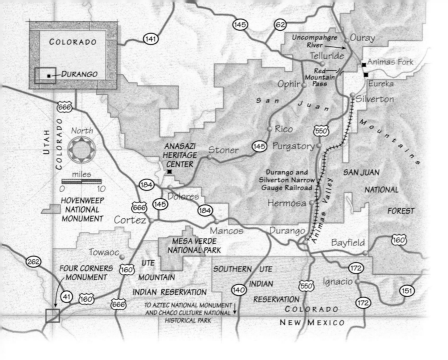

COLORADO
DURANGO
UTAH
COLORADO
North
miles
0   10
HOVENWEEP
NATIONAL
MONUMENT
Cortez
Towaoc
FOUR CORNERS
MONUMENT
UTE
MOUNTAIN
INDIAN RESERVATION
TO AZTEC NATIONAL MONUMENT
AND CHACO CULTURE NATIONAL
HISTORICAL PARK
ANASAZI
HERITAGE
CENTER
Stoner
Dolores
Mancos
MESA VERDE
NATIONAL PARK
SOUTHERN UTE
INDIAN
RESERVATION
Uncompahgre
River
Telluride
Red
Mountain
Pass
Ophir
San   Juan
Rico
Purgatory
Durango and
Silverton Narrow
Gauge Railroad
Hermosa
Durango
Bayfield
Ignacio
COLORADO
NEW MEXICO
Ouray
Animas Fork
Eureka
Silverton
Mountains
SAN JUAN
NATIONAL
FOREST
Animas Valley

non-Indian settlement; and that the story of the landscape itself begins with a battle of opposing rock masses.

On one side lies the **Colorado Plateau**, a province of sedimentary layers, brilliantly colored and carved into canyons and mesas and shimmering expanses of desert. Those sediments have lain flat and essentially undisturbed for hundreds of millions of years, one on top of the other in the order of their deposition. Beside them rise the young and brash **Rocky Mountains**, born of violence and drama some 70 million years ago, thrusting hard rocks skyward. Erosion ripped away the top layers. Volcanoes exploded. Glaciers mauled the heights. Rocks fell and rivers carried them away.

This meeting of old desert and young mountain explains much of the area's modern character. The city of **Durango**, perched as it is between the two, is influenced by both. Blessed by that particular luminous beauty of the high Southwest, it also feels like a mountain town. A happily hybrid community, it provides a natural base for exploration.

Hovenweep, and hundreds of other nearby sites. These Ancestral Puebloans were here before the horse, before the wheel, yet their sophisticated, networked society flowered across what is now called the Four Corners Region. Before them lived other cultures dating back thousands of years to nomadic hunter-gatherers.

History Embedded in Rock

This is an ancient land parched by the desert in its lower reaches, raked by wind and storm among the high peaks. Vegetation and soil cling thinly to the underlying stone. Over large areas, stone becomes the primary element in the landscape. It seems natural, then, that chipped stone tools are among the earliest evidence of human habitation; that stone buildings on high stone cliffs tell the story of early Indian civilization; that hard-rock mining built the foundation for

Railroad Town

In the beginning, Durango was a smelter town, built by the Denver and Rio Grande Railroad to process ore from the surrounding area. It must have been a smoky, hardfisted community, but today the smelters and most of the tailings have been removed. The town is driven by recreation, tourism, and the keen energy of recent immigrants eager to make a life in one of the country's more naturally blessed corners. The historic

License plates are nailed to a wall in Crested Butte (right), a former gold and coal mining camp.

The San Juan Mountains rise behind Telluride (opposite); the town is named after tellurium, an element found in gold and silver ore.

district – and tourist economy – centers on Main Avenue, where art galleries, saloons, bistros, gift shops, and restaurants occupy well-preserved buildings, many of which were put up at the turn of the century. Not by coincidence, the business district parallels the all-important railroad tracks.

Since the first streets were laid out, Durango has lived to the sound of the train whistle, a sweet call that echoes off the surrounding mountains and penetrates even the shadowy Victorian luxury of Durango's historic architectural anchor, the **Strater Hotel**. On a hot day, the parlor is a pleasant place to sit for a few minutes and let your mind wander to the time when swanky people rode in on the rails from Denver, a 30-hour journey if all went well. At the time, Denver was on the frontier, and Durango was deep in the Wild West. The Strater must have reassured newcomers that they need not abandon all hope of civilized comfort. Now it's a living museum. Don't miss the historic items on display in the lobby, including the expected rifles, coils of barbed wire, saddles, and Indian art; and a few surprises, like the elaborate corset found under the bed in Room 111 in June 1892, the night after "Diamond Jim" Brady and his flamboyant consort, singer-actress Lillian Russell, stayed there.

Inevitably, the steam whistle and sound of chuffing locomotives draws you to the south end of Main Street. Here, at its original wooden depot, the **Durango & Silverton Narrow Gauge Railroad** loads up for the 45-mile trip to Silverton (see sidebar). While the railroad tracks punch their way up the roadless Animas River Canyon, Highway 550 takes the alpine route. At 10,910-foot Molas Pass, it enters San Juan County, a territory so high that it contains more mountains than citizens and not a single acre of arable land. From the pass, it's all downhill to Silverton, which at 9,320 feet still feels pretty high.

Mining Remnants

Silverton huddles like a movie set on the treeless valley floor. It's been there more than a century, but seen from a distance it looks fragile, as if any day it could lose its long battle with the elements. Up close, however, it appears more solid, anchored by substantial structures like the **Grand Imperial Hotel**, the **Wyman Building**, and the 1907 **Telluride Courthouse** with its clock tower and gold dome. The courthouse shows that Silverton's founders had big hopes for the future. On the other hand, what sort of future did they expect would require the three-story jail that stands next door? The big pokey never saw much use, and now houses the **San Juan County Museum**.

Perhaps the town fathers just wanted to hedge their bets. Mining has never been a gentle occupation, and Silverton had its share of rotgut saloons, bordellos, con artists, and desperadoes. In the 1880s, the town marshal was killed in a gunfight. His replacement – none other than Dodge City's own Bat

Masterson – was hired to put a lid on things. He would have arrived by rail, just as in the old Westerns, a famous hired gun dismounting from a puffing train, pistols gleaming, ready to clean up another frontier trouble spot. Masterson was a movie hero before movies were invented.

Around Silverton, rough roads climb high into a landscape littered with the sometimes picturesque detritus of history. Only ghosts inhabit **Eureka** and **Animas Forks**, but experienced miners conduct guided tours of the **Old Hundred Gold Mine** and the **Mayflower Mill**. Jeep roads, some of which would frighten a mule, lead over the mountains to Lake City, Ouray, and more remote areas, but many routes can be negotiated in an ordinary passenger car. Seemingly inaccessible rock faces rise all around, but close inspection through binoculars reveals hundreds of prospect holes, tramlines, mine tunnels, and buildings, some quite substantial. It appears that no cliff was remote enough, no peak high enough, to defeat determined miners. Their workings are gradually weathering back into the rocks, and seem almost natural.

That's not the case a few miles north at **Red Mountain Pass**, where deadly brilliant tailings spill across the rust-colored surface, creeks paint their beds bright orange with mineral oxides, and crumbling headframes rise from the gradually recovering forest. It's a colorful place, and probably the most visually appealing Superfund cleanup site in America. Idarado Mining Company is attempting to remedy the environmental impact of some 100 mines near the head of the valley.

Far below the pass, in a rock-girded pocket, sits the town of **Ouray**, a tidy cluster of Victorian buildings hemmed in by high mountains on three sides. The highway and the Uncompahgre River squeak through the only exit, a narrow canyon to the north. Having gotten its start in 1875, Ouray was richer and less rowdy than Silverton. Big mining companies dominated the scene, among them **Camp Bird**, which turned a poor Irishman named Thomas Walsh into a rich, famous Irishman and owner of the Hope Diamond. You can get an in-depth view

Durango & Silverton Railroad

Pioneers would be puzzled by our delight in that clanking, smoky, iron contraption – the 19th-century steam engine. They'd see an automobile as being so much cleaner, so much more comfortable than a hard-backed seat on steel wheels. For that matter, diesel trains are a great improvement – quieter, more powerful, pulling clean air-conditioned cars on welded tracks. You can imagine an old-timer shaking his head, wondering why people would want to get cinders in their hair.

On the other hand, even the toughest old miner must have gotten excited seeing that column of smoke moving up the rugged canyon of the Animas River, whistle sounding, freight cars full of fancy goods from back East, hardware for the mines, and visiting relatives. Back then, passengers probably leaped aboard with the same enthusiasm as the tourists who today line up every morning to make the 45-mile journey from Durango to Silverton, truly a ride into history.

The Durango & Silverton Narrow Gauge Railroad has operated continually ever since it was established in 1882 as part of the Denver & Rio Grande Railway. Every summer morning, three (sometimes four) trains, consisting of original and rebuilt 1880s coaches pulled by locomotives built in the 1920s, leave the depot in downtown Durango and steam north, up the Animas Valley. After a few miles, the tracks veer away from the highway, and the train chuffs through a landscape of wild summits that rise on both sides, while the Animas River crashes along the canyon bottom.

The train steams into Silverton in time for lunch and a couple of hours of shopping. If you're still eager for historical romance, as most passengers are, you can ride back to Durango on the train. But if you find yourself thinking more like an old-timer, you can take the bus. The scenery is different, and there are no cinders.

An abandoned mine (opposite) clings to a mountainside in an aspen forest near Ophir.

The Durango & Silverton Railroad (left and below), one of the last operating narrow-gauge lines in western Colorado, steams through Animas Canyon. Narrow-gauge railways, built for traversing precarious mountain passes, connected remote mining towns to the outside world.

on the **Bachelor-Syracuse Mine Tour**, riding a mine train 3,350 feet into **Gold Hill**.

About 10 miles due west (but 58 miles by highway), **Telluride** is the third town of this alpine trio. It was named for a kind of gold ore containing the element tellurium. Miners drilled and blasted thousands of tunnels and shafts in the immediate area. Inevitably the mines played out, and Telluride, capitalizing on its splendid scenery, reinvented itself around skiing; gradually it has grown into a top-rank year-round resort. Like the other communities, it has stories to tell. Its **San Miguel County Bank** was Butch

Cassidy's first robbery, in 1889. He made off with $22,500 and launched a storied career. It's unlikely that his getaway route was any rougher than the Imogene Pass Jeep road, which leads back to Ouray through the alpine zone, topping out at 13,100 feet.

Cities in Stone

Up in that high country, there are places where if you look south and west, you can see a warm glow at midday, a reflection of the red and yellow rocks of the **Colorado Plateau**. Out there, gold is just a color, and history runs deeper than ore. A cowboy

Spruce Tree House (left) in Mesa Verde National Park sheltered as many as 125 people and included several underground ceremonial chambers known as kivas.

A trio of riders (opposite) splashes through a creek in the high country.

named Richard Wetherill discovered this one winter day in 1888 when he went looking for cattle on the mesa above his Mancos Valley ranch and where canyons ran in every direction like a maze. Through a curtain of snow, he saw what appeared to be a lost city hidden in a sandstone alcove.

So began one of America's great archaeological sagas. Wetherill had found **Cliff Palace**, in what is now **Mesa Verde National Park**. In subsequent years, thousands of sites have been uncovered, including dozens of cliff dwellings, the hauntingly beautiful homes of people who abandoned them in the late 1200s for reasons that remain a mystery. Was it drought that made them leave? Depletion of resources? Cultural changes? Questions outnumber answers, and puzzling over the matter is one of the main pleasures of touring the ruins. Their builders were dubbed the Anasazi, a Navajo term meaning "ancient enemies" or "ancient strangers." But Anasazi (a term used less and less these days) was not their own word; they were ancestors of modern puebloan people such as the Hopi and the Rio Grande tribes. They did not vanish. They moved south to join their relatives.

Cliff Palace is the largest and most famous alcove site. Nearby **Balcony House** is named for its unusual terrace and the narrow tunnel that provided the only entrance in ancient times. Both sites can be visited only on ranger-led tours (reservations and tickets required). Other tours, including **Spruce Tree House** and **Long House**, are self-guiding and offer you a chance to sit

and ponder at your own pace. Alcove sites tucked beneath the mesa rim are most picturesque, but the more spacious mesa top was home to far more people. Numerous reconstructed or stabilized structures tell the story of habitation, from pithouses built in AD 600 to the elaborate structures of the final phase. Among the last buildings was **Sun Temple**, a large rambling mass that may have been an astronomical observatory designed to mark the ceremonial year.

The wealth of archaeological sites in the region is dazzling. **Aztec National Monument**, over the state line in **Farmington, New Mexico**, features a restored great kiva, or ceremonial chamber. **Hovenweep**, west of **Cortez, Colorado**, is a small but beautifully designed village on the rim of a small canyon. North of Cortez, the **Anasazi Heritage Center** offers an excellent new museum that tells the Ancestral Puebloan story from the perspective of archaeological techniques. And although it's a rough drive, no interested person should miss **Chaco Culture National Historical Park**, south of Farmington; Chaco was the cultural capital of the Ancestral Puebloans in the San Juan Basin between roughly AD 900 and 1150. Scientists have only begun to understand its significance.

For a more personal experience, consider visiting the **Ute Mountain Tribal Park**, which adjoins Mesa Verde on the south. Unlike the heavily traveled national park, this section of the Ute Reservation is undeveloped and rarely visited. Tribal guides conduct custom tours of remote ruins where corncobs and potsherds lie among the ancient buildings, just as they did at Cliff Palace when Richard Wetherill first glimpsed it through falling snow.

TRAVEL TIPS

DETAILS

When to Go

The best time to visit the high country is between mid-May and October. Summer is warm and sunny, with highs in the 90s. Spring can be quite cool. Autumn colors are spectacular in the San Juan Mountains. Expect heavy snowfall in winter; back roads and trails remain impassable until June.

How to Get There

Commercial airlines serve Telluride Regional Airport and Four Corners Regional Municipal Airport in Farmington, New Mexico.

Getting Around

Car rentals are available at the airports. A four-wheel-drive vehicle may be necessary on mountainous backcountry roads.

INFORMATION

Durango Area Chamber Resort Association

111 South Camino del Rio, P.O. Box 2587; Durango, CO 81302; tel: 800-525-8855 or 970-247-0312.

Gateway Durango

2615 Main Avenue, Suite A; Durango, CO 81301; tel: 800-828-4228.

A free central reservation service for lodging and activities in Durango, Silverton, Ouray, and Telluride.

Silverton Chamber of Commerce

P.O. Box 565; Silverton, CO 81433; tel: 800-752-4494 or 970-387-5654.

Telluride Visitor Services

666 West Colorado, P.O. Box 663; Telluride, CO 81435; tel: 800-525-3455 or 970-728-4431.

LODGING

PRICE GUIDE – double occupancy

$ = up to $49 $$ = $50–$99

$$$ = $100–$149 $$$$ = $150+

Alma House

220 East Tenth Street; Silverton, CO 81433; tel: 970-387-5336.

Built in 1898, this elegant Victorian has 10 guest rooms, each furnished with antiques and named after a mine in the area. Rooms are provided with a history and photographs of their respective mine. Some rooms have shared baths. Open May through October. $$

Far View Lodge

1 Navajo Hill Road; Mesa Verde National Park, CO 81330; tel: 970-529-4421.

Situated near the top of Mesa Verde, this park lodge offers 150 guest rooms, many with balconies and 100-mile vistas. Native American food is served in the dining room. Tours of the nearby cliff dwellings are available. $$–$$$

Historic Western Hotel

210 Seventh Avenue; Ouray, CO 81427; tel: 970-325-4645.

Just off Main Street, this old clapboard hotel offers simple accommodations in an authentic Old West atmosphere. The hotel has 14 rooms and two suites, some with shared bath.

Leland House

721 East Second Avenue; Durango, CO 81301; tel: 800-664-1920 or 970-385-1920.

This tastefully refurbished 1927 brick apartment building has 10 suites with kitchen facilities. Decor features photos, memorabilia, and framed written biographies of historic figures associated with the place. A gourmet breakfast is served at the adjacent Rochester Hotel. $$$–$$$$

New Sheridan Hotel

231 West Colorado Avenue; Telluride, CO 81435; tel: 800-200-1891 or 970-728-5024.

Built in 1895, the New Sheridan is situated in the heart of old Telluride. The hotel has 38 restored and updated rooms, most with private bath. $$–$$$

Strater Hotel

699 Main Avenue; Durango, CO 81301; tel: 800-247-4431 or 970-247-4431.

This Victorian belle has been providing fine accommodations since 1887. The hotel features museum-quality antiques, period decor, 93 comfortable rooms, and its own melodrama theater and saloon, the Diamond Belle, one of the most famous honky-tonks in the Southwest. Fine dining is available. $$$–$$$$

TOURS & OUTFITTERS

America West Expeditions

P.O. Box 2975; Durango, CO 81302; tel: 800-247-1886.

Tours of archaeological sites and historic places in the Four Corners region.

Durango & Silverton Narrow Gauge Railroad

479 Main Avenue; Durango CO 81301; tel: 888-872-4607 or 970-247-2733.

Scenic 45-mile rail journey through the scenic Animas River Valley.

Mesa Verde Tours

109 South Main Street, P.O. Box 277; Mancos, CO 81328; tel: 970-529-4421.

The park concessionaire offers tours from May to mid-October.

MUSEUMS

Anasazi Heritage Center

Bureau of Land Management, 27501 Highway 184; Dolores, CO

81323; tel: 970-882-4811.

State-of-the-art exhibits make this an engaging place to learn about the ancient peoples of the Four Corners. Two significant archaeological sites adjoin the museum.

Animas Museum

3065 West Second Avenue; Durango, CO 81301; tel: 970-259-2402.

Exhibits on regional history are housed in a 19th-century school.

San Juan County Museum

P.O. Box 154; Silverton, CO 81433; tel: 970-387-5838.

Housed in the old three-story jail next to the courthouse, this museum is primarily devoted to Silverton's mining history.

Telluride Historical Museum

220 East Colorado Avenue; Telluride, CO 81435; tel: 970-728-3344.

Artifacts and photographs chronicle Telluride's mining history.

PARKS

Aztec Ruins National Monument

P.O. Box 640; Aztec, NM 87410; tel: 505-334-6174.

Large Chacoan pueblo featuring a rare, reconstructed great kiva.

Hovenweep National Monument

McElmo Route; Cortez, CO 81321; tel: 970-749-0510.

This remote site preserves pueblos built by people of the Mesa Verde culture.

Mesa Verde National Park

P.O. Box 8; Mesa Verde, CO 81330; tel: 970-529-4465.

The park protects the well-preserved cliff dwellings and pithouse ruins of the Mesa Verde culture.

Ute Mountain Tribal Park

P.O. Box 109; Towaoc, CO 81334; tel: 800-847-5485 or 970-565-3751.

Tribal guides conduct custom tours of remote ruins where corncobs and potsherds still lie among the ancient buildings.

Excursions

Denver

Denver Metro Convention and Visitors Bureau; 1555 California Street, Suite 300; Denver, CO 80202; tel: 800-645-3446 or 303-892-1505.

Denver went from an 1858 goldmining camp to a wealthy Victorian city to a modern metropolis in just one century. For a look at its history, stroll Larimer Square Historic District, where Victorian buildings have morphed into stylish shops and restaurants, and see how Denver's nobs lived at the Molly Brown House Museum, the elegant Capitol Hill home of the *Titanic*'s unsinkable heroine. The city has many excellent museums. The Denver Art Museum displays the works of Indian and Hispanic artists, while the Museum of Western Art houses masterpieces by Moran, Russell, and others. The Colorado History Museum focuses on the state's colorful past, and the Black American West Museum covers the history of African-Americans in the West. Just outside Denver, Four Mile Historic Park preserves a restored 1860s stock ranch, stagecoach stop, and working farm. A visit to Buffalo Bill's Memorial Museum and Grave on Lookout Mountain makes a fitting finale.

Montrose

Ute Indian Museum and Ouray Memorial Park; 17253 Chipeta Road; Montrose, CO 81401; tel: 970-249-3098.

Montrose is home to the Ute Indian Museum, where visitors learn the story of the Ute Tribe, which was pushed from the San Juan Mountains by gold-hungry settlers in the late 1800s. On display are many items belonging to Chief Ouray, the chief negotiator of the 1868 federal treaty that established Ute ownership of most of Colorado's western slope. Eighteen miles northeast is Black Canyon of the Gunnison National Monument, a dramatic, 2,000-foot-deep volcanic gorge carved by the Gunnison River.

Rocky Mountain National Park

Estes Park, CO 80517; tel: 970-586-1333.

More than 78 peaks soar above 12,000 feet in this 414-square-mile park, where lakes and fragile alpine tundra rival the dizzying heights. Mule deer, elk, moose, and bighorn sheep are a common sight, and the birding is quite good. Trail Ridge Road, the park's main thoroughfare, is one of the most scenic drives in the country.

Oregon Trail
Nebraska-Wyoming

CHAPTER **17**

t's a magical evening at Gordon and Patty Howard's ranch near Bayard, Nebraska. Several dozen visitors have already sat down to the best steaks they'll ever eat, accompanied by warm sourdough bread and homemade ice cream. Now it's campfire time, and after a couple rounds of "She'll Be Coming 'Round the Mountain" and "I've Been Working on the Railroad," Gordon Howard announces that he has a special surprise. He snaps his fingers and voilà: Chimney Rock – the most famous landmark along the Oregon Trail, maybe three miles away from the campfire – is bathed in floodlights. Everyone oohs and ahs, then all turn to friendly farewells amid the tall cottonwoods, the trees' flighty seeds swirling down like dervishes on the warm June evening. ◆ The modern-day visitors climb into their cars and pickup trucks and return to their motels in nearby Scottsbluff. Had they been here 150 years ago, however, they'd be stretching out by the fire, wagons circled – but not before taking some

Historic landmarks and modern-day wagon treks recall the epic journey across the plains.

time to record their impressions of the day and, specifically, their wonder at Chimney Rock. "A great part of the spire has lately fallen but still it strikes the beholder with astonishment," emigrant Winfield Scott Ebey wrote in 1854. ◆ From the early 1840s through the mid-1860s, more than 300,000 travelers walked west on the Oregon Trail, along a route previously used by Native Americans and fur trappers. The **Oregon Trail** was busiest during the tumultuous gold rush years of 1849 through 1852, when many emigrants followed the route as far as western Wyoming or Idaho before taking any of several shortcuts toward the goldfields of California. But nowhere along its 2,000 miles is the Oregon Trail as evocative of the past as in the Nebraska

Scotts Bluff in Nebraska's North Platte River Valley towers over Conestoga wagons similar to those used on the Oregon Trail.

panhandle and eastern Wyoming, where the trail still winds far from the interstate, and where landmarks such as Chimney Rock and Scotts Bluff and stark wagon ruts look much the same today as they did in the 19th century.

Mileposts and Monuments

Modern trail buffs like to leave Interstate 80 at **Ogallala, Nebraska**, not far from where first the 100th meridian line and then the beginning of the Mountain Time Zone assure travelers that they've really made it out west. From here, Highway 26 runs nearly 200 miles west until it joins Interstate 25 in Wyoming. The stretch can be driven in a day with a few hasty historical stops, although it's far better to plan on spending more time to savor the route's Old West flavor.

    Ash Hollow State Historical Park, about 25 miles northwest of Ogallala, is the first landmark along the way. Here, emigrants found shade, firewood, and exceptional water – "the best and purest ever drank ... a beverage prepared by God himself," one traveler wrote. But before they could enjoy these gifts, the pioneers had to negotiate **Windlass Hill**, among the trail's steepest descents. You can take the modern-day path to the top of the hill to see the slope as the emigrants did and to view the gashes left by their wagon wheels.

    The Oregon Trail continues to parallel Highway 26 across the Nebraska panhandle from **Lewellen** to **Bridgeport**. It's a straight, two-lane road that runs through a handful of small towns, the Union Pacific tracks and the North Platte River never far away (now, as in the 19th century, transportation corridors follow the well-watered paths of least resistance). Swing south at Bridgeport for a detour to **Courthouse** and **Jail Rocks**. These monoliths lay several miles off the emigrant trail, but few pioneers could fight the urge to see and climb them. Modern trail diarists might try to outdo this 1841 description of Courthouse Rock by Rufus Sage: "Occupying a perfect level site in an open prairie, it stands as the proud palace of solitude, amid boundless domains."

    Chimney Rock comes into view west of Bridgeport, and just as it served as a key milepost in many emigrants' journeys, it can be the focus of an Oregon Trail trek today. Plan to arrive in the afternoon to visit **Chimney Rock National Historic Site**, followed by the chuck-wagon dinner at the Howards' ranch. If you have more time, consider taking one of the Howards' overnight or longer Oregon Trail Wagon Train treks. Guests travel much as the emigrants did, sleeping under the stars, receiving mail via the Pony Express (as long as it's mailed to the Wagon Train two weeks ahead of time), square dancing on the prairie, and learning how to shoot a muzzle loader. Most treks last four days and three nights, with no itinerary after the first day. Life simply unfolds as it has for centuries on these prairies, and participants can be as busy – or as lazy – as they like, though most soon learn, as the real emigrants did, that it's more comfortable to walk than ride in a crowded, bumpy covered wagon.

Trail of Graves

West of Chimney Rock, **Scotts Bluff National Monument** promises sweeping views of the surrounding prairies. Plains Indians, most likely the Oglala Lakota, called this 800-foot-high landmark *Me-a-pa-te*, which whites later translated as "hill that is hard to go around." Today, however, visitors can go up the bluff, either under their own power on the 1.6-mile (one way) **Saddle Rock Trail** – one of Nebraska's best hiking experiences – or via private vehicle or park shuttle. The bluff is topped by two overlook trails, and visitors frequently catch sight of swifts, meadowlarks, mule deer, cottontail rabbits, and prairie rattlesnakes. Back on the plains, the monument's visitor center includes an outstanding collection of photos, sketches, and paintings by William Henry Jackson, one of the frontier's best-known artists. Another short trail outside leads to Jackson's 1866 campsite, as well as to ruts left by the pioneer's wagons. Park rangers are on hand most summer weekends to present living-history and interpretive programs.

Western Nebraska is also a good spot to consider the human toll of the Oregon Trail and its parallel routes, the California and Mormon Trails. Although a majority of the 19th-century wayfarers made it to their destinations, thousands did not, and the route is often called "the world's longest graveyard." Most burial sites are unmarked, but just east of **Scottsbluff-**

Gering, off Beltline Road in a small wayside park, the grave of Mormon pioneer Rebecca Winters is worth seeking out. She died of cholera in 1852, her resting place marked by an extra wagon wheel on which a family friend chiseled "Rebecca Winters. Aged 50 Years." The grave – recently relocated farther from the nearby railroad tracks – is still marked by that same wagon wheel, one of the most tangible, touching reminders of love and loss along the trail.

From Scottsbluff, it's 20 miles west to the Wyoming border. The peaks so long in the distance seem to grow closer as the geography swells from plains to mountains and back again. From here, trail life, frequently tedious, would get tougher, and emigrants, whose sights once fixed on wondrous landmarks, would now yearn to see the few outposts of the advancing westward movement,

A historic marker in Wyoming (left) commemorates the great migration to the West in the mid-1800s.

Wagon ruts, some several feet deep, are visible at Oregon Trail Ruts State Historic Site in Wyoming.

the forts established by those who earlier blazed the way.

Fort Laramie, some 30 miles west of the border, was one such place; in fact, until Nebraska's Fort Kearny was built in 1848, it was the first such outpost along the way west. Here at what was first known in the 1830s as Fort William, pioneers mingled with mountain men, fur traders, soldiers, and members of several tribes, notably the Oglala Lakota, Cheyenne, and Arapaho. These early visitors' lives are re-enacted today by volunteers who dress in period costumes and staff the bakery, officer's quarters, and other post facilities.

Pioneer Traces

It's a short drive west from Fort Laramie to **Guernsey**, where sights include **Register Cliff** and some of the best ruts on the Oregon Trail. Register Cliff's sandstone face is covered with the autographs of 19th-century emigrants (and, sadly, not a few modern-day graffiti artists). Travel down the pathway away from the parking lot, noting the large boulders to the left. Stop at the last one and look right, about three feet up the wall. There is the famous signature of Alva Unthank, who took the Oregon Trail west in 1850 but died just a week after signing Register Cliff. His autograph

A Pony Express rider speeds past a telegraph crew in this *Harper's Weekly* engraving (above). "Man and horse burst past our excited faces, and go winging away like a belated fragment of a storm," wrote Mark Twain of the courageous riders.

Mormon emigrants, portrayed in this reenactment (opposite, top), followed the Oregon Trail to South Pass, Wyoming, before heading southwest to Utah.

Register Cliff in Guernsey, Wyoming (opposite, bottom), features the inscriptions of Oregon Trail emigrants.

Pony Express

In its later years, the Oregon Trail was used by other travelers, including the intrepid riders of the Pony Express. Although it lasted only 18 months, from April 1860 through October 1861, the famous "lightning mail" service holds a prominent place in the lore of the American West.

The Pony Express was the brainchild of three free-wheeling entrepreneurs, William Russell, Alexander Majors, and William Waddell, who promised to deliver mail from St. Joseph, Missouri, to Sacramento, California, in just 10 days – about twice as fast as the speediest stagecoaches.

It was a risky venture, both financially and physically. The newspaper ads didn't mince words: "WANTED – Young skinny wiry fellows not over 18. Must be expert riders willing to risk death daily. Orphans preferred." Eighty riders were hired initially, including a fatherless 15-year-old named William F. Cody, later known as Buffalo Bill. Each rider took an oath, agreeing not to use profane language, not to get drunk, and not to fight with other employees, and all were given a Bible to go along with his weapons – two Colt revolvers, a knife, and a carbine.

Their route paralleled the Oregon Trail as far west as Fort Bridger, Wyoming, before arcing off across the high deserts of Utah and Nevada and over the Sierra Nevada to California, a total of nearly 2,000 miles. Riders covered about 75 miles per shift, changing horses every 10 to 15 miles at relay stations along the route. A few such stations remain standing; the **Hollenberg Ranch Station** near **Hanover, Kansas**, is one of the best preserved, and you couldn't ask for a better place for a picnic. A Pony Express Festival the last Sunday in August features re-enactments, a circuit-rider church service, and a buffalo barbecue.

For a comprehensive overview of the Pony Express era, visit the **Pony Express Museum** in **St. Joseph**. Housed in the original stables, the museum chronicles the operation of the service and explains why it ultimately failed. Financial losses and the coming of the transcontinental telegraph were the main culprits.

s accompanied by that of his nephew, O. N. Unthank, who passed by in 1869, and by his great-grandson, O. B. Unthank, who made a pilgrimage in 1931. The Unthank names, among the cliff's most famous, nearly vanished in recent decades after a leak sprang overhead. The state did nothing, so in stepped Oregon–California Trails Association member Randy Brown, who deepened the etchings for posterity by making a stencil from an enlarged 1931 photograph of the names. Brown is characteristic of the men and women all along the Trail who, often with their own time and money, make sure the historic routes are preserved.

Nearby **Oregon Trail Ruts State Historic Site** showcases perhaps the nation's best stretch of wagon ruts. Most remaining sections of the Oregon Trail are faint, but there's no mistaking these impressions. Rugged terrain here forced the wagons to follow a narrow path; their passages, coupled with erosion, carved ruts up to five feet deep in some places.

Crossing the Divide

Fifteen miles west of Guernsey, Highway 26 joins Interstate 25, and 100 miles or so to the northwest, the trail leaves the freeway again, heading west of Casper for the Continental Divide. The emigrants chose to cross the Rockies at **South Pass**, a broad valley that was exactly the opposite of the narrow, mountainous gap the pioneers expected. In fact, the crossing was so gentle that the pioneers scarcely knew they'd made it across until they saw streams running the "wrong" way on the other side.

But the emigrants were only about half-way to their destination, and there were more difficulties – and wonders – ahead. In the weeks and months to come, they'd climb up and down a much steeper mountain at Clover Creek; they'd endure drought along the Snake River Plain and brave the swift-water ford at Three Island Crossing. They'd rush to get over the Blue Mountains before the snow flew, then face the choice of a white-knuckled raft trip through the rapids of the Columbia River or an arduous pull around

the southern slopes of Mount Hood on the Barlow Road. But finally, they'd make the end of the trail, nearly 2,000 miles from its start. "Friday, Oct. 27: Arrived at Oregon City at the falls of the Willamette," emigrant James Nesmith wrote in 1843. "Saturday, Oct. 28: Went to work."

For the pioneers, the labors of making a new life weren't over. There were cabins to build, crops to plant, business-es to establish, and – for some – bad memories to forget. But they had taken part in history's greatest peacetime migration, and they had found, if not paradise,  most of what they'd been promised in the Oregon country. The pioneers had helped their nation, too. For many years, both Great Britain and the United States had made solid claims to the Northwest. But by 1849, so many Americans had come to Oregon that it was awarded territorial status. The United States stretched from sea to sea, its shores settled, its destiny secured.

DETAILS

When to Go

Although much of the trail parallels well-maintained roads, some parts are rugged and exposed. The best time to follow the trail is from mid-spring to early fall. Be prepared for changing conditions. As they say on the plains, "Don't like the weather? Wait a minute."

How to Get There

The trail can be picked up in Missouri, Kansas, Nebraska, Wyoming, Idaho, or Oregon. Major airlines fly to Lambert-St. Louis International and Mid-Continent International in Missouri; Lincoln Municipal Airport in Nebraska; Natrona County International in Wyoming; Boise Airport in Idaho; and Portland International in Oregon.

Getting Around

A car offers the most convenient means of following the trail; rentals are available at the airports.

INFORMATION

Nebraska Travel and Tourism Division

P.O. Box 98907, 700 South 16th Street; Lincoln, NE 68509-8907; tel: 800-228-4307 or 402-471-3796.

Oregon–California Trails Association

524 South Osage Street, P.O. Box 1019; Independence, MO 64050; tel: 816-252-2276.

Oregon Trail Museum Association

Scotts Bluff National Monument, Box 27; Gering, NE 69341-0027; tel: 308-436-2975 or 308-436-4340.

Wyoming Tourism

I-25 at College Drive; Cheyenne, WY 82002; tel: or 800-225-5996 or 307-777-7777.

LODGING

PRICE GUIDE – double occupancy

$ = up to $49 $$ = $50–$99
$$$ = $100–$149 $$$$ = $150+

Baker's Bar M Ranch

58840 Bar M Lane; Adams, OR 97810; tel: 888-824-3381 or 541-566-3381.

An 1864 stagecoach stop east of Pendleton, this popular wilderness lodge offers eight guest rooms, four apartments, and two cabins, all with private baths. Horseback riding, hot springs, square dancing, hiking, and a recreation barn are available. A six-night minimum is required in summer; a two-night minimum is required in May and September. $$$

Best Western Stagecoach Inn

201 Stagecoach Trail; Ogallala, NE 69153; tel: 800-662-2993 or 308-284-3656.

One hundred guest rooms are available at this inn, a few blocks from downtown Ogallala. A hiking trail leads to the Platte River. $$

Candlelight Inn

1822 East 20th Place; Scottsbluff, NE 69361; tel: 800-424-2305 or 308-635-3751.

This two-level modern hotel on the east side of Scottsbluff has 58 rooms with private baths. A lounge and outdoor heated pool are on the premises; a restaurant is next door. $–$$

Idanha Hotel

928 Main Street; Boise, ID 83702; tel: 208-342-3611.

Built in 1901, this six-story hotel has crenelated walls and four turrets. Recently renovated, the hotel's interior features claw-foot tubs, flock wallpaper, brass handrails and bedsteads, and velvet settees. Six suites and 70 guest rooms are available. $$–$$$

Geiser Grand Hotel

1996 Main Street; Baker City, OR 97814; tel: 888-434-7374 or 541-523-1889.

Built by the Geiser family in 1889, this Italian Renaissance Revival hotel was known as the finest hotel between Portland and Salt Lake City during Baker City's gold-rush era. Now restored, it features a grand staircase, wrought-iron and mahogany balustrade, 10-foot windows, crystal chandeliers, and the elegant Palm Court with its distinctive stained-glass ceiling. A restaurant and saloon are on the premises. $$$

TOURS & OUTFITTERS

Oregon Trail Wagon Train

Route 2, Box 502; Bayard, NE 69334; tel: 308-586-1850.

Two- to six-day wagon trips along the Oregon Trail include sleeping under the stars, square dancing, learning how to shoot a muzzle loader, and other pioneer activities. The outfit also offers nightly campfire cookouts.

Historic Trails Expeditions

P.O. Box 428; Mills, WY 82644; tel: 800-327-4052 or 307-266-4868.

Half-day to five-day wagon train treks in Wyoming.

MUSEUMS

End of the Trail Interpretive Center

1726 Washington Street; Oregon City, OR 97045; tel: 503-657-9336.

This handsome museum, housed in three 50-foot-high buildings shaped like covered wagons, offers trail exhibits and an impressive 17-minute multimedia presentation, "The Spirit Lives On."

National Oregon Trail Interpretive Center

P.O. Box 987; Baker City, OR 97814; tel: 541-523-1843.

Perched on Flagstaff Hill, this

museum features a 100-foot dio-
ama of trail life, pioneer diary
extracts, paintings, and photos,
and offers activities such as wagon
packing, living-history encampments, and hikes to wagon ruts.

PARKS

Ash Hollow State Historical Park
P.O. Box A; Lewellen, NE 69147;
tel: 308-778-5651.

Near Windlass Hill, 25 miles
from Ogallala, this landmark
commemorates the pioneers who
found shade, wood, and potable
water here.

**Chimney Rock National
Historic Site**
P.O. Box F; Bayard, NE
69334; tel: 308-586-2581.

The most famous landmark
on the Oregon Trail, 500-
foot Chimney Rock can be
seen from 30 miles away.

**Fort Laramie National
Historic Site**
HC 72, Box 389; Fort
Laramie, WY 82212; tel:
307-837-2221.

This 1830s park preserves
a trader's store, bakery,
officer's quarters, and
other post facilities.

**Oregon Trail Ruts State
Historic Site**
Platte County Chamber of
Commerce, 65 16th Street, P.O.
Box 427; Wheatland, WY 82201;
tel: 307-322-2322.

The best place to see preserved
Oregon Trail ruts, which run as
deep as five feet.

Scotts Bluff National Monument
Box 27; Gering, NE 69341-0027;
tel: 308-436-4340.

This 800-foot-high landmark offers
excellent trails, bird-watching,
living history, and a visitor center
with an outstanding collection of
photos, sketches, and paintings
by frontier artist William Henry
Jackson, whose 1866 campsite is
nearby, along with ruts left by
pioneer wagons.

Excursions

Baker City
Baker County Chamber of Commerce,
490 Campbell Street; Baker, OR
97814; tel: 541-523-5855.

Once a popular stop along the Oregon
Trail, where tall peaks surround a broad
valley, Baker City was dubbed "the
Queen City" during its gold-mining
days. Many of the buildings constructed
between 1880 and 1915 still stand, their
architecture encompassing Italianate,
Greek Revival, Carpenter Gothic, and Victorian styles. The
area's sites and activities include two Oregon Trail museums,
the landmark Geiser Grand Hotel, downtown trolley tours,
and nearby Sumter historic railroad.

Columbia River Gorge
Mount Hood National Forest, 902
Wasco Avenue, Suite 200; Hood River,
OR 97031; tel: 541-386-2333.

When the pioneers reached The Dalles, at
the eastern end of the 80-mile Columbia
River Gorge National Scenic Area, they
had either to take the rough Barlow
Road around Mount Hood or raft the
cascades of the mighty Columbia. Today,
you're in luck: dams have tamed the
river and paved roads traverse the only
sea-level pass through the Cascades.
Dawdle along Oregon or Washington
highways for breathtaking views of lava
cliffs, waterfalls, and both desert and
wetland wildlife.

Oregon City
Oregon City Chamber of Commerce, 1810 Washington Street;
Oregon City, OR 97045; tel: 800-424-3002 or 503-656-1619.

Now a Portland suburb, Oregon City's lush Willamette Valley
lured Oregon Trail pioneers in the mid-1800s, leading to the
settlement of the state. Oregon City was a vital fur-trading base
for the British-owned Hudson's Bay Company, whose Northwest
representative was John
McLoughlin. McLoughlin,
a Canadian, helped
Americans settle Oregon
and eventually became a
U.S. citizen, retiring to a
house here with his Swiss-
Cree wife, Marguerite.
The McLoughlin house is
open to the public.

Jackson Hole and Yellowstone
Wyoming

CHAPTER 18

From his cowboy boots to his wind-burnished face, Chuck Smith looks every inch the horseman, Wyoming born and bred. So it's a mite surprising to learn that he hired on in Jackson Hole just a few years ago after spending much of his life in southern Illinois. ◆ These days, Smith manages the Gros Ventre River Ranch with his wife, Buzzie. "We started coming here as guests in the 1970s," he said. "I was working in a coal mine and I told myself, 'As soon as I get my 20 years in, I'm quitting and moving to Wyoming.'" And he did. "It's a lot different being at 7,000 feet after working 850 feet below the ground." ◆ And how. When folks think of the West, and of cowboys, Jackson Hole is often the first place that springs to mind. That's ironic since most authentic Wyoming cattle spreads are east of the Continental Divide. But, pretty as they are, Douglas, Casper, and Riverton don't have the Tetons – among the most beautiful mountains in the world – at their back door. So Jackson has one of the West's

Ranch heaven and "Colter's Hell" draw tourists to Jackson Hole to experience two spectacular national parks and a taste of the Wild West.

highest concentration of guest ranches: some ruggedly rustic, some – like the Gros Ventre River Ranch – more upscale. At Gros Ventre (pronounced Gro-vont), guests have their choice of comfortable cabins or luxurious lodge quarters, the latter with gorgeous mountain views. The food is hearty western gourmet, with eggs Benedict, rack of lamb, and salmon among the bills of fare. ◆ Guests can ride horseback every day at most Jackson-area dude ranches. And with gentle mounts, expert guides, and stunning scenery as incentives, most visitors saddle up at least a few times. For one-time dude Chuck Smith, there's still nothing like riding across a meadow carpeted

Snowcapped peaks rise majestically behind the weather-beaten buildings and fences of Mormon Row in Grand Teton National Park.

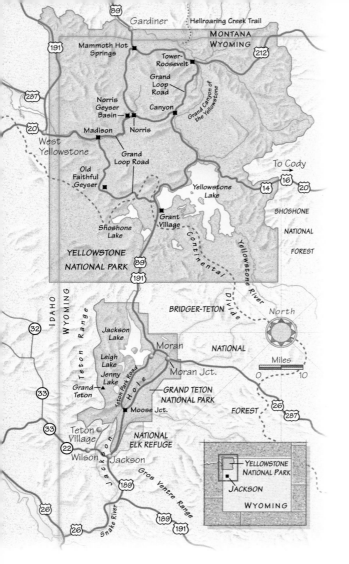

dents. Ah, but just when you think the Jackson Hole of yore has gone the way of glitz and Gore-Tex, you can stake yourself a spot on the town square for the mock Old West shoot-out, held every summer evening but Sunday. After the gunplay, many visitors fork over $5 for a stagecoach ride around town, while scores of others sidle up to a saddle seat in the **Million Dollar Cowboy Bar** for a shot of red-eye.

If it's western wear you want, you can find plenty of shops where you can get outfitted. Other emporiums hawk everything from fine art and log furniture to T-shirts and sunglasses. But one of the best deals is the walking tour that leaves three mornings a week in summer from the **Jackson Hole Museum**. On these treks, visitors learn that Jackson had the nation's first all-female city government circa 1920; that early saloon-keeper Joe Ruby was asked to leave town after a shooting in what is now the Million Dollar Cowboy Bar; and that you can sleep or eat in some of Jackson's oldest buildings at such spots as the Huff House Bed & Breakfast (built for the original town doctor), Jedediah's House of Sourdough, and the Sweetwater Restaurant.

Jackson offers a wide array of outdoor sports, from mountain climbing, river rafting, and golf in summer to skiing and snowmobiling in winter. The town also serves as a springboard for touring two of the best-loved U.S. national parks – Grand Teton and Yellowstone – which offer wildlife and natural wonders unlike any others on the planet.

Grand Teton National Park took its name from a signature 13,770-foot peak and its sublime sisters. When many people think of mountains, they think of the Tetons, even if they've never seen them in person. When, at last, visitors catch sight of these towering beauties, they are rarely disappointed.

Explorers and Settlers

The Jackson Hole–Yellowstone region was visited by numerous tribes in centuries past, chiefly the Shoshone, but also the Blackfeet, Flathead, Gros Ventre, Crow, Nez Percé, and Arapaho. Yet few people lingered in the area,

with wildflowers, cresting a ridge, and seeing the Tetons loom over the western horizon. "I've been doing it for 20 years and it seems like every time I look at 'em, I see something different."

Clash of Past and Present

Before, during, or after their ranch stay, most dudes venture into **Jackson**. Once there, reality may clash with expectation: With its Gap and Häagen-Dazs stores, Jackson can seem more a shopping destination than the frontier outpost many first-time visitors expect. The celebrity quotient is high, too, with actor Harrison Ford and lawyer-author Gerry Spence among the area's noted resi-

and only the Sheepeater band of Shoshone ever lived here year-round. Explorers from the outside world showed up around the beginning of the 19th century. John Colter, among the most famous alumni of the Lewis and Clark Expedition, may have been the first to enter the valley, probably from the west around 1808. Jim Bridger, Joe Meek, Osborne Russell, Jedediah Smith, and David Jackson were other early visitors. (The valley was named for the latter.) Fur trappers all, they came to make a living from beaver pelts, which were in great demand for the fashionable men's hats of the day.

When haberdashers substituted silk for beaver and the fur trade went into decline, Jackson Hole fell largely silent for decades. It wasn't until 1884 that permanent settlers began trickling in, eager to "prove up" on the land under the dictates of the Homestead Act. Most soon found that while the land was ill-suited to farming and ranching, other rewards were possible. "Dudes winter better than cattle," one wag said, and Jackson's tourism industry was born.

Spurs (left) are used to guide horses but are also part of the cowboy image. As one writer observed, a cowboy would "as soon appear in public without his pants as without his spurs."

Cowhands (bottom) drive the herd to a summer pasture east of Yellowstone National Park.

One of the area's most historic sites is just inside the south entrance of Grand Teton National Park at **Moose**. This land was homesteaded in 1894 by Bill Menor, who built a ferry to help his fellow pioneers cross the Snake River. Today, visitors can still ford the river on a replica of Menor's boat. Other sights at Menor's Ferry include his original homestead and general store and a cabin moved here by Maude Noble, who took over Menor's enterprises in 1918. By the 1920s, Jackson Hole's wilderness character was threatened by rampant development. Fortunately, area ranchers had the foresight to recommend that a park be established to preserve at least part of the Teton landscape.

Protecting Yellowstone

By the time Grand Teton National Park was created in 1929, **Yellowstone National Park** had been in business more than a half-century. Congress created the world's first national park in 1872, after hearing reports sent back by such early surveyors as David Folsom, who wrote in an 1869 issue of *Western Monthly* magazine: "As we were about departing on our homeward trip we ascended the summit of a neighboring hill and took a final look at Yellowstone Lake. Nestled among the forest crowned hills which bounded our vision, lay this inland sea, its crystal waves dancing and sparkling in the sunlight as if laughing with joy for their wild freedom." Folsom was prophetic enough to understand what park status would mean to Yellowstone and other natural treasures. The lake vista, he wrote, "is a scene of transcendent beauty which has been viewed by few white men, and we felt glad to have looked upon it before its solitude should be broken by the crowds of pleasure seekers which at no distant day will throng its shores."

The pleasure seekers did come, first on foot and horseback, later by stagecoach, railroad, and car. They were drawn by tales of the park's many spectacles – of geysers erupting in showers of water and steam; of fishermen cooking their catch in any of the park's 10,000 hot springs; of the largest mountain lake in North America; of more than two million acres of pristine wilderness.

Yellowstone's earliest tourists had to be as hearty as mountain men, for there were no amenities, and lawlessness was rampant. Most famous was a group of Montana tourists who had come to see the new park in 1877. The sightseers were kidnapped and temporarily held captive by Nez Percé Indians who were fleeing from federal troops. Poaching

Buffalo Bill Historical Center

Everything about the Buffalo Bill Historical Center is larger than life. From Gertrude Vanderbilt Whitney's monumental bronze statue of the center's namesake to the towering tipi at the entrance of the Plains Indian Museum to the epic paintings by Harry Jackson, this **Cody, Wyoming**, attraction is devoted to telling the whole sprawling story of the American West.

An orientation gallery helps visitors plan their time at the center. The **Buffalo Bill Museum** is packed with memorabilia from the life of William F. Cody, who won fame as a 19th-century adventurer, trapper, scout, and Wild West showman. The **Plains Indian Museum** re-creates a Sioux village of the 1890s and goes on to trace how tribal traditions have survived. The **Whitney Gallery of Western Art** has a world-class collection of historical and modern works by such notables as Albert Bierstadt, George Catlin, and Charles M. Russell. The **Cody Firearms Museum** has more than 4,000 weapons, along with exhibits explaining the role fire-arms have played in the history of the American West. Other attractions include Buffalo Bill's boyhood home, sculpture gardens, and screenings of classic western films.

No one could loom larger here than Buffalo Bill himself. William F. Cody made a pile of money with his touring Wild West shows, but he was at least as interested in promoting the West of the future. He founded the town of Cody in 1896 and instigated a host of ambitious projects, from the building of the Buffalo Bill Dam and Reservoir to the construction of a road from Yellowstone National Park to his fledgling town.

Toward the end of his life, Cody said: "I don't want to die and have people say, 'Oh, there goes another old showman.' ... I would like people to say, 'This is the man who opened up Wyoming to the best of civilization.'" After a day spent surveying the riches of the Buffalo Bill Historical Center, most visitors will agree that Cody got his wish.

The Rattlesnake (left), a sculpture by Frederic Remington, is housed at the Buffalo Bill Historical Center.

The steaming terraces of Mammoth Hot Springs (opposite, top) in Yellowstone National Park are the result of long-term limestone deposits made by hot springs.

Bighorn sheep (opposite, bottom) are adapted to living on the steep slopes of the Rocky Mountains.

was another major problem, with thousands of elk and bison slaughtered, often for sport.

By 1886, the U.S. Army was called in to protect and manage Yellowstone. Transportation had improved, too, with the completion of the **Grand Loop Road**, which, then as now, provided up-close access to the park's most famous features. Hotels sprang up along the route, from the modest Pleasant Valley Hotel, where patrons reportedly had to bribe owner John Yancey for clean sheets, to the grand Old Faithful Inn and Lake Yellowstone Hotel. Stagecoach travel boomed, as mostly wealthy tourists climbed aboard for the four- to five-day grand tour of "Wonderland," as Yellowstone was commonly called. Not everyone could afford stage travel, and many visitors continued to see the park under their own power. But today, just about everyone can afford the half-hour stagecoach rides from the stables at **Tower-Roosevelt** out the **Hellroaring Creek Trail**. As the horses' hooves kick up clouds of dust and the stagecoach heads west on the time-worn trail, it's as if you've time-traveled back to 1915.

Muir's Wonderland

If Grand Teton National Park is synonymous with its mountains, Yellowstone National Park is much more difficult to pin down. Jackson Hole can easily be seen and appreciated in a day or two, but discovering Yellowstone's geysers, canyons, waterfalls, and wildlife can take a lifetime. Travelers who don't have much time tend to speed through the park,

stopping only for quick peeks at the most famous attractions. With so much to see, this approach is understandable – but it won't bring a true appreciation of Yellowstone.

For that, you need to leave your car. Take the stagecoach ride, attend a ranger's evening program at a campground amphitheater, hike to the brink of a waterfall, or wander down to the shores of Lake Yellowstone. Rather than trying to see it all, claim one or two small pieces of Yellowstone and vow to get to know them as intimately as your time together allows. Heed the suggestions of naturalist John Muir, who in 1886 had this to say about the world's first national park: "The sun is setting; long violet shadows are growing out over... the western rim of the park.... but do not let your town habits draw you away to the hotel. Stay on this good-fire mountain and spend the night among the stars. Watch their glorious bloom until the dawn, and get one more baptism of light. Then, with fresh heart, go down to your work, and whatever your fate... you will remember these fine, wild views, and look back with joy to your wanderings in the blessed old Yellowstone Wonderland."

TRAVEL TIPS

DETAILS

When to Go

Jackson offers a variety of warm- and cold-weather pastimes. Many Western activities – chuck-wagon rides, the Town Square shoot-outs, most guest ranches – are available in summer only. Skiing is popular in winter, as are sleigh rides through the National Elk Refuge. The area is less crowded in spring and fall. Weather in July and August is warm and pleasant, with highs around 90°F and cool nights. Winter is harsh, with extremes well below freezing.

How to Get There

Commercial airlines serve Wyoming at Jackson Hole Airport and Cody Municipal Airport, and Montana at Bozeman International Airport and Logan International Airport in Billings.

Getting Around

Some guest ranches provide shuttles from the Jackson airport. Otherwise, you'll need a car to explore the area; rentals are available at the airports.

INFORMATION

Jackson Chamber of Commerce

532 North Cache Street, P.O. Box 550; Jackson, WY 83001; tel: 307-733-3316.

LODGING

PRICE GUIDE – double occupancy

$ = up to $49 $$ = $50–$99
$$$ = $100–$149 $$$$ = $150+

Huff House Inn

240 East Deloney Street; Jackson, WY 83001; tel: 307-733-4164.

This refined inn is set in a quiet spot just a short walk from the town square. Once the home of Charles Huff, a doctor in old Jackson, the inn offers guest rooms in both the main house and elegant cottages. $$–$$$$

Irma Hotel

1192 Sheridan Avenue; Cody, WY 82414; tel: 800-745-4762 or 307-587-4221.

Built by Buffalo Bill and named for his daughter, the Irma recently remodeled its rooms, all individually decorated with plenty of antiques and Western charm. On summer evenings, mock gunfights take place on the street out front. $–$$

Jackson Lake Lodge

P.O. Box 240; Moran, WY 83013; tel: 800-628-9988 or 307-543-2855.

Set on a bluff overlooking Jackson Lake, this chalet-style lodge offers stunning views of the Tetons, especially Mount Moran. There are more than 42 guest rooms in the main lodge and cottages scattered on the grounds. A restaurant, nightclub, and swimming pool are on the premises. Open June to October. $$$–$$$$.

Lake Yellowstone Hotel and Cabins

P.O. Box 165; Yellowstone National Park, WY 82190; tel: 307-344-7311.

This splendid four-story hotel, the park's oldest building, was erected on Yellowstone Lake in 1891 and recently renovated. Large hotel rooms have lake and mountain views; some of the 110 rustic cabins have private baths; all have two double beds. A lakeside dining room, bar, deli, marina, and guided tours are available. Open May through September. Make reservations well in advance. $$–$$$

Old Faithful Inn

P.O. Box 165; Yellowstone National Park, WY 82190; tel:

307-344-7311.

Completed in 1904, this 327-room lodge is the world's largest log building, with simple but comfortable accommodations and a monumental three-story fireplace in the lobby. A restaurant, bar, and nightclub are on the premises. Horseback riding and guided tours are available. Open May to mid-October. $$$$

Red Rock Ranch

P.O. Box 38; Kelly, WY 83011; tel: 307-733-6288.

This family-oriented ranch sits on the banks of Crystal Creek high in the Gros Ventre Valley, a favorite of horseback-riding enthusiasts. Cabins are rustic but comfortable. Guests are encouraged to participate in the fall stock roundups. A heated swimming pool and sauna are on the grounds. A minimum stay of one week is required. $$$$.

Wort Hotel

50 North Glenwood Street; Jackson, WY 83001; tel: 800-322-2727 or 307-733-2190.

Downtown Jackson's grand hotel blends an unusual Tudor style with Western flair. Guest rooms are spacious. The Silver Dollar Bar is a Jackson landmark with good live music. $$–$$$$

TOURS & OUTFITTERS

Jackson Hole Museum

105 North Glenwood Street; Jackson Hole, WY 83001; tel: 307-733-2414.

A walking tour of Jackson is offered several mornings a week in summer.

Yellowstone Institute

P.O. Box 117; Yellowstone National Park, WY 82190; tel: 307-344-2294.

Offers two- to five-day courses on a wide variety of topics. Most meet at the historic Lamar Buffalo Ranch in Yellowstone National Park's northeastern corner. Call for a current catalog.

MUSEUMS

Jackson Hole Museum

105 North Glenwood Street; Jackson Hole, WY 83001; tel: 307-733-2414.

Learn about Jackson's early days at this superb small museum. In addition to the usual guns and Native American artifacts, exhibits delve into the fascinating human history of Jackson Hole.

National Museum of Wildlife Art

P.O. Box 6825; Jackson, WY 83002; tel: 307-733-5771.

The museum exhibits some of the nation's finest wildlife art in a gallery overlooking the National Elk Refuge.

Norris Geyser Basin Museum

P.O. Box 168; Yellowstone National Park, WY 82190; tel: 307-344-7353.

Exhibits focus on Yellowstone's extraordinary geothermal features.

PARKS

Grand Teton National Park

P.O. Drawer 170; Moose, WY 83012; tel: 307-739-3300.

This 485-square-mile park encompasses the Grand Tetons, a portion of the Snake River, and prime habitat for moose, sandhill cranes, elk, and other species.

Yellowstone National Park

P.O. Box 168; Yellowstone National Park, WY 82190-0168; tel: 307-344-7381.

America's first national park pre-serves 10,000 hot springs, the largest mountain lake in North America, 2.2 million acres of wilderness, and glorious wildlife.

Excursions

Island Park

Island Park Area Chamber of Commerce, P.O. Box 83; Island Park, ID 83429; tel: 208-558-7755.

Fly-fishing, cross-country skiing, and snowmobiling are favorite pastimes in Island Park, west of Yellowstone. Nearby are Harriman State Park, an early-20th-century industrialists' retreat, which now protects abundant wildlife; Mesa Falls Scenic Byway, a paved alternative to U.S. Highway 20, with views of 114-foot Upper Mesa Falls; and a back road into Yellowstone's remote Bechler District. Over the Montana border, the Quake Lake site interprets a 1969 earthquake that killed 19 people and wreaked havoc on the Yellowstone ecosystem for years afterward.

Cheyenne

P.O. Box 1147, Cheyenne, WY 82003; tel: 307-638-3388.

The Wyoming state capital is host to the region's biggest Western shindig, Cheyenne Frontier Days, affectionately known as the "Big Daddy of 'em all." The event is held in the last week of July and includes a parade, powwow, carnival, and world-class rodeo. Visit the Wyoming State Museum and old Union Pacific Depot for a glimpse into the state's past.

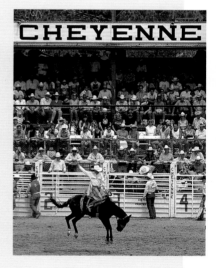

Shoshone National Forest

808 Meadow Lane; Cody, WY 82414; tel: 307-527-6241.

Stretching from the Yellowstone boundary east to Cody, and from the Montana-Wyoming state line south into the Absaroka Mountains and Wind River Range, the nation's oldest national forest offers two outstanding scenic drives: Chief Joseph Highway (Wyoming Highway 296, northwest of Cody) and the Wyoming portion of Beartooth Highway (U.S. Highway 212, from Red Lodge to Cooke City, Montana) – both highlighted by fascinating geology, mountain vistas, and plentiful wildlife. Good fishing and picnicking are available.

Black Hills
South Dakota

CHAPTER **19**

n the summer of 1874, Lt. Col. George Armstrong Custer led a thousand cavalrymen, scientists, and engineers through a gap in the western hogback of the Black Hills looking for gold and a possible site for a military post. They passed through a beautiful parklike area, which Custer named Floral Valley. The horses waded belly-deep in flowers. The troopers bedecked their bridles and slouch hats with garlands of colorful primrose, lupine, and flax. The regimental band serenaded the column with "The Blue Danube," arias from the opera *Il Trovatore*, and other popular favorites. ◆ During the last days of July, two prospectors from the expedition found solid evidence of gold along the banks of French Creek, southwest of Floral Valley. For five frantic days, scientists and soldiers attacked the creek with picks, shovels, tin dishes, and bowie knives. Even Aunt Sally, a black cook who was the only woman in the expedition, succumbed to the frenzy. The Black Hills had yielded their first trace of serious treasure, and everyone wanted a share.

Rumors of gold and adventure brought Custer's cavalry and waves of fortune seekers to the sacred hills of the Lakota Sioux.

◆ The Black Hills of South Dakota continue to yield treasure today, though of another kind. Tourists from all over the world flock here every summer to discover what it is about this isolated body of trees and hills – 120 miles long by 60 miles wide, a forested island surrounded by a sea of grass – that radiates such mystery and allure. ◆ The Lakota believe that all the buffalo in the world once emerged onto the plains through an opening in the surrounding hogback, known as Buffalo Gap. Today, a gravel road slices through the gap, following a route taken by early white explorers such as Jedediah Smith, who in 1823 reported that the hills were a "pleasant

Wranglers round up the bison herd at Custer State Park; the calves are vaccinated and branded in fall.

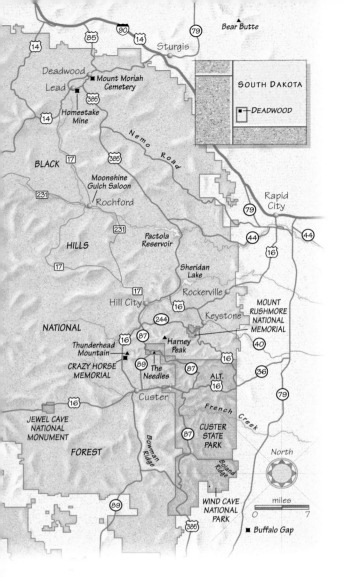

highest point (7,242 feet) in the Black Hills and the tallest peak between the Rockies and the Atlantic Ocean. They started up on horses; when the going got tough, they dismounted and led them through the thick brush. Thwarted by the steep acclivity, they continued on foot. Much to Custer's chagrin – he wanted to be the first white man to straddle the Harney summit – the towering cliffs at the top prevented them from reaching the apex.

It was in a vision atop Mount Harney that Lakota holy man Black Elk experienced his singular and encompassing view of the universe, so memorably described in John Neihardt's transcription of his life, *Black Elk Speaks*: "Then I was standing on the highest mountain of them all, and round about beneath me was the whole hoop of the world." Today, from a lookout tower at the top, hikers are rewarded for their two-hour climb with a spectacular panorama of the Black Hills: forests, lakes, valleys; the fluted spires and columns of the granite formations, flashing between the trees like the flanks of surfacing whales.

North of Custer State Park, within a half-hour's drive of each other, are two major tourist draws: **Mount Rushmore** and **Crazy Horse Monument**. The grandiose proportions of both these massive rock sculptures seem jingoistic and excessive in the politically correct atmosphere of the present day. Gutzon Borglum, architect of the Rushmore profiles, believed that America deserved a colossal art, worthy of the Egyptian Sphinx and the classic monuments of Greece and Rome. From 1927 to 1941 he labored to complete his epic frieze of four of America's notable leaders: Washington, Jefferson, Lincoln, and Teddy Roosevelt. Less well known, but even more ambitious in size and scope, is sculptor Korczak Ziolkowski's rendition of Crazy Horse, begun in 1947 and still in the process of being blasted out of the side of **Thunderhead Mountain**, a few miles north of the town of Custer. When completed, the figure of the famed Lakota war chief will measure 563 feet high by 641 feet long, dwarfing the Rushmore profiles.

undulating pine Region cool and refreshing, so different from the hot dusty plains we have been so long passing over."

The area where Custer's expedition found gold is north of Buffalo Gap and is now preserved as **Custer State Park**, the largest state park in the United States. Custer, in a military report dated August 2, 1874, waxed enthusiastic about the scenery, the spectacular views, the luxurious grass, the delicious wild berries. He said nothing about gold until the end, in which he warned that no conclusions could be reached "until all the facts were in." Was it gold he was interested in, or other treasures? One day he and his officers tried to climb **Mount Harney**, the

The Northern Hills

Highway 17 winds northwest out of nearby Hill City, through the sparsely populated west-central section of the hills. This is the heart of the Black Hills, glitz-free, untouched by tourism, where ranchers and farmers pursue traditional vocations. Forest Service Road 231 coils north through quiet country, dotted with the crumbling remains of old mining camps. The road passes through narrow gorges and over purling streams to **Rochford**, population 25, a cluster of false-fronted buildings that includes the historic **Moonshine Gulch Saloon**.

In 1878, Rochford was a full-fledged gold camp with 500 settlers and 300 log cabins. Crowds of swindlers, shysters, and claim jumpers competed for precious turf along the banks of Rapid Creek. Fed up with the poaching, two grizzled prospectors from Montana posted a blunt warning: "We, the undersigned, knowing our racket, take up this tree. We claim 1,500 feet upwards and

Millions of bison (left) once roamed the prairie, but by the late 1800s the great beasts were nearly extinct.

Park Service workers (below) inspect the granite face of Thomas Jefferson at Mount Rushmore in South Dakota.

a radius of 300 feet from branches to spread and the first son-of-a-bitch who disturbs our stakes is liable to be cannibalized immediately thereafter."

At the north end of the Hills lies the legendary town of **Deadwood**, a national historic landmark. Deadwood: boomtown, mining town, town of desperados and fortune seekers. Today, especially in summer, it's packed with tourists doing the sights or looking to strike it rich in one of the 80 casinos located within the city limits.

Rumors of fabulous wealth in the Black Hills abounded throughout the 19th century. Following Custer's 1874 expedition, those rumors fanned into a full-scale stampede. The

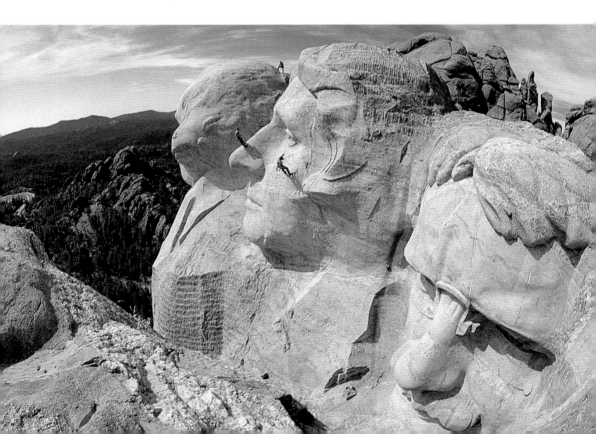

U.S. Army tried to honor its obligations to the Lakota as set forth in the 1868 Treaty, but when President Ulysses Grant ordered the troops to depart in late 1875, thousands of prospectors stormed the hills, most bustling into a narrow, tree-choked valley along Deadwood Creek to stake their claims. By fall 1876, Deadwood boasted 27 saloons, 21 grocery stores, 14 gambling houses, and 11 haberdasheries. A bevy of colorful character accompanied the onslaught. Calamity Jane and Wild Bill Hickok were the most famous but the notoriety of the place hardly rested on their shoulders alone. Wild Bill was a resident for barely six weeks when he was shot in the back of the head while playing cards

Calamity Jane

Nowhere is the American capacity for reinventing oneself better demonstrated than in the memorable life of Martha Jane Canary, alias Calamity Jane, born in Princeton, Missouri, around 1850. In her spurious autobiography, ghosted by an anonymous writer, she claims to have been a scout for Colonel Custer and the lover of Wild Bill Hickok, neither of which was true. Nonetheless, during her tempestuous life she was a bullwhacker, a bona fide scout (for Gen. George Crook), a teamster, a prostitute, a drunk, a crack shot, a prospector, and a dime-novel heroine. "I was considered the most reckless and daring rider and one of the best shots in the western country," she declared. "And I was at all times with the men where there was excitement and adventure to be had."

Excitement and adventure – and men – abounded in the Black Hills in the 1870s. Calamity arrived in the town of Deadwood in June 1876 in the company of Wild Bill Hickok. Despite her claim that they were lovers, the fastidious Wild Bill could never bring himself to consort with such a vulgar bawd; he was happily married and spent his few weeks in Deadwood indulging in his favorite passions: gambling, prospecting, and writing love letters to his wife.

The origin of Calamity's famous name is unknown. In her autobiography, she says it was bestowed upon her after a daring rescue of a cavalry officer during an Indian ambush. The fact that she helped nurse countless victims of a deadly smallpox scourge in Deadwood in the summer of 1878 might be another source. Still another version suggests that she received the nickname as a result of the venereal calamities she inflicted upon her many paramours.

When she died in 1903, she lay in state with a six-shooter in each hand. So many mourners clipped souvenir locks from her hair that the undertaker had to construct a wire cage over her face. A long procession of people followed her coffin through the main street of Deadwood up to Mount Moriah Cemetery, where she was interred in a plot next to Wild Bill Hickok. Her gravestone says simply "Calamity Jane, Mrs. M. E. Burke, died August 1, 1903, Aged 53 Years." But her real epitaph might be the rejoinder she once gave to a party of well-intentioned people who tried to reform her profligate ways: "Why don't the sons of bitches leave me alone and let me go to hell my own route?"

Calamity Jane, Gen. Crook's Scout.
Copyrighted by H. R. Locke, 1895.

Calamity Jane (above) was famous for brawling and bragging. After one incident in Montana, it took three burly deputies to drag her to jail.

Wild Bill Hickok (left) once boasted that "No man gets the drop on me." He came to Deadwood in 1876 hoping to be elected marshal and was shot and killed only six weeks later.

The eroded peaks of Cathedral Spires (opposite, emerge from morning fog

by a surly misfit named Jack McCall. Hickok was holding black aces and eights, known forever after as "The Deadman's Hand."

A walking tour of downtown Deadwood is perhaps the best way to insinuate oneself into the ambience of the place. The walk covers less than a mile and takes about 30 minutes to complete. Of special note are the **Adams Museum**, with its outstanding collection of artifacts and historical photos, and the **Old Style Saloon #10**, where Wild Bill met his fate – the saloon is the only museum in the world that's also a bar. No trip to Deadwood is complete without a stroll through **Mount Moriah Cemetery**. Three of Deadwood's most famous residents are buried here: Bill Hickok, Calamity Jane, and Potato Creek Johnny.

In the nearby town of **Lead** (pronounced "Leed") sits the **Homestake Mine**, the most productive gold mine in the

Western Hemisphere. As the rewards for surface miners operating with gold pans and sluice boxes began to wane, hard-rock mining – extracting gold from the quartz in which it was embedded – took over. Hard-rock mining involved a tremendous outlay of capital, and in 1877 George Hearst, father of newspaper tycoon William Randolph Hearst, bought the fledgling mine from the Manuel Brothers for $70,000. Hearst struck it rich indeed: between 1878 and 1962, the mine produced $715 million worth of bullion.

Sacred Site

A few miles east of the town of **Sturgis**, famous for the motorcycle rally held there every summer, is **Bear Butte** (*Mato Paha*, in the Lakota language), one of Native North America's premier holy sites. For centuries,

Plains Indians have journeyed there for solace and inspiration. The Cheyenne prophet Sweet Medicine received the four sacred arrows, holiest of all the relics of his people, on the slopes of Bear Butte. Crazy Horse's father had a vision at the top of the butte about the promising future of his light-skinned, light-haired son Curly. So promising was the vision that the father bestowed his own name, Crazy Horse, onto his son.

One man's promise is another man's curse. Against the advice of his Arikara scouts, George Custer rode a horse to the summit of Bear Butte in 1874. To this day, many Indians believe that Custer and his entourage violated the sanctity of the butte and were doomed to die. Two years later they did indeed die – along the banks of the Little Big Horn River in Montana.

TRAVEL TIPS

DETAILS

When to Go

Summer is warm and pleasant, with highs in the 90s and occasional afternoon thunderstorms. Spring and fall are brisk and breezy. Expect heavy snowfall and temperatures well below freezing in winter.

How to Get There

Commercial airlines serve Rapid City Regional Airport, about 30 miles from the Black Hills.

Getting Around

You'll need a car to explore the area; rentals are available at the airport.

INFORMATION

Black Hills, Badlands and Lakes Association

1851 Discovery Circle; Rapid City, SD 57701; tel: 605-355-3600.

Deadwood-Lead Chamber of Commerce

735 Main Street; Deadwood, SD 57732; tel: 605-578-1876.

South Dakota Department of Tourism

711 East Wells Avenue; Pierre, SD 57501; tel: 800-732-5682 or 605-773-3301.

LODGING

PRICE GUIDE – double occupancy

$ = up to $49 $$ = $50–$99
$$$ = $100–$149 $$$$ = $150+

Angostura State Resort

HC 52, Box 125; Hot Springs, SD 57747; tel: 800-364-8831 or 605-745-6665.

The resort's four modern cabins are situated on scenic Angostura Reservoir and offer a panoramic view of the Black Hills. Private cabins have two bedrooms, two full baths, a living room, and a full kitchen. $$$

Blue Bell Lodge and Resort

Custer State Park Resort Company; HC 83, Box 74; Custer, SD 57730; tel: 800-710-2267 or 605-255-4531.

Built in the early 1920s by a Bell Telephone executive – hence the name – the lodge is located at the base of Mount Coolidge. The resort has 29 cabins, with fireplaces and open-beamed ceilings; some are more rustic than others. Restaurant dining, western chuck-wagon cookouts, hayrides, horseback riding, and pack trips are available. $$–$$$

Historic Franklin Hotel

700 Main Street; Deadwood, SD 57783; tel: 800-688-1876 or 605-578-3452.

Guests at this gracious hotel have included Teddy Roosevelt, Babe Ruth, Pearl Buck, and Kevin Costner. Opened in 1903, 11 years after its foundation was laid, the hotel recently underwent a five-year, $2-million renovation. Its four-story Greek Revival architecture is magnificently preserved, while the interior features an assortment of precious woods, ceramic mosaic tiles, fluted columns, and pressed tin. Amenities include a restaurant, casino, and sports bar. $–$$$$

Historic Town Hall Inn

215 West Main Street; Lead, SD 57754; tel: 605-584-2147.

This Italianate-style inn, built in 1912, has 14-foot vaulted ceilings and Victorian decor. Each of the 12 guest rooms has a private bath. $$–$$$$

State Game Lodge

Custer State Park Resort Company; HC 83, Box 74; Custer, SD 57730; tel: 800-710-2267 or 605-255-4541.

This lodge served as President Coolidge's "Summer White House." Built in 1920, the stone-and-timber building is set in a beautiful mountain valley surrounded by pine forest. Seven rooms retain their stately historic charm; 40 separate motel units afford basic comfort. The lodge also has cabins, some with kitchenettes. $$–$$$$

TOURS & OUTFITTERS

Custer State Park Resort Co.

HC 83, Box 74; Custer, SD 57730; tel: 800-658-3530 or 605-255-4772.

Hayrides, chuck-wagon cookouts, horseback trail rides (day or overnight), and Jeep safaris.

Dakota Badlands Outfitters

P.O. Box 85; Custer, SD 57730-0085; tel: 605-673-5363.

Trail rides in the Black Hills.

Original Deadwood Tour

P.O. Box 363; Deadwood, SD 57732-0363; tel: 605-578-1546.

Motor tours investigate historic Deadwood.

MUSEUMS

Adams Museum

54 Sherman Street; Deadwood, SD 57732; tel: 605-578-1714.

This excellent little museum is filled with memorabilia of historic Deadwood and Lead.

Crazy Horse Memorial and Indian Museum

Avenue of the Chiefs; Crazy Horse, SD 57730-9506; tel: 605-673-4681.

A museum at the base of the memorial displays Plains Indian artifacts.

High Plains Heritage Center and Museum

825 Heritage Drive; Spearfish, SD 57783; tel: 605-642-9378.

he museum features antique
ools, a sod dugout, a one-room
choolhouse, corrals with live
uffalo and longhorn, and cow-
oy music and poetry between
Memorial Day and Labor Day.

omestake Gold Mine

60 West Main Street; Lead, SD
7754; tel: 605-584-3110.

ead's mining history is traced
vith interactive exhibits at this
ne new museum.

ld Style Saloon No. 10

57 Main Street; Deadwood, SD
7732; tel: 605-578-3346.

he saloon where Wild Bill Hickok
vas gunned down is said to be
ne only museum in America
vith a working bar.

ioux Indian Museum

22 New York Street, P.O.
ox 1504; Rapid City, SD
7709; tel: 605-394-2381.

. superb museum run by
ne Sioux featuring a collec-
on of beadwork, ceremo-
ial pipes, and other
andicrafts.

ARKS

lack Hills National Forest

R2, Box 200; Custer, SD
7730; tel: 605-673-2251.

he region's cool piney
orests, creeks, and coulees can
e explored on forest roads and
 fine network of trails.

uster State Park

IC 83, Box 70; Custer, SD 57730;
el: 605-255-4515.

he largest state park in the
nited States preserves the site
vhere Custer found gold in the
9th century. Bison, prairie dogs,
nd pronghorn antelope are often
een along the Wildlife Loop Road.

Iount Rushmore National Iemorial

.O. Box 268; Keystone, SD
7751; tel: 605-574-2523.

culptor Gutzon Borglum's
nonumental portrait of four
.S. presidents.

Excursions

Badlands National Park

P.O. Box 6; Interior, SD 57750-0006; tel: 605-433-5361.

The prairie takes on a completely different aspect about 60 miles east of the Black Hills. This is the Badlands, an immensely rugged country of furrowed cliffs, gnarled spires, and deep, branching ravines torn from the plains by a half-million years of erosion. Haunting the dramatically desolate park are eagles, owls, vultures, coyotes, prairie rattlers, bison, pronghorn, and bighorn sheep. Wildlife watching is particularly good in the Sage Creek Wilderness Area. The White River Visitor Center, situated in the Stronghold Unit of the park, interprets Oglala Sioux Indian culture and history.

Devils Tower National Monument

P.O. Box 10; Devils Tower, WY 82714; tel: 307-467-5283.

Devils Tower rises above the Belle Fourche River Valley in northeast Wyoming about 110 miles northwest of Rapid City. The formation stands 865 feet tall and is held sacred by Native Americans. One legend tells of a giant bear that clawed the deep grooves in its sides while chasing children to the top.

Theodore Roosevelt National Park

P.O. Box 7; Medora, ND 58645; tel: 701-623-4466.

About 250 miles north of Rapid City, this North Dakota park encompasses an eroded prairie landscape of deep ridges and dry streambeds, or coulees, that are covered by isolated stands of juniper and ash and thick growths of cactus, sage, and yucca. A young Theodore Roosevelt made his first attempt at ranching here in the late 1880s. His tiny cabin has been restored. A half-day drive through the North or South Unit offers superb views of rugged badlands and prairie wildlife.

Northern Rockies
Montana-Idaho

CHAPTER **20**

The locals in **Nevada City, Montana** – population 15 – see it happen all the time. Nevada City lies in a mountain valley on U.S. Highway 287 about 90 miles northwest of Yellowstone National Park. "Many blow through, say 'whoa' about a quarter-mile out of town, and come back," said one local. To hell with the schedule, the drivers seem to say; let's check this out.   ◆   Why do they stop? Most western towns have a museum, but **Nevada City** *is* a museum: to prospectors like Bill Fairweather and Henry Edgar, who first found gold in Alder Gulch in 1863; to the Chinese miners who doggedly worked the gold diggings long after others had taken the easy claims; to sodbusters who accepted hard lives in a harsh environment; even to the outlaws who were hanged from makeshift gallows in a barn. Once you've seen Nevada City, it's hard to shake it from your soul.   ◆   The feeling is the same throughout the **Northern Rockies**, from the storied battlefields of the Little Bighorn and the Big Hole to the mining

Ghost towns, forsaken cabins, abandoned mines, and haunting battlefields testify to tough frontier life in Big Sky country.

capitals of Nevada City, Helena, and Butte. The quest for mineral wealth made the region a rollicking, often lawless place to be throughout the 1860s and 1870s. The push for gold and other riches also fostered misunderstandings and mayhem among the Indian tribes, who had long shared the bounty of the area, and the newcomers, who wanted to stake their own claims to the land.   ◆   Perhaps this is why, for a region whose history is so recent, civilization's imprint on Montana and Idaho seems decidedly tenuous. Abandoned cabins list heavily against the prairie winds. Clouds cling to mountain peaks, emptying in an afternoon thundershower before setting sail

Cowboy country. The setting sun illuminates a spray of water as horsemen race across a mountain stream.

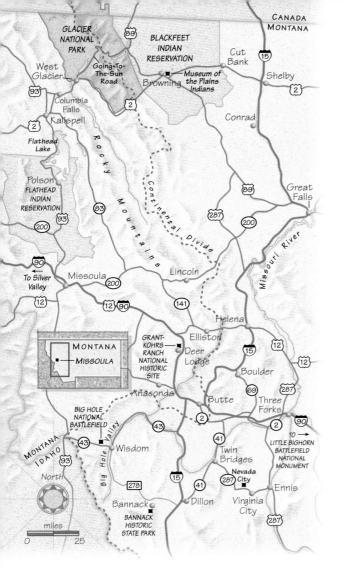

CANADA
MONTANA

GLACIER NATIONAL PARK

89

BLACKFEET INDIAN RESERVATION

Cut Bank

15

West Glacier

Going-To-The-Sun Road

Browning · Museum of the Plains Indians

Shelby

2

93

Columbia Falls

2

Kalispell

Conrad

Flathead Lake

Rocky

Polson
FLATHEAD INDIAN RESERVATION

83

Great Falls

89

200

93

Mountains

Continental Divide

287

200

To Silver Valley

Missoula

200

Lincoln

Missouri River

12

12

90

141

Helena

GRANT-KOHRS RANCH NATIONAL HISTORIC SITE

Elliston

MONTANA

MISSOULA

Deer Lodge

15

12

12

Boulder

Anaconda

Butte

69

287

BIG HOLE NATIONAL BATTLEFIELD

43

2

Three Forks

2

90

TO → LITTLE BIGHORN BATTLEFIELD NATIONAL MONUMENT

MONTANA
IDAHO

43

Wisdom

41

Twin Bridges

Big Hole Valley

93

North

15

Nevada City

41

287

Ennis

278

Bannack

Dillon

Virginia City

287

BANNACK HISTORIC STATE PARK

miles

0   25

the 50 or so other buildings on view are Montana's oldest public school, built in 1867 at **Twin Bridges**; the fine old **Sedman Mansion** from **Granite Creek**; even a Chinese fish market and a Buddhist temple. All of Nevada City is wonderfully photogenic, whether your camera captures flowers twisting through the spokes of a wizened wagon wheel, a grandfather and his grandchild resting on the front porch of the post office, or pots and pans hung outside a settler's small cabin.

From Nevada City, Highway 287 follows the Ruby River to **Twin Bridges**, where it's a short drive south to **Dillon**, then west to **Bannack** via Highways 41 and 278. Now a state park, Bannack was the site of the first Montana gold rush in 1862 and the state's first territorial capital. It was also the bailiwick of Sheriff Henry Plummer, a corrupt lawman accused of leading a thieving band of thugs that roamed the road between Bannack and Virginia City. Bannack is a true ghost town, with about 60 buildings still standing along Grasshopper Creek, including a two-story building that housed a Masonic lodge and a school. Past the Bannack turnoff, Highway 278 continues west and then north into the **Big Hole Valley**, which stands a mile and a half above sea level, nearly twice the average elevation in Montana.

The "hole" – an old mountain man's term – is surrounded by the Bitterroots, the Pioneers, and the Anaconda-Pintlers, their peaks rising 10,000 feet and more. The superlatives don't stop there: Big Hole River is considered one of America's top fly-fishing waters, with thousands of trout per mile and plenty of local guides to help visitors master the sport. Others in this isolated valley make their living the same way their ancestors did decades back, running cattle and baling hay. The homes and shops of their small communities are low-slung and closely built, as if huddling together might diminish the vastness of their surroundings. It's tempting to believe that nothing has changed in a century, until you see the sign in Wisdom promising Internet access, or the out-of-state license plates outside the Wisdom River

across the big sky. Urban visitors feel their hearts pound as never before – partly because of the elevation and the dizzying mountain roads, all hairpin turns and steep drop-offs, but also because the Northern Rockies are a place where you can hear yourself breathe, and where the past has a firm hold on the imagination.

This is certainly true in **Nevada City**, which is easily worth a few hours of exploration. Get a copy of the town brochure and just set off. Many visitors begin at the famous two-story outhouse behind the **Nevada City Hotel**. The hotel and its adjacent cabins still accept guests, but the once-operational outhouse now stands strictly for laughs. Among

Gallery, a showcase for fine western and wildlife art.

Battlefield of Regrets

West of Wisdom, it's not far to **Big Hole National Battlefield**, a key site in **Nez Percé National Historical Park**. In a region noted for its ghost towns, Big Hole National Battlefield may be the most haunting place of all. A short, level trail leads to a solemn tipi village, the naked poles arrayed much as they were on August 9, 1877, when about 750 Nez Percé were camped here. The Nez Percé thought they were well ahead of the federal troops who were charged with forcing them onto a reservation; they did not know that soldiers closing in for a surprise attack would wind up claiming the lives of 60 to 90 Nez Percé, about two-thirds that number women, children, and elders. (Some 29 U.S. soldiers died, too.) It was the turning point in the Nez Percé War, which ended two months later near Chinook, Montana. There, just 42 miles from sanctuary at the Canadian border, Chief Joseph of the Nez Percé made his famous "I will fight no more forever" speech before surrendering to the U.S. Army.

These killing fields are sad, but they also feel like places of reconciliation. The beauty is stunning, for one thing. With mountains rimming the horizon, wildflowers erupting in colorful bunches, and an occasional moose ambling along the river, the scene is as serene today as it was bloody in 1877. But it's the silence here that really heals. Unlike other major U.S. battlefields, where large group tours congregate and bus engines drone, Big Hole is well off the beaten path and incredibly quiet. Silence, in turn, brings reflection, understanding, perhaps even acceptance.

People of all races and faiths seem to recognize the spiritual nature of the Big Hole, and many Nez Percé still sense the presence of those who fought and died at the site. But non-Indian people can also be heard singing or praying on the battlefield, and some even return to the visitor center with tears in their eyes. The main request the Nez Percé make is that visitors treat the site with respect and honor the ground on which their ancestors fell.

Bannack, now a ghost town (right), sprang to life in 1862 after gold was discovered in nearby Grasshopper Creek. Within a few months the town had 500 residents.

Mining and Ranching

From the Big Hole, it's a scenic trip on Highway 43 and Interstate 15 northeast to **Butte**. Butte was built on the "richest hill on Earth," and as emigrants from many lands poured in to work its copper mines, it became Montana's most international city. But when the Anaconda Company tightened its grip on labor and global competition gutted the copper market, battered Butte went into a decline it has yet to fully escape. It's telling that the **Berkeley Pit**, a huge abandoned copper mine that sprawls more than a mile across the northeast side of town, is among Butte's most popular tourist attractions and its biggest eyesore.

Yet Butte also has one of the best examples of another byproduct of mining wealth. Copper magnate William A. Clark spared no expense in the construction of his mansion, which took four years to build. The **Copper King Mansion** is filled with priceless antique furniture, Tiffany windows, frescoed ceilings, and a massive pipe organ. Unlike most historical mansions, however, this one offers overnight accommodations, making it one of the West's most unusual bed-and-breakfasts.

Though mining fueled the settlement of the Northern Rockies, cowboys staked their claims on the land, too. Just outside **Deer Lodge**, **Grant-Kohrs Ranch National Historic Site** showcases what once ranked among the biggest cattle operations in the West. Started by Johnny Grant in the 1850s, the spread was later bought by Conrad Kohrs. The ranch flourished, and at one point, Kohrs and his partner, John Bielenberg, were running cattle on more than a million acres across four states and Canada. The ranch stayed in the Kohrs family until 1972, when it was purchased by the National Park Service. Today, it's a fine place to see how ranching evolved in the Rockies. Other Deer Lodge attractions include the **Old Montana Prison**, which dates to 1893.

Helena, back across the Continental Divide on U.S. Highway 12, is Montana's capital city, a seat of government, education, and the arts. But Helena was a wild place in the mid-19th century. It was here in 1864 that four weary Confederate soldiers-turned-prospectors, ready to give up, finally struck gold on Prickly Pear Creek. They dubbed their find Last Chance Gulch, and Helena was on its way to great wealth and power – in the 1880s, the town had more millionaires per capita than anywhere else in the United States. Take the **Last Chance Tour Train** for a look at Helena's fabulous architecture and for a chance to hear some great stories, such as the one about the

Mountain Men

They were free spirits and dreamers, gritty survivalists, incidental explorers, occasional Indian fighters, and, once a year, hell-raisers. They were fearless, radiating west from the Missouri River without roads, maps, or guarantee of safe passage from the native property owners. They exemplified American initiative at its best and American rapacity at its worst; they all but exterminated the source of their own livelihood in 30 years.

The era of the mountain man was a flicker in history, 1807 through the mid-1830s, and fewer than a thousand men actually ventured into the Rocky Mountain wilderness to trap beaver. But their impact was profound. Their presence formed a wedge between the Spanish in the Southwest and the British in the Northwest, which stretched the ambitions of the expanding United States. They inspired books and paintings that spiked the nation's fascination with the West. And they aggravated Anglo-American relations with tribes from the northern plains Blackfeet to the southwestern desert Mohaves, spreading white people's diseases and spraying lead when they felt it necessary. As Kit Carson said, "We determined to trap wherever we pleased, even if we had to fight for the right."

The irony was that for all the risk and hardship, few if any mountain men ever made money. Merchants back in civilized St. Louis devised a system to neatly relieve them of any profits. Once each summer, from 1825 to 1840, mountain men converged for a rendezvous, usually in Wyoming, where they drank, feasted, brawled, gambled, fornicated, and generally squandered everything. A beaver pelt sold for $6, but a pint of whiskey, thinned with Green River water, cost them $5. (Wholesale price in St. Louis: 30 cents a gallon.) Even essential supplies carried a markup of 1,000 to 2,000 percent. Nursing their rendezvous hangovers, historian Hiram Chittenden wrote, the trappers "betook themselves with heavy hearts but light pockets to their lonely retreats in the mountains, there to pass another three hundred and sixty days in peril and toil, that they may spend five in drunken frolic."

Although drunken frolic is quite politically incorrect today, the Museum of the Mountain Man in Pinedale, Wyoming, stages an annual rendezvous pageant with a cast of 150 on the second weekend of July. In March the National Festival of the West in Scottsdale, Arizona, presents a mountain-man encampment, with costumed "interpreters" demonstrating pioneer survival skills. The revivals confirm what historian Bernard DeVoto concluded: "To be a mountain man, you had to be something of a savage but you had to be something of a hero, too." – *Lawrence W. Cheek*

Chief Joseph (opposite, top) was never permitted to return to his homeland after the Nez Percé War. He was said by his physician to have died of a broken heart.

Tipis (opposite bottom) were carried on a *travois*, or sled, allowing Indians to move camp easily.

Mountain men (left and below) adopted Indian techniques, tools, dress, and attitudes, and frequently took Native wives.

barnstorming pilot who flew between the twin spires of the Cathedral of St. Helena.

The town of **Great Falls**, just to the north, on Interstate 15, has two historical claims to fame: Lewis and Clark were forced to camp here for several weeks while portaging an unexpected series of Missouri River waterfalls, and Charles M. Russell hung his hat here in the early years of the 20th century. The famous cowboy artist's home and studio serve as highlights of the **C. M. Russell Museum Complex**.

Beyond Great Falls, U.S. Highway 89 crosses the plains to **Browning**, center of the **Blackfeet Indian Reservation**. If you arrive in mid-July, you can experience North

American Indian Days. The event features powwow dancing, singing, and Indian rodeo and attracts participants from all over North America. If not, consider a stop in the **Museum of the Plains Indian** or noted bronze sculptor Bob Scriver's studio-gallery.

Browning is one of the main gateways to **Glacier National Park**, among the grandest mountain landscapes in North America. Here, the "Wild West" includes grizzly and black bears, mountain goats, moose, and bald eagles. More than 700 miles of hiking trails make Glacier a walker's paradise, but the scenery from the famous **Going-To-The-Sun Road** is mighty spectacular, too. The Great Northern Railroad was instrumental in Glacier's development as a destination, pouring $1.5 million into lodges, chalets, and tent camps. In the 1920s, visitors commonly spent a week seeing Glacier, traveling on horseback from one accommodation to the next.

Little Bighorn Battlefield

To many people from all over the world, a mass grave atop a rise near **Hardin, Montana**, is the ultimate symbol of the Wild West. Here in 1876, Lieutenant Colonel George Armstrong Custer and every last one of the more than 200 men under his command fell fighting Sioux, Cheyenne, and Arapaho warriors angered by federal violations of the 1868 Fort Laramie Treaty. The Battle of the Little Bighorn was indeed a great victory for the tribes, but it turned out to be their last stand, too: within months, they were forced to abandon the nomadic way of life they'd lived for centuries and return to government-decreed reservations.

Much of what happened along the Little Bighorn remains obscure, but the markers scattered around **Last Stand Hill** tell the tale well enough. All eyes are naturally drawn to the tablet memorializing Custer, but the dozens surrounding it – engraved simply with "U.S. Soldier, 7th Cavalry, Fell Here June 25 1876" – really show the magnitude of the losses. Memorials to the 100 or so Indian losses are conspicuously absent, but plans are in the works for a "Peace Through Unity" monument. As designed, the memorial would include a "spirit gate" to welcome the cavalry dead and recognize "the mutual understanding of the infinite all the dead possess," according to a rendering now on view at the visitor center.

For further insights on the battle, listen in on one of the frequent ranger talks, with such topics as "The Road to the Little Bighorn" and "Life in the 7th Cavalry." After that, retrace the battle on your own, starting about five miles southeast at the **Reno-Benteen Battlefield**, or take the guided tour offered by Crow-run Apsaalooke Tours.

The last weekend of each June, a series of Custer's Last Stand Re-enactments, held six miles west of Hardin, serves as the centerpiece of Little Bighorn Days, a five-day "celebration of cultural heritage." An Anniversary Days commemoration is also held at the national monument itself.

Brash and eager for glory, Custer (left) once boasted that "There are not Indians enough in the country to whip the Seventh Cavalry."

A gravestone (below) marks the final resting place of an unidentified soldier killed at the Little Bighorn battlefield.

Beaded buckskin gloves (opposite, top) are worn for protection from rope burns, barbed wire, branding irons, and winter cold.

A rancher feeds his herd at a spread near Idaho's Pioneer Mountains.

Valley of Silver and Bordellos

West of the Rockies, Idaho's panhandle is characterized by big lakes and towering trees. Canadian explorer David Thompson built the first fur trade post in the U.S. Northwest on the shores of Lake Pend Oreille in 1809, and Kullyspell House signaled the white entrance into a regional economy that would long be based on natural resources. Today, however, North Idaho communities are looking to travelers and adventurers to replace logging and mining as economic bedrock.

But mining's legacy lingers. **Silver Valley**, centered in **Wallace** and **Kellogg**, was to silver what Butte was to copper. More than $5 billion worth of silver, lead, and zinc was mined in the region's heyday. Experienced miners serve as guides on **Wallace's Sierra Silver Mine Tour**, which features a walk underground into what was once a working shaft. Another fascinating local attraction, the **Oasis Rooms Bordello Museum**, details an industry that was important to the Silver Valley well into the 20th century.

Highway 90 bisects the Idaho panhandle along the old **Mullan Road**, an army route built in the mid-19th century from Fort Benton, Montana, to Walla Walla, Washington. Its vistas reveal the wide impact people have had on this region, from the scars of mine tailings and clearcut forests to such sublime statements of faith as Father Antonio Ravalli's **Old Mission** at **Cataldo**, completed in 1853.

But ultimately, nothing that's happened in the Northern Rockies in the past 150 years can compete with the land itself. Here along the backbone of the continent, you can almost see forever and begin to understand the lure of the West: the majestic mountains, the crystalline rivers, and the rolling prairies with grass thigh-high and meadowlarks making the soundtrack.

TRAVEL TIPS

DETAILS

When to Go

The Northern Rockies are at their best in summer and early fall. Temperatures vary according to elevation. Summer is sunny but often cool and prone to thunderstorms, with temperatures ranging from the 40s to the 80s. Winter temperatures can drop well below freezing, and snow leaves much of the region impassable from October through May.

How to Get There

Commercial airlines serve the following Montana cities: Billings, Missoula, Great Falls, and Bozeman.

Getting Around

You'll need a car to traverse the vast, often desolate stretches in this region. Car rentals are available at the airports.

INFORMATION

Idaho Travel Council

700 West State Street; Boise, ID 83720; tel: 800-635-7820 or 208-334-2470.

Travel Montana

1424 9th Avenue, P.O. Box 200533; Helena, MT 59620; tel: 800-847-4868.

LODGING

PRICE GUIDE – double occupancy

$ = up to $49 $$ = $50–$99
$$$ = $100–$149 $$$$ = $150+

Beaverhead Rock Ranch

4325 Old Stage Road; Dillon, MT 59725; tel: 800-338-0061 or 406-683-2126.

The ranch offers guest houses near the Beaverhead River south of Dillon. Stay in a two-bedroom farmhouse or a restored 19th-century cabin. Both are comfortably furnished with private baths, kitchens, and appliances. A two-night minimum stay is required. Open March through November. $$

Copper King Mansion

219 West Granite Street; Butte, MT 59701; tel: 406-782-7580.

The beautifully restored three-story mansion of copper baron William A. Clark has four guest rooms furnished with museum-quality antiques, glassware, and china. $–$$$

Diamond J Ranch

P.O. Box 577; Ennis, MT 59729; tel: 406-682-4867.

This 70-year-old dude ranch, 12 miles east of Ennis in Jack Creek Canyon, offers rustic comfort and a wide range of activities. Guests can choose one of 11 cabins or a room in the main house. The weekly rate includes meals, horseback riding, fly-fishing, birding, barn dancing, and more. $$$$

Goldsmith's Inn

809 East Front Street; Missoula, MT 59802; tel: 406-721-6732.

This brick mansion was built in 1911 and is set on the Clark Fork River, with scenic views of the Bitterroot Mountains. Goldsmith's has seven rooms, including a honeymoon suite with its own riverfront porch and Japanese soaking tub. $$$

Jackson Hot Springs Lodge

P.O. Box 808; Jackson, MT 59736; tel: 406-834-3151.

Built around the same hot springs that members of the Lewis and Clark Expedition visited in 1806, the lodge features a dozen snug cabins and home-cooked meals. Cabins are simply furnished; some have private baths. $$

Sanders Bed-and-Breakfast

328 North Ewing Street; Helena, MT 59601; tel: 406-442-3309.

This three-story 1875 Victorian mansion, built by one of Montana's first U.S. senators, has hardwood floors, bay windows, beveled glass, and high ceilings. Helena's premier bed-and-breakfast offers seven spacious guest rooms, all with private bath, some with fireplace. $$$

Scott Bed-and-Breakfast

15 West Copper; Butte, MT 59701; tel: 800-844-2952 or 406-723-7030.

This restored three-story brick inn, formerly a boardinghouse for miners, has seven small rooms and a well-appointed sitting and dining area on the second floor. Elaborate breakfasts are served. $$

Stonehouse Inn

306 East Idaho; Virginia City, MT 59755; tel: 406-843-5504.

This fine Gothic Revival house was built in 1884 and now serves as a bed-and-breakfast. Five guest rooms are furnished with brass beds and antiques and have shared baths. $$

TOURS & OUTFITTERS

Last Chance Tour Train

225 North Roberts Street; Helena, MT 59601; tel: 406-442-1023.

Trains operate from mid-May through September and depart in front of the Montana Historical Society Museum.

Sierra Silver Mine Tour

420 Fifth Street; Wallace, ID 83873; tel: 208-752-5151.

Mine tours are available from mid-May to mid-October.

MUSEUMS

C.M. Russell Museum Complex

400 13th Street North; Great Falls, MT 59401; tel: 406-727-8787.

The home, studio, paintings, and sculptures of cowboy artist Charlie Russell.

Museum of the Plains Indian

P.O. Box 400, Browning, MT 59417; tel: 406-338-2230.

Exhibits interpret Plains Indian tribes of the region.

Oasis Rooms Bordello Museum

605 Cedar Street; Wallace, ID 83873; tel: 208-753-0801.

An unusual museum with displays of lingerie, magazines, and other items from the brothel that operated here until 1988.

World Museum of Mining and Hell Roarin' Gulch

Montana Tech University, West Park Street; Butte, MT 59701; tel: 406-723-7211.

A chronicle of Butte's mining history and raucous frontier days.

PARKS

Bannack State Park

4200 Bannack Road; Dillon, MT 59725; tel: 406-834-3413.

Site of Montana's first gold rush in 1862, later state capital, Bannack is now a preserved ghost town with 60 buildings.

Big Hole National Battlefield

P.O. Box 237; Wisdom, MT 59761; tel: 406-689-3155.

Part of Nez Percé National Historical Park, this is the site of a fatal clash between the Nez Percé and U.S. Army troops in 1877.

Glacier National Park

West Glacier, MT 59936; tel: 406-888-7800.

Spectacular high country in northern Montana.

Grant-Kohrs Ranch National Historic Site

P.O. Box 790; Deer Lodge, MT 59722; tel: 406-846-2070.

A chronicle of ranch life at one of the biggest cattle operations in the Old West.

Excursions

Boise

Boise Convention and Visitors Bureau; 168 North 9th Street, Suite #200; Boise, ID 83702; tel: 800-635-5240 or 208-344-7777.

Visit Idaho's vibrant capital city to see the Old Penitentiary, built in the 1870s to house Idaho Territory's most notorious inmates. Also in town is the World Center for Birds of Prey and the Basque Museum and Cultural Center, which tells the story of Basque settlers and sheepherders in the Great Basin region.

Sun Valley

Sun Valley-Ketchum Chamber of Commerce; 411 North Main Street, P.O. Box 2420; Ketchum, ID 83340; tel: 800-634-3347 or 208-726-3423.

Long before the Sun Valley ski resort opened, Idaho's Wood River Valley was a mining and sheep-ranching stronghold. The towns of Hailey and Ketchum were among the first in Idaho to get telephones and electricity during the 1880s lead-silver boom. In addition to skiing, today's Sun Valley has excellent cycling, fishing, golf, and tennis, as well as more exotic pursuits like llama trekking and paragliding. Hailey has a big rodeo on July 4.

Salmon Valley

Salmon Valley Chamber of Commerce; 200 Main Street, Suite #1; Salmon, ID 83467; tel: 800-727-2540 or 208-756-2100.

Take your time on Highway 93, much of which follows Idaho's famed Salmon River (the "River of No Return"), a great place for a float trip. At Challis, swing southwest on Highway 75 to the alpine lakes of Sawtooth National Recreation Area or remain on Highway 93 as it unfurls below the Lost River Range. The stark volcanic landscape of Craters of the Moon National Monument near Arco contrasts with lush mountain surroundings.

Lewis and Clark Trail
Montana-Idaho

CHAPTER **21**

Wind whips the small encampment near the **Missouri River**, and the travelers scan the darkening western sky. No doubt, there'll soon be a thunderstorm, perhaps even hail. But at least they have made camp; at least they won't be out on that infernal prairie as they were during the storm a few days ago, dodging rattlesnakes, prickly pear cactus, and deep ruts left by wandering bison. ◆ After moving swiftly upriver since leaving **Fort Mandan**, the travelers – several dozen men, one young woman, a baby, and a dog – are made restless by the need to stay so long in one place. They need to move on; they need to find horses; they have to get over the approaching mountains before winter. Capts. Meriwether Lewis and William Clark expected to find just one waterfall here, easily portaged in a day. Instead, they found five formidable cascades, one after the other. It will take a month to make the portage. ◆ Because the Corps of Discovery spent so much time on its river-

Persevering through blizzards, risky portages, and unknown territory, the Corps of Discovery recorded the glorious sights of the West.

banks, **Great Falls, Montana**, has evolved into a major destination for anyone eager to trace the Lewis and Clark Trail, the 7,500-mile route explored by the captains and their team in 1804–06. For two and a half years, interrupted by winter camps in North Dakota and Oregon, Lewis and Clark and their party followed the instructions of President Thomas Jefferson, who was eager to learn what the United States had acquired in the 800,000-square-mile Louisiana Purchase. Most of all, Jefferson hoped they'd find the long-sought Northwest Passage, an easy water route across the continent to the Pacific Ocean. But the president also expected details of everything else the party

A canoeist traces the route of the Corps of Discovery through the Missouri Breaks region of the Missouri River in Montana.

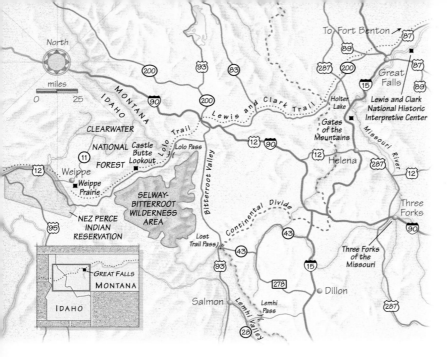

relive the events of nearly 200 years ago. Ask them anything about events beyond July 1805 and your question will be met with a blank stare. But ask them how to prepare suet dumplings from buffalo meat, or how to fashion a dug-out canoe, or how to treat ailing travelers with sulfur water, and they'll tell you all they know.

From Great Falls, modern travelers with time to spare can choose to backtrack up Highway 87 to **Fort Benton**, where you can arrange a guided boat trip or rent your own gear

encountered, from Indian tribes and trade opportunities to animal and plant life.

Legendary Path Retraced

All of these details are richly described at Great Falls' new **Lewis & Clark National Historic Interpretive Center**, built on a hillside overlooking Black Eagle Falls. Here, visitors learn how the expedition moved west and how its members interacted with the many native peoples they met along the way. Great Falls also is the site of an annual Lewis and Clark Festival, held each year in late June about the same time the expedition camped in the area. Well worth timing a vacation around, the festival features Missouri River float trips, a children's day camp, and a fascinating Lewis and Clark encampment, with scenes such as the one described above. Just like their Civil War-reenacting brethren in the eastern and southern United States, the festival's modern-day Lewis and Clark stand-ins pay strict attention to detail as they

for a float down the **Wild and Scenic Missouri River**. Lewis waxed rhapsodic over the riverbanks' white cliffs and dark buttes: "... elegant ranges of lofty freestone buildings having their parapets well stocked with statuary.... As we passed on it seemed as if those scenes of visionary enchantment would never have an end."

Whether on a guided trip or floating alone, take your time on the river. A portable copy of *The Journals of Lewis and Clark* is a must, so you can compare your experiences with those of the captains. Make camp early so you'll have time to climb the magnificent surrounding bluffs before dusk falls. It was here in the **Missouri River Breaks** that the Corps of Discovery encountered many grizzly bears and other creatures: "We can scarcely cast our eyes in any direction without perceiving deer, elk, buffalo, or antelope," Lewis wrote. The grizzlies are gone now, but other wildlife remains abundant, and campfires are often accompanied by the distant serenade of coyotes.

Approaching the Divide

At Great Falls, their portage complete, the corps drank the last of their whiskey on the Fourth of July, 1805. Soon after, they pushed on toward modern-day **Helena, Montana**, losely paralleling what is now Interstate 15. The historical highlight along this stretch is t **Upper Holter Lake**, home of the **Gates of he Mountains**. Lewis, traveling separately rom Clark at the time, wrote that the 1,200-oot-high cliffs here appeared to close in on he party, with scarcely a spot on shore vhere "a man could rest the sole of his foot." Jinety-minute boat tours take visitors hrough a handsome canyon to this spot, as vell as to a picnic area where the expedition probably camped. Blackfeet Indian pictographs are evident on the canyon walls, and sharp eyes may spy an osprey, a bald eagle, or even an occasional bighorn sheep or mountain goat.

By late July, the explorers had reached the **Three Forks of the Missouri River**. Here, the corps had no trouble deciding which fork to take. It had to be the westernmost, which they named the Jefferson in tribute to "the author of our enterprise," as Lewis noted in

Meriwether Lewis
(opposite, top) served as Thomas Jefferson's secretary before embarking on his epic journey. He chose William Clark (opposite, bottom), an old army comrade, as his second-in-command. "My friend," wrote Lewis, "I do assure you that no man lives with whom I would prefer to take such a trip."

Sacagawea uses sign language to communicate with potentially hostile Indians in Charles M. Russell's *Lewis and Clark on the Columbia* (above).

Sacagawea

There are no pictures of her. No one is sure where or when she died, or even how to say her name. Her life has been endlessly mythologized and misrepresented, but Sacagawea was a real person who made real contributions to the Lewis and Clark Expedition.

The biggest misunderstanding about Sacagawea (most historians pronounce her name Sah-CAH-ga-we-a) is that she guided the expedition westward. The truth is, the Shoshone teenager had been kidnapped near the Three Forks of the Missouri several years earlier, then sold to a trapper named Charbonneau, and she knew little of the country between there and Fort Mandan. But if she didn't exactly serve as a pathfinder, she contributed in countless other ways.

Sacagawea was an expert on plants and herbs, and that knowledge proved invaluable to the Corps of Discovery. Her very presence on the trip, together with that of her baby boy, Jean Baptiste Charbonneau, nicknamed Pompey, served as notice to all that the expedition came in peace. Most critically, it was that chance meeting at Camp Fortunate – where Sacagawea was reunited with her brother, the Shoshone chief Cameahwait – that ensured the party would get the horses they so badly needed to cross the Northern Rockies. Some Native Americans rue that day, since that contact ultimately led to the loss of traditional ways. But others celebrate Sacagawea for her strength, intelligence, and fortitude. Many Lewis and Clark journal entries show Sacagawea to be someone who acted calmly amid chaos, and someone who stood up for herself.

Much about Sacagawea is a mystery. Many historians believe that she died in 1812 at Fort Manuel in what is now South Dakota; she would have been only in her early twenties. Others believe that she lived to be quite old, traveling widely and finally making a home in western Wyoming, where a grave said to be hers can be seen on the Wind River Indian Reservation. Whatever the truth, it was Sacagawea's life, not her death, that we remember.

his journal. The captains were also heartened that Sacagawea, the young Shoshone woman in their midst, finally recognized the area through which they were traveling. They hadn't seen Indians for months, but Sacagawea's recollections gave the corps hope they'd soon find her people – and that the Shoshones would have the horses they'd need to get over the mountains before winter descended on the Rockies.

Latourel Falls (left) tumbles into the Columbia River along the last leg of the Corps of Discovery's route.

Lewis and Clark, shown in the far right of the canvas, attempt to convey their peaceful intentions in Charles M. Russell's *Lewis and Clark Meeting Indians at Ross' Hole* (below).

Of course, at that point they still had no idea how formidable a barrier those mountains would be. By mid-August 1805, Lewis and an advance party were again ahead of the main Corps of Discovery southwest of present-day **Dillon, Montana**, following what Lewis described as a "large and plain Indian road... I therefore did not despair of shortly finding a passage over the mountains and of tasting the waters of the great Columbia this evening." But when they reached the pass, Lewis was stunned to see not just one mountain range and the fabled Northwest Passage beyond it, but ridge after ridge of snow-capped peaks.

Today, travelers can take a rough ranch road up to **Lemhi Pass** and over the Continental Divide. A small campground just east of the Montana state line is dedicated to Sacagawea. A fence straddles the border, a few utility lines graze the horizon, and

nterpretive signs tell of the Corps of Discovery's visit. Other than that, things haven't changed a lot at Lemhi Pass. You can't help but stand at the divide and think: This is very nearly the same scene Lewis saw 200 years ago.

Early Winter and Near Starvation

In Idaho's **Lemhi Valley**, the corps met a large band of Shoshones. Incredibly, the chief of the group, Cameahwait, was none other than Sacagawea's long-lost brother, and the expedition easily got the horses it needed to continue over the mountains. From **Lost Trail Pass**, the expedition made its way into Montana's **Bitterroot Valley**. To find a navigable river leading west, they had to cross the **Lolo Trail**, and they had to do it soon. It was already mid-September, and here in the high country, winter was fast on the way. On September 16, 1805, the expedition's members woke to find their beds covered with several inches of new snow. "I have been wet and as cold in every part as I ever

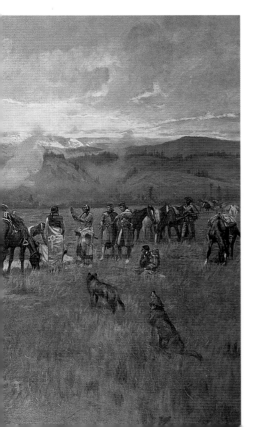

was in my life," Clark lamented in his journal. "Indeed I was at one time fearful my feet would freeze in the thin moccasins I wore." To make things worse, there was little game, and the explorers were reduced to killing and eating horses and even candles. The **Lolo Trail** can still be followed today, by automobile, mountain bike, or on horseback, though the land it traverses is both fragile and sacred to the Nez Percé; visitors must tread gently and with respect.

Lewis and Clark believed that the Lolo Trail crossing would take five days. It wound up taking twice as long, and they nearly starved in the process. But when they descended onto the **Weippe Prairie**, they were warmly greeted by the Nez Percé, who fed them, helped them build canoes, and sent the explorers on their way to the **Columbia River**. Here they encountered large numbers of Columbia River Indians encamped on the banks of the river or living in tightly knit longhouse villages, their lives revolving around the vast numbers of seasonally spawning salmon returning along the river from the ocean. The Indians, skilled canoeists, helped the Corps negotiate the dangerous swirling cascades of the Columbia as it plunged through the Gorge to the Pacific Ocean.

The expedition arrived back in St. Louis in September 1806, and word of their safe return soon spread east to Washington, D.C. Jefferson was surely disappointed to learn that there was no Northwest Passage, but he told Congress that "it is but justice to say that Messrs. Lewis and Clark and their brave companions have by this arduous service deserved well of their country." For the Corps of Discovery had succeeded in many other ways: in learning about plants and animals previously unknown to science, in mapping a land once cloaked in mystery, and in forging relationships with tribal peoples who, for a while at least, were warm and positive. Lewis and Clark and their companions not only lived one of history's greatest adventures; they gave their nation an insatiable wanderlust and a penchant for dreaming big – two traits that, 200 years later, still define the American experience.

TRAVEL TIPS

DETAILS

When to Go

Weather along the trail varies depending on elevation and exposure. Summer is sunny but often cool, with temperatures ranging from the 40s to the 80s. Winter is frigid, and heavy snowfall makes some mountain roads impassable.

How to Get There

Commercial airlines serve Great Falls International, Missoula International, and Bozeman International in Montana; Boise Airport and Lewiston Nez Perce County Airport in Idaho.

Getting Around

You'll need a car to follow the trail. Car rentals are available at the airports.

INFORMATION

Lewis and Clark National Historic Trail

National Park Service, 700 Rayovac Drive, Suite 100; Madison, WI 53711; tel: 608-264-5610.

Lewis and Clark Trail Heritage Foundation

P.O. Box 3434; Great Falls, MT 59403; tel: 406-454-1234.

LODGING

PRICE GUIDE – double occupancy

$ = up to $49 $$ = $50–$99
$$$ = $100–$149 $$$$ = $150+

Best Western Heritage Inn

1700 Fox Farm Road; Great Falls, MT 59404; tel: 800-548-0361or

406-761-1900.

Montana meets New Orleans at this Mardi Gras-themed hotel near downtown. In addition to regular casino action and many conventions, the inn hosts the annual Charlie Russell Art Auction each March. A restaurant and lounge and two indoor pools are on the premises. $$

Carriage House

611 Fifth Street; Lewiston, ID 83501; tel: 208-746-4506.

Within walking distance of downtown Lewiston, this Victorian-style bed-and-breakfast offers four guest rooms and an indoor spa. $$

Circle Bar Guest Ranch

P.O. Box K; Utica, MT 59452; tel: 406-423-5454.

About 90 miles southeast of Great Falls, this comfortable ranch has nine log cabins with woodstoves or fireplaces, and four modern suites in the main lodge. The annual highlight is September's five-day Charlie Russell Ride, where up to 15 guests are given a private tour of the C.M. Russell Museum, then spend several days riding trails painted by the artist. Horseback riding, cattle drives, ranch activities, a pool, and a hot tub are available. $$$

Rosebriar Hotel

636 14th Street; Astoria, OR 97103; tel: 800-487-0224 or 503-325-7427.

This big, white-frame Classic Revival home was built in 1902 on a hill overlooking Astoria, the West's first permanent American settlement west of the Mississippi. It is now a charming hotel with landscaped grounds and 11 suites, some with a Jacuzzi and fireplace. Gourmet breakfasts are served. $$–$$$

Sanders Bed-and-Breakfast

328 North Ewing Street; Helena, MT 59601; tel: 406-442-3309.

This three-story 1875 Victorian mansion, built by one of Montana's first U.S. senators, has hardwood floors, bay windows, beveled glass, and high ceilings. The inn offers seven spacious

guest rooms, all with private bath, some with fireplace. $$$

Three Rivers Resort

HC 75, P.O. Box 61; Kooski, ID 83539; tel: 888-926-4430 or 208-926-4430.

This resort offers eight motel rooms and 16 cabins with private baths, kitchens, and fireplaces. Old No. 1, a former ranger's cabin has a hot tub on its deck. A swimming pool and three hot tub are on the premises. $$–$$$

TOURS & OUTFITTERS

Missouri River Outfitters

P.O. Box 762; Fort Benton, MT 59442; tel: 406-622-3295.

Canoe and boat trips trace the Lewis and Clark Trail along the Wild and Scenic Missouri River near Fort Benton.

Montana River Outfitters

1401 5th Avenue South; Great Falls, MT 59405; tel: 406-761-1677

Float trips on the Missouri River near Great Falls recall the passage of the Corps of Discovery.

Triple 'O' Outfitters

P.O. Box 217; Pierce, ID 83546; tel 208-464-2349 or 208-464-2761.

Horseback trips venture along the Lolo Trail and through Clearwater National Forest.

MUSEUMS

Columbia Gorge Discovery Center and Wasco County Historical Museum

5000 Discovery Drive North; The Dalles, OR 97058; 541-296-8600.

Housed in an airy barnlike structure on a bluff overlooking the Columbia River, this impressive new interpretive center tells the rich story of the area through state-of-the-art, interactive exhibits, scale models, and videos.

Lewis and Clark Interpretive Center

P.O. Box 488; Ilwaco, WA 98624; tel: 360-642-3029.

Near Fort Clatsop National Memorial, this coastal interpretive center showcases the expedition through informative displays and memorabilia.

Lewis and Clark National Historic Trail Interpretive Center

P.O. Box 1806; Great Falls, MT 59403; tel: 406-727-8733.

This interpretive center, opened in 1998, gives a comprehensive look at the Lewis and Clark expedition's 1804–06 journey, paying particular attention to its encounters with Native American tribes along the route.

North Dakota Lewis and Clark Interpretive Center

North Dakota Lewis and Clark Bicentennial Foundation; P.O. Box 607; Washburn, ND 58577; tel: 701-462-8535.

Highlights here include a complete set of Karl Bodmer prints depicting Plains Indian life and exhibits explaining how explorers survived the harsh North Dakota winter of 1804–1805.

PARKS

Gates of the Mountains

P.O. Box 4478; Helena, MT 59624; tel: 406-458-5241.

This park preserves 1,200-foot-high cliffs at Upper Holter Lake covered in Blackfeet Indian pictographs, and the Corps' probable campsite, now a picnic ground.

Lolo Trail

Clearwater National Forest, Lochsa Ranger District; Kooskia, ID 83539; tel: 208-926-4275.

A high-country trail over the Bitterroot Mountains taken by the Corps in September 1805.

Missouri Headwaters State Park

Montana Fish, Wildlife and Parks, Region 3 HQ; 1400 South 19th; Bozeman, MT 59715; tel: 406-994-4042 or 406-285-3198.

Preserved here are the Three Forks of the Missouri River, a key spot where the Corps took the Jefferson fork west.

Excursions

Fort Clatsop National Memorial

92343 Fort Clatsop Road; Astoria, OR 97103; tel: 503-861-2471.

Fort Clatsop, near Astoria, Oregon, the site of the Corps of Discovery's 1805–06 winter camp, is one of the best interpretive sites on the Trail. Discuss trail lore with the knowledgeable park staff in the furnished fort replica and browse fascinating exhibits in the visitor center that detail both the expedition and its aftermath.

Pompey's Pillar

Montana Bureau of Land Management, 810 East Main Street; Billings, MT 59105; tel: 406-875-2233 or 406-238-1541.

East of Billings, Pompey's Pillar contains the only known physical evidence of the Lewis and Clark Expedition. Traveling apart from Lewis in July 1806, Clark and his party found this "remarkable rock" beside the Yellowstone River and christened it Pompey's Pillar, the nickname for Sacagawea's son, then 17 months old. Clark's dated signature is still visible beneath protective glass.

Washburn, North Dakota

North Dakota Lewis and Clark Bicentennial Foundation, P.O. Box 607; Washburn, ND 58577; tel: 701-462-8535.

Washburn is the town nearest Fort Mandan, where Lewis and Clark spent the winter of 1804–05 and hired interpreter Toussaint Charboneau and his wife Sacagawea. Fort Mandan has been reconstructed 10 miles upriver from its original site. There's also a fine new North Dakota Lewis and Clark Interpretive Center in Washburn. For a comprehensive look at area tribal traditions, visit Knife River Indian Villages National Historic Site, near Stanton, and Fort Abraham Lincoln State Park near Mandan.

Gold Country
California

CHAPTER **22**

oloma, California, hasn't changed much in the last 150 years. It's a small town set on the banks of the **American River**, amid the foothills of the **Sierra Nevada**. Even today, Coloma looks too pretty, too gentle, to be a place where so much boisterous and brawling history was made. ◆ But history was made there on January 24, 1848. Early that morning, a carpenter named John Marshall was inspecting the sawmill he had constructed for John Sutter, a Swiss immigrant who had amassed vast land holdings in northern California. Marshall peered into the American's shallow waters. "I reached my hand down and picked it up," he recalled later. "It made my heart thump, for I was certain it was gold." ◆ Eureka! The California Gold Rush had begun. Marshall and his employer Sutter tried to keep the discovery secret, but that proved futile. Within a year, gold- **A nugget of gold, pulled from** seeking "forty-niners" by the thousands **a Sierra Nevada riverbed,** were braving trails across the frontier **shaped the destiny of California** West or the perilous voyage around Cape Horn – **and a young nation.** all to reach the California goldfields. They seemed to come from everywhere – eastern cities and midwestern farms, England and Ireland and China and Chile. "It was the only population of the kind that the world has ever seen," Mark Twain wrote in *Roughing It*, "and it is not likely that the world will ever see its like again." ◆ Historians estimate that in the 50 years following the strike at Coloma some 125 million ounces of gold ($50 billion worth in present dollars) were pulled from these oak-studded foothills. Still, as the sharp-eyed observer of Gold Country mores, Dame Shirley (Louise Clapp), observed, "Gold mining is nature's great lottery scheme." Far more miners failed than succeeded. Neither John Marshall nor John Sutter profited from

Marshall Gold Discovery State Historic Park is the site where John Marshall discovered gold in 1848.

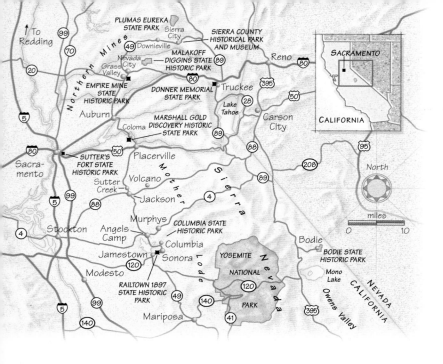

not just California but the West and the entire United States.

Determined prospectors still draw nuggets from California's mountains and streambeds. But for travelers, the Golden State offers much more than mere ore. With its 12,000-foot-high Sierra Nevada, its 1,700-mile-long Pacific coastline California boasts some of the most astonishingly varied geography on the planet. Great national parks – Yosemite, Sequoia, Death Valley – preserve both incomparable landscapes and a human history of exploration and enterprise, triumph and tragedy. While cities like Los Angeles, San Francisco, San Diego, and San Jose have grown into urban powerhouses, ranching regions like the Owens Valley, on the eastern slope of the Sierra, and the Santa Ynez Valley north of Santa Barbara, still allow visitors to live out western fantasies of ropin' and ridin'.

As for the place where it all started – California's Gold Country itself – it holds some of the prettiest small towns, most entrancing countryside, and most vivid history to be experienced anywhere in the West. Gold Country is a land for all seasons: tawny yellow in hot summer, tinged with fall color come autumn, moody and misty in winter, and dazzling in spring with displays of California poppy and wild lupine.

Marshall's momentous discovery. Marshall was booted off his mining claim and ended his days a blacksmith. Sutter fared worse: his lands were stolen from him by squatters – much of his acreage became the new city of Sacramento – and he died penniless. Likewise, many forty-niners went home broke.

But the Gold Rush started by Marshall and Sutter and thousands of other argonauts helped to wrest California from Mexico, make it briefly an independent republic, and then join it with the United States. Later California miners would fan out across the West to follow new booms in places like Jacksonville, Oregon; Leadville, Colorado; and Virginia City, Nevada. In short, the California Gold Rush was an event that changed, utterly,

A Capital History

Gold Country extends about 300 miles along the Sierra Nevada's western foothills, from Sierra City in the north to Mariposa in the south. It's often divided into two regions: **The Mother Lode**, which runs from Coloma south to Mariposa, and the **Northern Mines**, which extends from Auburn north to Sierra City. To the west lies California's capital, Sacramento – not quite part of Gold Country geologically but tied to it by culture and history.

Steel wheels (left): vintage trains at California State Railroad Museum commemorate the golden age of the "iron horse."

Gold pans like this one (opposite, top) and the specks of gold that turned up in them made some men wealthy while thousands went empty-handed.

The Prospector (opposite, bottom), by N. C. Wyeth, portrays a familiar sight in mid-19th-century California.

Today's Sacramento is a fast-growing center for agricultural and high-tech industries. But the city has also done a good job of restoring and preserving its past, which makes it a logical place to start a Gold Country tour. Sacramento's history is inextricably linked with John Sutter, who built a fort and founded a settlement he called New Helvetia (New Switzerland) here at the confluence of the American and Sacramento Rivers. Sutter's story of early success and later failure is well displayed at **Sutter's Fort State Historic Park**, not far from downtown.

Next door, the **California Indian Museum** focuses on the state's large and diverse Native American population. California's tribes suffered greatly after Spanish and American settlement, but surviving tribes, like the Hoopa on the state's North Coast and the Miwok in the Sierra foothills, have become increasingly vocal in state culture and politics. Housed in the California Archives building, the new **Golden State Museum** offers engagingly high-tech looks at California life since 1850. For fine art, the **Crocker Art Museum** is particularly strong in the works of Albert Bierstadt and other 19th-century masters of American landscape painting.

Sacramento is above all a river town, and most of its other historic attractions are clustered on the east bank of the Sacramento River in the district called **Old Sacramento**. Here, restored 19th-century buildings line wooden sidewalks and cobblestone streets, and shopping and dining choices are considerable, if mostly tourist-oriented. The single best stop is undoubtedly the **California State Railroad Museum**, the biggest railroad museum in the country. Or you can take to the water and cruise the Sacramento River on a vintage paddlewheeler.

Gold Rush Beginnings

As you head east from Sacramento on either Interstate 80 or U.S. 50, you'll see the foothills rumbling up gracefully before the snowy peaks of the Sierra Nevada. Now you're in true Gold Country. California's growth has made itself felt here, too: some of Gold Country's historic small towns have sprouted modern annexes with strip malls and subdivisions. But they're the exception; most remain remarkably enjoyable places to visit.

Coloma, where the big rush for gold began, is an essential stop on any tour of Gold Country. On a typical Sunday morning back then, according to argonaut Charles Gillespie, "the principal street of Coloma was alive with crowds of moving men, passing and repassing, laughing, talking, and all appearing in the best of humor." Today those

moving crowds are more likely to be tourists than miners, but Coloma still puts most of them in the best of humor. **Marshall Gold Discovery State Park** holds a replica of Sutter's Mill and a good museum. Visitors can try their hand at gold panning on the banks of the American River or attend the World Gold Panning Championships in late September. And the river that runs through town is good for more than gold. A number of outfitters run whitewater rafting trips through the American's rapids in spring and summer.

From Coloma, you can wind south on Highway 49, the mainly two-lane, often twisting route that links all 300 miles of Gold Country. A few turns of highway bring you to **Placerville**. Once called Hangtown – a testimonial to its fondness for vigilante justice – the town takes its present name from placer mining, a technique of panning or sluicing gold deposits found in river gravel. Notable attractions here include the **Gold Bug Park and Mine**, the only city-owned gold mine in the nation; **El Dorado County Museum**; and

Placerville Hardware, founded in 1852 and said to be the oldest hardware store west of the Mississippi.

Sutter Creek, just below Placerville, sometimes calls itself the Carmel of Gold Country. It is an undeniably pretty little place. Downtown holds an engaging collection of tin-roofed, balconied 19th-century buildings, and a number of Victorian homes have been turned into bed-and-breakfast inns. Sutter Creek also makes a good base for exploring Amador County's growing crop of wineries. Winemaking has a long history in Gold Country. Some of the first vines were planted shortly after the gold miners arrived, and some contemporary wineries, like **Boeger Winery**, near Placerville, occupy cellars that date back to the 1870s.

Mark Twain Lives

It's easy to tell when you've reached **Jackson**, four miles south of Sutter Creek: looming against the sky are the immense forms of the **Kennedy Tailings Wheels** – two 58-foot-diameter wheels that date from the early 20th century, when the search for gold had shifted to hard-rock mines bored deep into the earth. The wheels were used at the Kennedy and Argonaut Mines, among the deepest (one mile) and richest ($70 million of gold were found here) mines in the United States. Jackson is also the site of the **Amador County Museum**. Tucked into a valley to the east of Jackson, **Volcano** is a particularly appealing little town, its star attraction the 1863 vintage **St. George Hotel**, now a good bed-and-breakfast inn.

"I'll risk forty dollars that he can outjump any frog in Calaveras County," Jim Smiley bragged in "The Celebrated Jumping Frog of Calaveras County." Mark Twain set his famous yarn in **Angel's Camp**, and even now the amphibian antics live on in the town's annual Frog Jumping Jubilee held each May. A few miles east, the town of **Murphys** has tree-lined streets, well-maintained 19th-century buildings, and a pleasant sense of separation from the bustle of Gold Country.

The town of **Columbia** was once called "The gem of the southern mines." Now set aside as **Columbia State Historic Park**, it's one of the top two or three sites in Gold Country, successfully combining genuine history with a certain amount of tourist-savvy entertainment. Here you can tour the town on an antique stagecoach, try your hand at gold panning, applaud a stage show at the **Fallon Theater**, or retreat to the comforts of 1857 at the restored **City Hotel**.

A covered bridge (opposite) spans the Stanislaus River in the Mother Lode country of Knight's Ferry.

The Donner Party monument (right) at Donner Lake conveys the anguish and longing for survival that gripped the ill-fated party of emigrants.

The Donner Party

"Snowd. all night and snows yet rapidly ... the prospect is appalling but hope in God. Amen." So reads Patrick Breen's journal entry for Christmas Day of 1846. By then he had been trapped for two months in the blizzard-battered Sierra Nevada of California. Breen would remain there two months more. He was a member of the Donner Party, the group that has come to represent every terrifying aspect of America's migration west.

The party was named for two of its leaders, George and Jacob Donner, Illinois farmers who dreamed of better lives in California. In Wyoming, the Donners joined other wagonloads of immigrants headed for the California Trail. But below **Fort Bridger**, the Donners made a miscalculation: they set off on a newly mapped trail, the Hastings Cutoff, an ill-plotted route that left them wandering lost for three weeks. The party became worn out and beset by internal squabbling. By the time the Donners rejoined the main **California Trail** and reached its most fearsome obstacle – the Sierra Nevada – it was near the end of October, dangerously late to attempt a crossing.

The party pressed on into the mountains – and into disaster. The season's first storm struck October 28. Early November saw the party completely snowbound. Food supplies dwindled, and the snow made hunting impossible. The party ate its horses, ate boiled hides, ate nothing. As the frozen, hungry weeks wore on, men, women, and children sickened and died. And then the unspeakable occurred: the remaining members of the party cannibalized their own dead to survive.

"Are you men from California, or do you come from heaven?" cried one woman to the rescue party that reached them on February 18, 1847. But for many, rescue came too late. Of the 89 Donner Party travelers, only 45 survived. Among the living were Patrick Breen and his family; among the dead both George and Jacob Donner.

Today the scene of the Donner Party's nightmare is a popular resort area. The **Emigrant Trail Museum** in Truckee, California, preserves artifacts from the journey. At **Donner Memorial State Park**, you can hike in the Donners' footsteps. As you do, you will feel, even on a summer day, a chill to freeze you to your bones.

California Missions

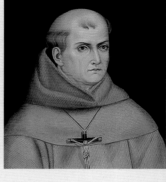

Father Junípero Serra (right), a Spanish Franciscan priest, founded the California missions.

Mission San Juan Capistrano (below), north of San Diego, is famous for its beauty and the yearly return of the swallows.

Lotta Crabtree (opposite) began her acting career as a child performer in the California gold camps and later became one of the richest performers of her day.

San Juan Capistrano, San Francisco de Asís, La Purísima Concepción: for more than 200 years these and their sister churches have commanded California's hills and valleys, their adobe walls and red-tiled roofs as graceful as their sweetly assonant names. They are California's chain of 21 missions, and the Golden State is what it is today because of them.

Outposts of the Spanish empire, the missions were the dream of Father Junípero Serra, a Franciscan priest born on the island of Majorca. Serra's goal was to create a line of churches that would run 600 miles along the California coast, each mission a day's horseback ride from the next. Serra founded the first, **San Diego de Alcalá**, in 1769; the last he would personally oversee was **San Buenaventura**, in 1782. But the dream would continue after Serra's death, with 12 more churches – the final one, **San Francisco Solano**, established in 1823 in what is now Sonoma County.

Architecturally, the missions were simple – adobe churches with living quarters, workshops, and storerooms grouped around a central courtyard. But the missions' religious and political goals were more complex. Certainly, Serra and his Franciscans hoped to bring Christianity to the Chumash, Ohlone, and other native tribes of coastal California. But the missions also served as a means of cementing Spanish rule on the North American frontier.

Today Father Serra and his missions have a mixed reputation. They helped transplant European civilization onto North America's Pacific shore, but they also hastened the nearly total destruction of California's indigenous culture. Still, one can no more imagine California without its missions than one can imagine Paris without Notre Dame. Each of the 21 remains a wonderfully resonant place to visit, and most still serve as parish churches. Some, like San Francisco or San Diego, stand in the middle of the large cities they helped nurture. Others, like **San Antonio de Padua**, maintain the rural solitude they possessed in Serra's day. All reflect an era when faith and work could unite in creating architecture of enormous and enduring grace.

"When I arrived at the commencement of 1849," miner William Perkins recorded of Sonora, "I thought I had never seen a more beautiful, a wilder, or more romantic spot." **Sonora**, just south of Columbia, was settled initially by miners from Sonora, Mexico – hence the name. While the 20th century has brought an invasion of gas stations and shopping centers to Sonora's outskirts, downtown retains much of the appeal it had in Perkins's day, with a number of restored historic buildings on Washington Street. Nearby is **Jamestown**, whose **Railtown 1897** is a shrine to traindom, with three steam locomotives that offer weekend excursions.

Mariposa marks the southern end of the Mother Lode. It's home to the **California State Mining and Mineral Museum**, an ideal place to learn the geology and technology behind the gold mining of yesterday and today. A number of local tour operators will take you out and show you how to pan local streams.

Gold Country Gems

To explore Gold Country's **Northern Mines**, head north from Coloma on Highway 49. First stop is **Auburn**, a gold town rapidly becoming a Sacramento suburb – but its **Old Town**, dominated by an 1891 Firehouse, maintains a walkable charm. Keep on Highway 49, 25 miles north, and you come to the neighboring towns of **Grass Valley** and **Nevada City**. While all Gold Country boasts interesting history, these two are in their own league. Grass Valley was founded in 1850, allegedly when an argonaut tripped over a quartz outcropping while chasing a cow. Its famous residents included notorious 19th-century dancers Lola Montez and Lotta Crabtree. The town's true heyday came late in the Gold Rush era, when placer mining had been replaced by hard-rock mines; **Empire Mine State Park** is one of the best places in Gold Country to get a feel for this tough business.

Nevada City (a popular name in the Old West) was, for a brief time in the 1850s, California's third largest city. Now this town of 3,000 is one of the most attractive in Gold Country, drawing artists and craftspeople. Many of Nevada City's Victorians have been converted to bed-and-breakfast inns, including the **Emma Nevada House** (childhood home of 19th-century opera star Emma Nevada) and the **Red Castle Inn**. Just outside town, **Malakoff Diggins State Park** shows a darker side of the mining era. It demonstrates the lasting effects of hydraulic mining, where enormous sprays of water were blasted against riverbanks to uncover precious gold. Efficient but ecologically disastrous, the practice was outlawed in 1884.

North of Nevada City on Highway 49, Gold Country becomes less touristy and more wild, and the road winds spectacularly along the Yuba River. **Downieville** is slow-paced, and **Sierra City** has as its backdrop the craggy Sierra Buttes. It's home to the **Sierra County Historical Park and Museum**, the former Kentucky Mine now turned into a historic park, with a stamp mill and working water wheel. A little to the north, **Plumas Eureka State Park** also has a museum and stamp mill, not to mention 6,700 acres of lakes and forests and hiking trails.

Though Gold Country is rich in history, it doesn't tell the whole story of the California Gold Rush. Miners and mines eventually swarmed over much of the state. Far to the north, **Shasta State Historic Park**, west of **Redding**, is as genuine a gold town as any in the Sierra foothills, as is nearby **Weaverville**; both still hold numerous historic treasures. And northwest of the Owens Valley – east of the Sierra Nevada, on the Nevada line – Bodie sprang up after a gold strike in 1859. Just 20 years later, it boasted 10,000 inhabitants and a reputation for wickedness: one minister condemned it as "a sea of sin, lashed by the tempests of lust and passion." Now **Bodie State Historic Park**, it's one of California's most hauntingly lovely ghost towns – its worn, battered buildings a testimony to the power of the gold-seekers' dreams and also to their transience.

TRAVEL TIPS

DETAILS

When to Go

Weather in Gold Country depends largely on elevation. In general, summer and fall are agreeable, with temperatures in the 70s and low 80s. Winter and early spring are wet and cool. Expect heavy snowfall and road closings in the High Sierra.

How to Get There

Commercial airlines serve San Francisco, Fresno, and Sacramento.

Getting Around

You'll need a car to travel from town to town in Gold Country; rentals are available at the airports.

INFORMATION

California Department of Parks and Recreation

P.O. Box 942896; Sacramento, CA 94296; tel: 800-444-7275 or 916-653-6995.

California Tourism

801 K Street, Suite 1600; Sacramento, CA 95814; tel: 800-462-2543 or 916-322-2881.

LODGING

PRICE GUIDE – double occupancy

$ = up to $49 $$ = $50–$99
$$$ = $100–$149 $$$$ = $150+

City Hotel

Main Street, P.O. Box 1870; Columbia, CA 95310; tel: 209-532-1479.

This 1856 hotel has been by turns an opulent mining-era hostelry, gold-assay shop, and dance hall. Now carefully restored, the hotel has 10 guest rooms with half-baths. A restaurant and bar are on the premises. $$$

Court Street Inn

215 Court Street; Jackson, CA 95642; tel: 209-223-0416.

This inn is comprised of three buildings – two Victorian houses built in the 19th century and the Indian House, a cottage built in 1930. Six suites are available in the main buildings, with four-poster or brass beds, some with a whirlpool tub or fireplace. The two-story cottage, furnished with vintage antiques, has two bedrooms and bathrooms, one with a claw-foot tub. $$$

Foxes in Sutter Creek

77 Main Street, P.O. Box 159; Sutter Creek, CA 95685; 209-267-5882.

Built in 1857, this bed-and-breakfast offers seven spacious guest rooms with private baths and queen-sized beds, some with fireplaces. Gourmet breakfasts are served. $$$–$$$$

Murphy's Inn

318 Neal Street; Grass Valley, CA 95945; tel: 530-273-6873.

Gold baron Edward Coleman built this house as a wedding present for his wife in 1866. Now a bed-and-breakfast, the house retains its opulence and serenity, not to mention the shade of a towering Sequoia. The inn has eight rooms with private baths. Amenities include two elegant sitting rooms with fireplaces. $$$–$$$$

Red Castle Inn Historic Lodgings

109 Prospect Street; Nevada City, CA 95959; tel: 530-265-5135.

This brick, four-story Gothic Revival house was built in 1857. Romantic footpaths, lit by fairy lights, wind past fountains and ponds on the inn's landscaped grounds. Four rooms and three suites have private baths and porches. $$–$$$

TOURS & OUTFITTERS

Gold Prospecting Expeditions

P.O. Box 974; Jamestown, CA 95327; tel: 209-984-4653.

Gold panning in local streams.

Railtown 1897

Columbia State Historic Park, P.O. Box 151; Columbia, CA 95310; tel: 209-984-3953.

Weekend steam-train excursions depart hourly from April to January and on Saturdays in November and December.

MUSEUMS

Amador County Museum

225 Church Street; Jackson, CA 95642; tel: 209-223-6386.

Exhibits examine hardrock mining.

California Indian Museum

2618 K Street; Sacramento, CA 95816; tel: 916-324-0971.

The state's Indian population, past and present, is interpreted at this museum.

California State Mining and Mineral Museum

P.O. Box 1192; Mariposa, CA 95338; tel: 209-742-7625.

Learn the geology and technology behind gold mining.

El Dorado County Historical Museum

100 Placerville Drive; Placerville, CA 95667; tel: 530-621-5865.

Exhibits on gold-mining history.

Golden State Museum

1020 O Street; Sacramento, CA 95814; tel: 916-653-7524.

The museum features interactive exhibits on California life since 1850.

PARKS

Bodie State Historic Park

P.O. Box 515; Bridgeport, CA 93517; tel: 760-647-6445.

This well-preserved ghost town

is situated in the Owens Valley near the Nevada border.

Columbia State Historic Park
P.O. Box 151; Columbia, CA 95310; tel: 209-532-0150.

The park, which preserves buildings in the old business district, gives visitors a chance to pan for gold, ride a stagecoach, and visit a museum.

Empire Mine State Historic Park
10791 East Empire; Grass Valley, CA 95945; tel: 530-273-4255.

This is one of the best places in Gold Country to get a feel for the tough business of mining.

Gold Bug Park and Mine
549 Main Street; Placerville, CA 95667; tel: 530-642-5232.

An old gold mine and stamp mill in Placerville.

Malakoff Diggins State Park
23579 North Bloomfield-Graniteville Road; Nevada City, CA 95959; tel: 530-265-2740.

The old mine demonstrates the effects of efficient but ecologically disastrous hydraulic gold mining.

Marshall Gold Discovery State Historic Park
P.O. Box 265; Coloma, CA 95613; tel: 530-622-3470.

This gold discovery site includes a replica of Sutter's Mill.

Plumas Eureka State Park
310 Johnsville Road; Blairsden, CA 96103; tel: 530-836-2380.

This old mine site has a museum and stamp mill.

Shasta State Historic Park
P.O. Box 2430; Shasta, CA 96087; tel: 530-243-8194.

A genuine gold town in the Sierra foothills.

Sutters Fort State Historic Park
111 I Street; Sacramento, CA 95814; tel: 916-445-4422.

The park commemorates the site where gold was first discovered in California, in 1848.

Excursions

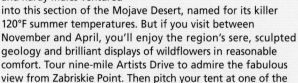

Death Valley National Park

Death Valley National Park, Box 579; Death Valley, CA 92328; tel: 760-786-2331.

Once only borax miners and hardy mules ventured into this section of the Mojave Desert, named for its killer 120°F summer temperatures. But if you visit between November and April, you'll enjoy the region's sere, sculpted geology and brilliant displays of wildflowers in reasonable comfort. Tour nine-mile Artists Drive to admire the fabulous view from Zabriskie Point. Then pitch your tent at one of the park's campgrounds or loll in the desert luxury of Furnace Creek Inn.

Nevada Ghost Towns

Greater Austin Chamber of Commerce, Box 212; Austin, NV 89310; tel: 702-964-2418. Eureka County Chamber of Commerce, Box 14; Eureka, NV 89316; tel: 702-237-5484. Virginia City Chamber of Commerce, Box 464; Virginia City, NV 89440; tel: 702-847-0311.

Any trip to the Mojave Desert should include a tour of Nevada ghost towns. On U.S. Highway 50, the silver and lead mining towns of Austin and Eureka remain vibrant today, with a brace of historic buildings, including the elegantly restored Eureka Opera House. Liveliest and most touristy of them all is Virginia City, queen of the Comstock.

Yosemite National Park

P.O. Box 577; Yosemite National Park, CA 95389; tel: 209-372-0200.

One of California's crown jewels, this 1,169-square-mile, glacier-gouged park in the Sierra Nevada has a rich human history. Miwok and Yokut Indians, California gold-seekers, and famed conservationist John Muir have lived here. To discover more, head to the Indian Cultural Museum, which displays a reconstructed Miwok village, and to Wawona, on the southern boundary, where the Pioneer Yosemite History Museum contains log cabins, a blacksmith shop, and other remnants of 19th-century settlement.

◆

Resource
Directory

FURTHER READING

Western Culture and History

Along the Ramparts of the Tetons, Robert B. Betts (University Press of Colorado, 1978).

Along the Santa Fe Trail, Marc Simmons (University of New Mexico Press, 1986).

The American Heritage History of the Great West, David Lavender (American Heritage Publishing Co., Inc., 1965).

America, New Mexico, Robert Leonard Reid (University of Arizona Press, 1998).

The Arizona Rangers, Bill O'Neal (Eakin Press, 1986).

Art of the Golden West, Alan Axelrod (Abbeville Press, 1990).

Bad Land: An American Romance, Jonathan Raban (Pantheon, 1996).

The Best of the West: An Anthology of Classic Writing from the American West, Tony Hillerman, ed. (HarperCollins, 1991).

Beyond the Hundredth Meridian: John Wesley Powell and the Second Opening of the American West, Wallace Stegner (Houghton Mifflin, 1954).

Big Bend: A Homesteader's Story, J. O. Langford Austin (University of Texas Press, 1981).

Billy the Kid: A Short and Violent Life, Robert M. Utley (University of Nebraska Press, 1989).

Black Elk Speaks, John Neihardt (University of Nebraska Press, 1961).

The Black West, William Loren Katz (Doubleday, 1971).

The Book of the American West, Jay Monaghan, ed. (Bonanza Books, 1963).

A Bride Goes West, Nannie T. Alderson (Farrar and Rinehart, Inc., 1942).

British Gentlemen in the Wild West: The Era of the Intensely English Cowboy, Lawrence M. Woods (Free Press, 1988).

Buckaroo, Hal Cannon and Thomas West, eds. (Callaway, 1993).

Bury My Heart at Wounded Knee, Dee Brown (Bantam Books, 1971).

Butch Cassidy and the Wild Bunch, Pearl Baker (Abelard Schuman, 1971).

Cadillac Desert: The American West and Its Disappearing Water, Marc Reisner (New York: Penguin, 1987).

Cities of Gold, Douglas Preston (Simon & Schuster, 1992).

The Contested Plains: Indians, Goldseekers, & the Rush to Colorado, Elliott West (University of Kansas Press, 1998).

Covered Wagon Women: Diaries and Letters from the Western Trails, 1840-1849, Kenneth L. Holmes, ed. (University of Nebraska Press, 1995).

Cowboy Gear, David Stoecklein (Dober Hill, 1993).

The Cowboys, William H. Forbis (Time-Life Books, 1973).

Cowboys & the Trappings of the Old West, William Manns and Elizabeth Clair Flood (Zon International, 1997).

The Cowgirls, Joyce Gibson Roach (Cordovan Corporation, 1977).

Crossing the Next Meridian: Land, Water, and the Future of the West, Charles F. Wilkinson (Island Press, 1992).

Custer Died for Your Sins, Vine Deloria (Avon, 1969).

Daughters of Joy, Sisters of Misery: Prostitutes in the American West, 1865-1890, Anne Butler (University of Illinois, 1985).

Denizens of the Desert, Elizabeth W. Forster (University of New Mexico Press, 1988).

The Desert Reader, Peter M. Wild, ed. (University of Utah Press, 1991).

Desert Solitaire: A Season in the Wilderness, Edward Abbey (Ballantine, 1968).

Downcanyon, Ann Zwinger (University of Arizona Press, 1995).

Encyclopedia of Western Gunfighters, Bill O'Neal (University of Oklahoma Press, 1979).

The Fur Trade of the American West, 1807-1840, David J. Wishart (University of Nebraska Press, 1992).

Grand Canyon: An Anthology, Bruce Babbitt (Northland Publishing, 1978).

A Great and Shining Road: The Epic Story of the Transcontinental Railroad, John Hoyt Williams (University of Nebraska Press, 1996).

The Great West, David Lavender (American Heritage Publishing, 1985).

Growing up with the Country: Childhood on the Far Western Frontier, Elliott West (University of New Mexico Press, 1997).

Hispanic Culture in the Southwest, Herbert Eugene Bolton (University of Oklahoma Press, 1979).

The Indian Frontier, Robert M. Utley (University of New Mexico Press, 1984).

Indian Removal: The Emigration of the Five Civilized Tribes of Indians, Grant Foreman (University of Oklahoma Press, 1972).

It's Your Misfortune and None of My Own: A New History of the American West, Richard White (University of Oklahoma Press, 1991).

The Journals of Lewis and Clark, Bernard de Voto, ed. (Houghton Mifflin, 1953).

Lasso the Wind: Away to the New West, Timothy Egan (Knopf, 1998).

The Last Best Place: A Montana Anthology, William Kittredge and Annick Smith, eds. (Falcon Press, 1994).

The Last Conquistador: Juan de Onate and the Settling of the Far Southwest, Marc Simmons (University of Oklahoma Press, 1991).

The Legacy of Conquest: The Unbroken Past of the American West, Patricia Nelson Limerick (W.W. Norton & Company, 1987).

Legends of the American Desert, Alex Schoumatoff (Knopf, 1997).

The Man Who Listens to Horses, Monty Roberts (Random House, 1996).

Montana, High, Wide and Handsome, Joseph Howard (University of Nebraska Press, 1983).

The Mountain Meadows Massacre, Juanita Brooks (University of Oklahoma Press, 1950).

My Life on the Plains, George Armstrong Custer (University of Nebraska, 1966).

National Parks: The American Experience, Alfred Runte (University of Nebraska Press, 1979).

Native American Testimony, Peter Nabokov, ed. (Viking, 1991).

The New Encyclopedia of the American West, Howard Roberts Lamar, ed. (Yale University Press, 1998).

The Oregon Trail Revisited, Gregory M. Franzwa (The Patrice Press, 1997).

Out West, Dayton Duncan (Penguin, 1988).

An Overland Journey, Horace Greeley (Knopf, 1963).

The Oxford History of the American West, Clyde A. Milner II, Carol A. O'Connor, and Martha A. Sandweiss, eds. (Oxford University Press, 1994).

The People: Indians of the American Southwest, Stephen Trimble (School of American Research Press, 1993).

People of the Southwest, Peter H. Welsh (Southwest Museum, 1984).

Roughing It, Mark Twain (Penguin, 1981).

A Sand County Almanac, Aldo Leopold (Oxford University Press, 1949).

A Short History of Santa Fe, Susan Hazen-Hammond (Lexikos, 1988).

A Shovel of Stars: The Making of the American West, Ted Morgan (Simon & Schuster, 1995).

The Solace of Open Spaces, Gretel Ehrlich (Penguin Viking, 1985).

Texas Cowboys, David Stoecklein (Dober Hill, 1997).

This House of Sky, Ivan Doig (Harcourt Brace Jovanovich, 1978).

This Reckless Breed of Men, Robert Cleland (Knopf, 1952).

Traveling the Lewis & Clark Trail, Julie Fanselow (Falcon Press, 1994).

Traveling the Oregon Trail, Julie Fanselow (Falcon Press, 1992).

Undaunted Courage: Meriwether Lewis, Thomas Jefferson, and the Opening of the American West, Stephen Ambrose (Simon & Schuster, 1996).

Under Western Skies: Nature and History in the West, Donald Worster (Oxford University Press, 1992).

Walking Down the Wild: A Journey Through the Yellowstone Rockies, Gary Ferguson (HarperCollins, 1995).

The West: An Illustrated History, Geoffrey C. Ward (Little, Brown and Company, 1996).

Western Culture and History Across the Wide Missouri, Bernard deVoto (Boston, 1947).

Western Women in History and Literature, Sheryll and Gene Patterson-Black (Cottonwood Press, 1978).

The Westward Movement: A Short History, Kent L. Steckmesser (McGraw-Hill, 1969).

Where the Bluebird Sings to the Lemonade Springs, Wallace Stegner (Random House, 1992).

Wilderness Essays, John Muir (Peregrine Smith Books, 1982).

The Winning of the West, 4 vols., Theodore Roosevelt (Putnam's, 1889-1896).

The Women Who Made the West, Western Writers of America (Doubleday & Co., Inc., 1980).

FICTION

All the Pretty Horses, Cormac McCarty (Knopf, 1992).

The Best of the American West: Outstanding Frontier Fiction by Louis L'Amour, Loren D. Estleman, Richard Matheson, Luke Short and Many Others, Edward Gorman and Martin H. Greenberg, eds. (Berkeley Publishing Group, 1998).

The Big Rock Candy Mountain, Wallace Stegner (Penguin, 1991).

Blood Trails, Rod McQueary (Dry Oak Press, 1993).

Bowdrie, Louis L'Amour (Bantam, 1983).

Cowboy Curmudgeon, Rod McRae (Peregrine Smith, 1992).

Cowboys are My Weakness, Pam Huston (W.W. Norton, 1992).

The Dance Hall of the Dead, Tony Hillerman (Harper and Row, 1982).

Death Comes for the Archbishop, Willa Cather (Knopf, 1927).

Fool's Crow, James Welch (Viking, 1986).

Great Stories of the American West, Martin H. Greenberg, ed. (Jove Publishing, 1996).

The Horse Whisperer, Nicholas Evans (Random House, 1997).

House Made of Dawn, N. Scott Momaday (Harper and Row, 1966).

Lonesome Dove, Larry McMurtry (Simon & Schuster, 1985).

The Loop, Nicholas Evans (Random House, 1998).

Luck of Roaring Camp, Bret Harte (Houghton Mifflin, 1903).

My Antonia!, Willa Cather (Houghton Mifflin Co., 1918).

New Hope: Western Stories, Ernest Haycox (Five Star, 1998).

North of 36, Emerson Hough (Grosset & Dunlap, 1923).

O Pioneers!, Willa Cather (Houghton Mifflin Co., 1913).

The Ox-Bow Incident, Walter Van Tilburg Clark (New American Library, 1996).

Ramona, Helen Hunt Jackson (Penguin, 1990).

Riders of the Purple Sage, Zane Grey (Penguin, 1990).

Ride the Dark Trail, Louis L'Amour (Bantam Books, 1972).

Shane, Jack Warner Schaefer (Bantam Starfire, 1983).

So Far from Spring, Peggy Simpson Curry (Viking, 1956).

Tales of the Gold Rush, Bret Harte (Heritage, 1929).

Twenty Tales of California: A Rare Collection of Western Stories, Hector Lee (Rayve Productions, 1996).

The Virginian, Owen Wister (G&D, 1929).

Magazines

American Cowboy
650 Westdale Drive, Suite 100; Wichita, KS 67209; tel: 316-946-0600.

American Indian Art
7314 East Osborn Drive; Scottsdale, AZ 85251; tel: 602-994-5445.

Arizona Highways
2039 West Lewis Street; Phoenix, AZ 85009; tel: 602-258-6641.

Cowboys and Indians
P.O. Box 538; Mount Morris, IL 61054; tel: 800-982-5370.

Native Peoples
P.O. Box 36820; Phoenix, AZ 85067-6820; tel: 602-277-7852.

New Mexico Magazine
Lew Wallace Building, 495 Old Santa Fe Trail; Santa Fe, NM 87503; tel: 505-827-7447.

Range
43 Bellevue Road; Carson City, NV 89704; tel: 702-882-0121.

Trail Dust Magazine
407 West Rosemary Lane; Falls Church, VA 22046.

Wild West
Cowles History Group, 741

Miller Drive SE, Suite D-2; Leesburg, VA 22075.

ORGANIZATIONS

The Dude Ranchers Association
P.O. Box F-471; LaPorte, CO 80535; tel: 970-223-8440.

International Professional Rodeo Association
2304 Exchange Avenue; Oklahoma City, OK 73108; tel: 405-235-6540.

National Bison Association
4701 Marion Suite, Suite 100; Denver, CO 80216; tel: 303-292-2833.

Professional Rodeo Cowboys Association,
101 Pro Rodeo Drive; Colorado Springs, CO 80919; tel: 719-593-8840.

Western Action Shootists Association
4719 Quail Lakes Drive, Suite 140; Stockton, CA 95207.

Women's Professional Rodeo Association
Route 5, Box 698; Blanchard, OK 73010; tel: 405-485-2277.

GOVERNMENT AGENCIES

Bureau of Land Management
U.S. Department of the Interior, 1849 C Street NW; Washington, D.C. 20240; tel: 202-208-5717.

Fish and Wildlife Service
U.S. Department of the Interior, 1849 C Street NW; Washington, D.C. 20240; tel: 202-208-5717.

Forest Service
U.S. Department of Agriculture, 14th and Independence Avenue SW, Agriculture Building; Washington, D.C. 20250; tel: 202-205-8333.

National Park Service
Office of Public Inquiries, P.O. Box 37127; Washington, D.C. 20013; tel: 202-208-4747.

TOURISM INFORMATION

Arizona Office of Tourism
1100 West Washington Street; Phoenix, AZ 85007; tel: 800-842-8257 or 602-542-8687.

California Deserts Tourism Association
P.O. Box 2881; Palm Springs, CA 92264; tel: 888-200-4469.

California State Division of Tourism
801K Street, Suite 1600; Sacramento, CA 95814; tel: 800-462-2543 or 916-322-2881.

Colorado Travel and Tourism Authority
1625 Broadway, Suite 1700; Denver, CO 80202; tel: 800-265-6723.

Idaho Travel Council
700 West State Street; Boise, ID 83720; tel: 800-635-7820.

Travel Montana
Deptartment of Commerce, 1424 9th Avenue; Helena, MT 59620; tel: 800-541-1447 or 406-444-2654.

Nevada Tourism
Capital Complex; Carson City, NV 89710; tel: 800-237-0774 or 702-687-4322.

New Mexico Tourism
Lamy Building, 491 Old Santa Fe Trail; Santa Fe, NM 87503; tel: 800-545-2040 or 505-827-7400.

North Dakota Tourism
Liberty Memorial Building, State Capitol Grounds, 604 East Boulevard; Bismarck, ND 58505; tel: 800-435-5663 or 701-328-2525.

Oklahoma Travel and Tourism
P.O. 52002; Oklahoma City, OK 73152-2002; tel: 800-652-6552 or 405-521-2409.

South Dakota Department of Tourism
711 Wells Avenue; Pierre, SD 57501; tel: 605-773-3301.

Texas Tourism
P.O. Box 12728; Austin, TX 78711; tel: 512-478-0098.

Utah Travel Council
Council Hall, Capitol Hill; Salt Lake City, UT 84114; tel: 800-200-1160 or 801-538-1030.

Wyoming Division of Tourism
I-25 at College Drive; Cheyenne, WY 82002; tel: 800-225-5996 or 307-777-7777.

CALENDAR OF EVENTS

January

Arizona National Livestock Show
1826 West McDowell Road; Phoenix, AZ 85007; tel: 602-258-8568.

Cowboy Poetry Gathering,
Western Folklife Center P.O. Box 888; Elko, NV 89801; tel: 702-738-7508.

National Western Stock Show Festival
1325 East 46th Avenue; Denver, CO 80216; tel: 303-297-1166.

Southwestern Exposition and Livestock Show
Fort Worth Convention and Visitors Bureau, 415 Throckmorton; Fort Worth, TX 76102-7410; tel: 817-336-8791 or 800-433-5747.

February

Houston Livestock Show and Rodeo
P.O. Box 20070; Houston, TX 77225; tel: 713-791-9000.

Los Comanches Dance
Taos Pueblo, P.O. Box 1846; Taos, NM 87571; tel: 505-758-8626.

San Antonio Stock Show and Rodeo
P.O. Box 200230; San Antonio, TX 78296-0230; tel: 210-225-5851.

Tucson Rodeo & La Fiesta de los Vaqueros
Tucson Convention & Visitors Bureau, 130 South Scott Avenue; Tucson, AZ 85701; tel: 520-624-1817.

March

Heard Museum Indian Fair and Market
22 East Monte Vista Road; Phoenix, AZ 85004; tel: 602-252-8848.

April

Cowboy Poetry Gathering
National Cowboy Hall of Fame and Western Heritage Center, 1700 NE 63rd Street; Oklahoma City, OK 73111; tel: 405-478-2250.

Gathering of Nations Powwow
Albuquerque Convention and Visitors Bureau, P. O. Box 26866; Albuquerque, NM 87125; tel: 505-243-3696 or 800-284-2282.

May

Buckskinner Rendezvous
Arizona Office of Tourism, 1100 West Washington Street; Phoenix, AZ 85007; tel: 602-542-8687 or 800-842-8257.

Calaveras County Fair and Jumping Frog Jubilee
Calaveras Lodging and Visitor Association, 1211 South Main; Angels Camp, CA 95222; tel: 209-736-0049.

Cinco de Mayo Celebration
Albuquerque Convention and Visitors Bureau, P.O. Box 26866; Albuquerque, NM 87125; tel: 505-243-3696 or 800-284-2282.

Fiesta de Santa Fe Baile de Mayo
Santa Fe Convention & Visitors Bureau, P.O. Box 909; Santa Fe, NM 87501; tel: 505-984-6760.

June

Chisholm Trail Round-Up
Stockyards Historic Area, Visitor Center, 130 East Exchange Street; Fort Worth, TX 76106; tel: 817-625-9715.

Durango Pro Rodeo Series
Durango Chamber Resort Association, 111 South Camino del Rio; Durango, CO 81301; tel: 970-247-0312. Through August.

Indian Fair
San Diego Museum of Man, 1350 El Prado, Balboa Park; San Diego, CA 92101; tel: 619-239-2001.

Old Fort Days
Fort Sumner State Monument, P.O. Box 356; Fort Sumner, NM 88119; tel: 505-355-2573.

Old Miners Day in Chloride
Arizona Office of Tourism, 1100 West Washington Street; Phoenix, AZ 85007; tel: 602-542-8687 or 800-842-8257.

Plains Indian Museum Powwow
Buffalo Bill Historical Center, P.O. Box 1000; Cody, WY 82414; tel: 307-587-4771.

San Juan Feast Day
Taos Pueblo, P.O. Box 1846; Taos, NM 87571; tel: 505-758-8626.

July

Bannack Days
Bannack State Park, 4200 Bannack Road; Dillon, MT 59725; tel: 406-834-3413.

Cody Stampede Parade and Rodeo
Cody Country Visitors & Convention Council, 836 Sheridan Avenue; Cody, WY; 27777; tel: 307-587-2297.

Days of '47 Celebrations
Utah Travel Council, Council Hall, Capitol Hill; Salt Lake City, UT 84114; tel: 800-200-1160.

Durango Cowgirl Classic
Durango Chamber Resort Association, 111 South Camino del Rio; Durango, CO 81301; tel: 970-247-0312.

Green River Rendezvous
Museum of the Mountain Man, 700 East Hennick; Pinedale, WY 82941; tel: 307-367-4101.

North American Indian Days
Blackfeet Tribal Council, P.O. Box 850; Browning, MT 59417; tel: 406-338-7522.

Soldiering on the Santa Fe Trail
Fort Union National

Monument, P.O. Box 127; Watrous, NM 87753; tel: 505-425-8025.

Spanish Market
Spanish Colonial Arts Society, P.O. Box 1611; Santa Fe, NM 87504; tel: 505-983-4038.

Taos Fiesta
Taos County Chamber of Commerce, P.O. Drawer 1; Taos, NM 87571; tel: 505-758-3873 or 800-732-8267.

August

American Indian Exposition
P.O. Box 908; Anadarko, OK 73005; tel: 405-247-2733.

Boom Days
Leadville Chamber of Commerce, P.O. Box 861; Leadville, CO 80461; tel: 719-486-3900.

Crow Fair
Crow Tribal Council, P.O. Box 159; Crow Agency, MT 59022; tel: 406-638-2601.

Indian Market
Santa Fe Convention & Visitor Bureau; PO Box 909, Santa Fe, NM 87501; tel: 505-984-6760.

Nez Percé Cultural Days
Nez Percé National Historical Park, P.O. Box 93; Spalding, ID 83551; tel: 208-843-2261.

Old Lincoln Days
New Mexico Tourism, Lamy Building, 491 Old Santa Fe Trail; Santa Fe, NM 87503; tel: 800-545-2040.

Palace Mountain Man Rendezvous and Buffalo Roast
Museum of New Mexico, Palace of the Governors, 105 West Palace Avenue; Santa Fe, NM 87501; tel: 505-827-6483.

September

Fort Bridger Rendezvous
Fort Bridger State Historic Site, P.O. Box 35; Fort Bridger, WY 82933; tel: 307-782-3842.

Navajo Nation Fair
Navajo Nation Tourism Office, P.O. Box 663;

Window Rock, AZ 86515; tel: 520-871-6436.

New Mexico State Fair and Rodeo
New Mexico Tourism, Lamy Building, 491 Old Santa Fe Trail; Santa Fe, NM 87503; tel: 800-545-2040.

Pendleton Round-Up
P.O. Box 609; Pendleton, OR 97801; tel: 503-276-2553.

Pioneer Days Celebration and Rodeo
Stockyards Historic Area, Visitor Center, 130 East Exchange Street; Fort Worth, TX 76106; tel: 817-625-9715.

San Geronimo Feast Day
Taos Pueblo, P.O. Box 1846; Taos, NM 87571; tel: 505-758-8626.

October

Old West Rodeo
Durango Chamber Resort Association, 111 South Camino del Rio; Durango, CO 81301; tel: 970-247-0312.

November

Death Valley Encampment
Death Valley Chamber of Commerce, P.O. Box 157; Shoshone, CA 92384; tel: 619-852-4524.

Grand National Rodeo
Horse and Livestock Exhibition, Cow Palace, PO Box 34206; San Francisco, CA 94134; tel: 415-469-6000

Indian National Finals Rodeo
New Mexico Tourism, Lamy Building, 491 Old Santa Fe Trail; Santa Fe, NM 87503; tel: 800-545-2040

December

Gilcrease Rendezvous
Gilcrease Museum, 11400 Gilcrease Museum Road; Tulsa, OK 74127; tel: 918-596-2700.

National Finals Rodeo in Las Vegas
Nevada, Pro Rodeo Cowboys Association, 101 Pro Rodeo Drive; Colorado Springs, CO 80919; tel: 719-593-8840.

PHOTO AND ILLUSTRATION CREDITS

Dan Abernathy 33B, 62B

Academy of Motion Picture Arts and Sciences 24B

Adstock Photos 40T, 113, 133T, 165T

Tom Algire/Tom Stack & Associates 148

Amon Carter Museum 79B, 195

Anschutz Collection 12-13, 30B

Sue Bennett/Adstock Photo 41, 210-211

Craig Blacklock/Larry Ulrich Stock Photography 132-133B

Matt Bradley 34T

Steve Bruno 97B, 110, 145, 179

Buffalo Bill Historical Center 22, 27, 170, 178B

Charles Chanley/Adstock Photos 117T

Richard Cummins/Viesti Collection 112

John Drew 48-49, 52T, 52B, 53B, 54B, 55T, 55B, 56T, 56 (2nd from top), 56 (3rd from bottom), 56 (2nd from bottom), 56B, 57T, 57 (2nd from bottom), 100, 124T, 131B, 147T, 150, 153T, 203T

Jeff Foott 82, 86T, 124-125B, 171T, 173B, 181M, 209T, 209B

Jeff Foott/Tom Stack & Associates 160, 163B

Michael H. Francis 89B, 177T

Francois Gohier 92

Ira Mark Gostin 61T, 68

Susan Hazen-Hammond 1, 35, 103T

Paul Horsted 174, 177B

George H.H. Huey 8L, 85B, 117M, 122B, 127M, 132T, 134M, 134B, 137T, 137 (2nd from top), 140, 144B, 151

Independence National Historical Park Collection 194T, 194B

Kansas State Historical Society 45L, 45R

Jeff Kida/Adstock Photos 120

Bill Lea 173T

J. C. Leacock 114B

Library of Congress 10-11, 18T, 26T, 26B, 31T, 34B, 94, 121T, 135, 162, 178T, 188T, 207

Robert J. MacDonald 57 (3rd from top)

Bill Manns 5T, 5B, 8R, 9B, 24T, 76B, 114T

John Marshall/Adstock Photos 121B

Fred W. Marvel/Oklahoma Tourism 81M

Buddy Mays/Travel Stock 69T, 105B, 165B, 169B, 191T

Montana Historical Society 25, 42, 46T, 87, 196-197B

Museum of Fine Arts, Boston (Gift of the William H. Lane Foundation) 19

Museum of Texas Tech University, Lubbock, Texas 203B

William Neill/Larry Ulrich Stock Photography 125T

Oakland Museum of California 47

Laurence Parent 72, 74, 78

Brian Parker/Tom Stack & Associates 75

Jack Parsons 18B, 31B, 54T, 56 (3rd from top), 66T, 66B, 67, 85T, 89T, 93, 103B, 109T, 117B, 122T, 188B

Don Pitcher 166, 173M

Bob Pool/Tom Stack & Associates 60, 69B

Larry Rice 192

John Running 9T, 28, 40B, 46B, 186B

Santa Barbara Mission Archive-Library 206T

Mike Scully/Adstock Photos 58, 187T

Jerry Sieve/Adstock Photos 109M

Allen B. Smith/Tom Stack & Associates 187B

Smithsonian Institution 79T, 123T, 186T

Tom Stack & Associates 64, 171B

David R. Stoecklein 2-3, 62T, 77T, 77B, 169T, 189B

David R. Stoecklein/Adstock Photos 6-7, 14-15, 16, 30T, 32, 76T, 86B, 127B, 142B, 155, 182, 189T

Tom Till 20-21, 44, 50, 53T, 81T, 89M, 90, 97T, 97M, 105T, 107B, 109B, 115, 127T, 128, 137 (2nd from bottom), 137B, 138, 141, 142T, 143T, 143B, 144T, 147M, 147B, 154, 157B, 161, 165M, 181T, 181B, 191B, 199B

Stephen Trimble 36, 38, 39T, 39B, 57 (3rd from bottom), 57B, 61B, 63, 95, 98, 101, 102T, 102B, 104T, 104B, 106T, 106B, 107T, 130, 131T, 157T, 157M, 163T, 191M, 196T, 202, 205, 209M

Larry Ulrich 4, 57 (2nd from top), 70-71, 84, 118, 123B, 134T, 152, 153B, 158, 200, 204, 206B

Union Pacific Museum Collection 144M

Steve Warble 199T, 199M

Western Folklife Center 33T

Will Rogers Memorial Commission 81B

Ted Wood 185

Maps by Karen Minot

Design and layout by Mary Kay Garttmeier

INDEX

Note: page numbers in italics refer to illustrations